Prohibitions

Prohibitions

EDITED BY JOHN MEADOWCROFT

WITH CONTRIBUTIONS FROM
RALF M. BADER
SIMON W. BOWMAKER
MARK J. CHERRY
K. AUSTIN KERR
GARY A. MAUSER
JOHN MEADOWCROFT
ALBERTO MINGARDI
MARTIN RICKETTS
ROBERT SIMMONS
NADINE STROSSEN
ALEXANDER TABARROK
MARK THORNTON
GEOFFREY E. WOOD

The Institute of Economic Affairs

First published in Great Britain in 2008 by
The Institute of Economic Affairs
2 Lord North Street
Westminster
London SW1P 3LB
in association with Profile Books Ltd

The mission of the Institute of Economic Affairs is to improve public understanding of the fundamental institutions of a free society, by analysing and expounding the role of markets in solving economic and social problems.

A CIP catalogue record for this book is available from the British Library.

ISBN 978 0 255 36585 7

Many IEA publications are translated into languages other than English or are reprinted. Permission to translate or to reprint should be sought from the Director General at the address above.

Typeset in Stone by MacGuru Ltd
info@macguru.org.uk

Printed and bound in Great Britain by Hobbs the Printers

CONTENTS

ABOUT THE AUTHORS

Ralf M. Bader

Ralf M. Bader read Philosophy, Politics and Economics at the University of Oxford (St Edmund Hall), gaining a First Class degree. While at Oxford, he refounded the Oxford Hayek Society. Having completed an MLitt with Distinction in philosophy at the University of St Andrews, he is now working on his PhD at St Andrews and is currently a visiting researcher in the philosophy department at Stanford University. His research focuses on metaphysics, ethics and libertarianism, and he is presently writing a book on Robert Nozick for the Major Conservative and Libertarian Thinkers series to be published by Continuum.

Simon W. Bowmaker

Simon W. Bowmaker is a Visiting Lecturer in Economics at New York University. Prior to pursuing an academic career, he worked as an economist at HSBC Markets, the Government Economic Service and Cambridge Econometrics. For several years, Simon taught economics at the University of Edinburgh and has held visiting teaching positions at a number of universities in the United States, including Florida State University, State University of New York at Buffalo, University of Colorado at Denver and Georgia Institute of Technology. His research interests include the economics of marriage, crime and drug policy, and these topics feature in a book he recently edited, *Economics Uncut: A Complete Guide to Life, Death, and Misadventure* (Edward Elgar, 2005). He received his economics training from Aberdeen, Cambridge and St Andrews universities.

Mark J. Cherry

Mark J. Cherry is the Dr Patricia A. Hayes Professor in Applied Ethics at St Edward's University, Austin, Texas. He is author of *Kidney for Sale by Owner: Human Organs, Transplantation, and the Market* (Georgetown University Press, 2005). He serves as editor of the *Journal of Medicine and Philosophy*, editor of *Christian Bioethics*, editor-in-chief of *Health-Care Ethics Committee Forum* and book series co-editor of the *Annals of Bioethics*. He is editor or co-editor of the books: *Persons and Their Bodies: Rights, Responsibilities, Relationships* (Kluwer, 1999), *Allocating Scarce Medical Resources: Roman Catholic Perspectives* (Georgetown University Press, 2002), *Regional Perspectives in Bioethics* (Taylor and Francis, 2003), *Religious Perspectives in Bioethics* (Taylor and Francis, 2004), *Natural Law and the Possibility of a Global Bioethics* (Springer, 2004), *The Death of Metaphysics; The Death of Culture* (Springer, 2005) and *Pluralistic Casuistry* (Springer, 2007). He is also credited with numerous articles, book chapters and other publications.

K. Austin Kerr

K. Austin Kerr is a Professor Emeritus of History at Ohio State University. His writings include *Organized for Prohibition: A New History of the Anti-Saloon League* (Yale University Press, 1985), 'In the shadow of Prohibition: domestic American alcohol policy Since 1933', *Business History*, July 2005 (with Pamela E. Pennock) and 'The rebirth of brewing and distilling in the United States in 1933: government policy and industry structure', *Business and Economic History On Line*, Business History Conference, 2005. He has served as President of the Alcohol and Drugs Historical Society and of the Business History Conference. In addition to his service at Ohio State University, Professor Kerr has been a Fulbright Professor at Waseda University, the University of Tokyo and the University of Hamburg.

Gary A. Mauser

Gary Mauser is a professor at the Institute for Canadian Urban Research Studies, Faculty of Business Administration, Simon Fraser University, in British Columbia, Canada. He received his PhD from the University of California, Irvine. Recent publications include, 'Would banning firearms reduce murder and suicide? A review of international evidence', *Harvard Journal of Law and Public Policy* (co-author Don B. Kates, 2007) and *Hubris in the North: The Canadian Firearms Registry* (Fraser Institute, 2007). He has made invited presentations to the United Nations Conference on Small Arms and Light Weapons, the Canadian House of Commons, and he has testified as an expert witness before the Supreme Court of Canada. For more information please see his website, *www.gary-mauser.net*.

John Meadowcroft

John Meadowcroft is Lecturer in Public Policy at King's College London. He is the author of *The Ethics of the Market* (Palgrave, 2005), which won an Intercollegiate Studies Institute Templeton Enterprise Award, co-author with Mark Pennington of *Rescuing Social Capital from Social Democracy* (Institute of Economic Affairs, 2007), which won the Arthur Seldon CBE Award for Excellence, and co-editor with Philip Booth of *The Road to Economic Freedom* (Edward Elgar, 2006). Since 2004 he has been a Deputy Editor and Book Review Editor of the IEA journal *Economic Affairs*. He is Series Editor of the Major Conservative and Libertarian Thinkers series to be published by Continuum.

Alberto Mingardi

Alberto Mingardi is managing director of the Istituto Bruno Leoni, the Italian free market think tank, which he helped to establish in 2003. He is also a Senior Fellow with the Centre for the New Europe. In 2002, he was a Calihan Fellow at the Acton Institute for the Study of Religion and

Liberty. He is the translator into English of Antonio Rosmini Serbati's masterpiece *The Constitution under Social Justice* (Lexington Books, 2007). He has also contributed to a wide range of publications, in Italian as well as in English, including the *Wall Street Journal*, the *Washington Post*, the *Financial Times*, *Economic Affairs* and the *Journal of Markets and Morality*.

Martin Ricketts

Martin Ricketts is Professor of Economic Organisation and Dean of Humanities at the University of Buckingham. He has published in professional journals on the Theory of the Firm, Public Choice and the New Institutional Economics. He is author of *The Economics of Energy* (Macmillan, 1980) (with Michael G. Webb), *British Economic Opinion* (Institute of Economic Affairs, 1990) (with Edward Shoesmith) and is sole author of *The Many Ways of Governance* (Social Affairs Unit, 1999) and *The Economics of Business Enterprise* (Edward Elgar, 3rd edition, 2002). He was Economic Director of the National Economic Development Office (UK) (1991–92), Dean of the School of Business at the University of Buckingham (1993–97) and is chairman of the Academic Advisory Council and a managing trustee of the Institute of Economic Affairs.

Robert Simmons

Rob Simmons is Senior Lecturer in Economics at Lancaster University Management School. He has a PhD from the University of Leeds. His research interests include sports economics and the economics of gambling. Recently published articles on the economics of gambling have covered topics in sports betting and lottery play. These have appeared in *Applied Economics*, the *International Journal of Forecasting* and the *Oxford Review of Economic Policy*. He has served as an expert adviser to the UK House of Commons Select Committee for

Culture, Media and Sport. He also serves on the editorial boards of the *International Journal of Sport Finance* and the *Journal of Sports Economics*.

Nadine Strossen

Nadine Strossen, Professor of Law at New York Law School, has written, lectured and practised extensively in the areas of constitutional law, civil liberties and international human rights. In 1991, she was elected President of the American Civil Liberties Union, the first woman to head the largest and oldest civil liberties organisation in the USA (since the ACLU presidency is non-paid, Strossen continues in her faculty position as well). The *National Law Journal* has named Strossen one of America's '100 Most Influential Lawyers'. She makes approximately two hundred public presentations per year, before diverse audiences, and she also comments frequently on legal issues in the national media. Strossen's more than 250 published writings have appeared in many scholarly and general-interest publications.

Alexander Tabarrok

Alexander Tabarrok is Associate Professor of Economics at George Mason University and Director of Research for the Independent Institute. Professor Tabarrok is co-author of the website FDAReview.org, an extensive resource on the history, policies and potential reform of the FDA. He is also the editor of the books *Entrepreneurial Economics: Bright Ideas from the Dismal Science* (Oxford University Press, 2002), *The Voluntary City: Choice, Community, and Civil Society* (University of Michigan Press, 2002) (with David Beito and Peter Gordon) and *Changing the Guard: Private Prisons and the Control of Crime* (Independent Institute, 2002). His papers have appeared in the *Journal of Law and Economics*, *Public Choice*, *Economic Inquiry*, the *Journal of Health Economics*, the *Journal of Theoretical Politics*, the *American Law and Economics Review*, *Kyklos* and many other journals. Popular articles by Professor Tabarrok have appeared in magazines and newspapers throughout the United States, and he writes regularly for the blog MarginalRevolution.

Mark Thornton

Mark Thornton is Senior Fellow at the Ludwig von Mises Institute. He serves as the Book Review Editor of the *Quarterly Journal of Austrian Economics* and as a member of the editorial board of the *Journal of Libertarian Studies*. He has served as the editor of the *Austrian Economics Newsletter* and as a member of the graduate faculties of Auburn University and Columbus State University. He has also taught economics at Auburn University in Montgomery and Trinity University in Texas. Mark served as Assistant Superintendent of Banking and economic adviser to Governor Fob James of Alabama (1997–99) and was awarded the University Research Award at Columbus State University in 2002. His books include *The Economics of Prohibition* (University of Utah Press, 1991), *Tariffs, Blockades, and Inflation: The Economics of the Civil War* (Rowman and Littlefield, 2004), *The Quotable Mises* (Ludwig von Mises Institute, 2005) and *The Bastiat Collection* (Ludwig von Mises Institute, 2007). He has over sixty articles published in academic journals and books. He is a graduate of St Bonaventure University and received his PhD in economics from Auburn University.

Geoffrey E. Wood

Geoffrey Wood is Professor of Economics at the Sir John Cass Business School in London and Professor of Monetary Economics at the University of Buckingham. He is a graduate of Aberdeen and Essex universities, and has worked in the Federal Reserve System, the Bank of England and at several universities in Britain and overseas. He has authored, co-authored or edited over twenty books, and has published over one hundred academic papers. His fields of interest are monetary economics, monetary history and financial regulation.

TABLES AND FIGURES

FOREWORD

In the New Zealand of my youth, we suffered high inflation. The prime minister of the time, Robert Muldoon, lighted upon an idea that really was a 'no brainer'. If we wanted to be rid of inflation, why not simply ban it? In July 1982, New Zealand's parliament passed a law making it illegal to increase the prices of the goods you sold.

Alas, Mr Muldoon was not also prime minister of the many countries from which New Zealand businesses imported materials they used in production. Although he could prevent these businesses from increasing their revenues, he could not hold down their costs. Output declined, unemployment increased and inflation still ran at 11 per cent!

Most contemporary politicians would laugh at such economic Canutism. But few are entitled to. Though they may not favour price freezes, many share Muldoon's enthusiasm for achieving their policy goals by imposing legislative limitations on voluntary transactions.

Take a mundane example, of a kind now so common that it hardly raises an eyebrow. It is illegal in Britain, and in the rest of the European Union, for an employee voluntarily to forgo a day of his holiday entitlement in return for an extra day's pay. This prohibition is justified on the fashionable pretext of 'protecting the vulnerable'; it prevents employers from coercing employees into working when they would prefer to use their holiday entitlement.

Yet, to avoid the small risk of such a breach of contract, for which remedies already exist, this prohibition forces employees who might prefer an extra day's pay to take a holiday instead. It imposes the preferences of legislators (who certainly seem to enjoy their holidays) on the entire population, including those who do not share them. Knowing nothing of your circumstances or tastes, they still believe they know how many days' holiday you should take.

And not only that. They also know how you should while away your leisure time (not in a private cigar bar, for example), how you should earn a living (not by selling sex to willing buyers, for example) and all manner of other things that you might think individuals were better able to decide for themselves.

The cost of this oppression falls not only on those whose preferred choices are outlawed, but also often on the wider population. The War on Drugs provides the most obvious example. The abstemious also pay for our governments' attempts to ensure that all intoxication is caused by alcohol. Their taxes fund the enforcement and healthcare costs (illegally produced drugs are more dangerous), and they suffer from the violence produced by criminals battling for control of local black markets. Then, after all this, prohibitions often fail to achieve their goals. Ecstasy pills are so readily available in London that their price has fallen to £3 or less. Since Britain's restrictive gun laws were introduced in 1997, handguns have become cheaper and the number of people shot by them has increased.

Despite its manifest failings, prohibiting voluntary transactions remains popular not only with politicians but also with the voting public. If you doubt it, just spend an afternoon listening to talk radio. You will come away feeling fortunate to have any remaining liberties; if the government took the punters' advice, it would 'put a stop' to everything.

Where does this authoritarian tendency come from? Perhaps our genetic and social programming for parenthood predisposes us to it. Perhaps it is because most of us are educated by the state. Perhaps it is the result of a lingering tribalism, whereby we like to see our own values dominate those who differ from us.

Whatever the root cause, the error can only be encouraged by the bizarre misrepresentation of contemporary prohibitionists, both by themselves and by journalists. Right-wing advocates of moralistic legislation are correctly described as authoritarians. But left-wing advocates of inefficient prohibitions, such as Gordon Brown and Hillary Clinton, are systematically and uncritically described as liberal rather than as authoritarian.

Which is why this book is so important. *Prohibitions* is a corrective to the prevailing sympathy for paternalistic authoritarianism. It is a part of the intellectual resistance movement. Each chapter considers a significant prohibition on voluntary transactions, from prostitution to recreational drugs to gambling. They are fascinating individually, employing a combination of economic theory, statistics and historical fact to show that the prohibition concerned is a costly mistake. Taken together, they are devastating. The cumulative effect of reading *Prohibitions* has been to render me even more sceptical about the possibility of making us better off by preventing our voluntary transactions. And that is saying something.

JAMIE WHYTE

Consultant, Oliver Wyman

Auckland, New Zealand

November 2007

Prohibitions

1 INTRODUCTION
John Meadowcroft

This collection examines prohibitions – the outlawing of the manufacture, distribution, sale or provision of particular goods and services by consenting adults. After this introduction, the book begins with an overview of the economics of prohibition and then the subsequent chapters analyse the prohibition of the following goods, services and activities:

- recreational drugs, in particular cocaine, heroin and marijuana;
- boxing;
- firearms;
- advertising;
- pornography;
- medicinal drugs;
- prostitution;
- gambling;
- body parts for transplant;
- alcohol.

The above goods, services and activities are all prohibited in some part of the world, and in some cases – such as those of alcohol, gambling and prostitution – in large parts of the world.

The chapters in this collection are written by an international cast of authors from across the social science disciplines. The authors include economists, lawyers, political scientists, philosophers and sociologists, who have applied their expertise to the problems posed by the provision of these particular goods and services both outside and inside the law.

Although the authors are drawn from throughout the social sciences, all have considered the economics of prohibition (broadly defined) within their contributions. The economics of prohibition implies an analysis of the pecuniary costs and benefits of prohibition, but it also entails much more than this. First, the relevant costs and benefits are far more than simply monetary – they include all the individual and social costs and benefits. Second, at its heart economics is the study of property rights and the consequences that arise from different regimes for the ownership of property. Owning a property title involves owning a bundle or collection of rights. A person who owns a property can do what he or she wants with it: they may use it, rent it, donate it, transfer it, sell it or even destroy it. If, however, another entity may prevent an individual from using their property as they wish, then that other entity has a partial right of ownership of that property. Hence, when planning laws prevent a person from demolishing a listed building, the government obtains part-ownership of that property because it has a say in its use. Similarly, when government prevents an individual from choosing to imbibe cocaine or engage in prostitution, it may be said to have taken part-ownership of that person as it has a say in how they use their body. Slavery and military conscription are examples of other people taking almost complete ownership of a person, but all prohibitions involve government assuming at least partial ownership rights in its citizens.[1]

By assigning partial ownership rights in citizens to the state, prohibitions necessarily involve a diminution of individual liberty. People without the power to choose what they do with their bodies cannot be said to be as free as people with such a choice, and a society in which many activities are prohibited cannot be considered a free society. For this reason, prohibitions must be carefully justified. It must be shown that the benefits of prohibition outweigh the costs. But the most important cost may be the most difficult to measure and to quantify: the

---

1   This understanding of individual self-ownership is derived from a Lockean approach to property rights (Locke 1698 [1993]). For a more complete discussion, see McGee (1993) and/or Nozick (1974).

cumulative cost of many small and seemingly unimportant restrictions on individual liberty. Freedom is rarely lost in one dramatic incident, but is more commonly gradually taken away as many seemingly minor restrictions on personal freedom cumulatively take effect. It was on this basis that the English constitutional theorist A. V. Dicey (1914 [1981]: 257–8) wrote:

> The beneficial effect of State intervention, especially in the form of legislation, is direct, immediate, and, so to speak, visible, whilst its evil effects are gradual and indirect, and lie out of sight ... Hence the majority of mankind must almost of necessity look with undue favour upon government intervention. This natural bias can be counteracted only by the existence ... of a presumption or prejudice in favour of individual liberty – that is, of *laissez faire*.

According to Dicey, then, individual liberty can be saved from the crushing weight of a multitude of well-intentioned government interventions only if there is a general presumption in favour of laissez-faire – that is, an assumption that government will not intervene, even if a good case for intervention can be made, other than as an absolute last resort. If such an approach is not adopted, freedom may be gradually eroded in the name of many seemingly worthwhile interventions until it has completely disappeared.

Prohibition and the harm principle

Prohibition is usually justified in order to prevent harm – the invocation of 'the harm principle'. Hence, recreational use of heroin and cocaine is prohibited in most countries to prevent harm to users (and perhaps to the wider society), boxing is prohibited in some countries to prevent harm to pugilists, and the manufacture, distribution and sale of alcohol was prohibited in the United States from 1920 to 1933 to prevent drinkers (and others) being harmed by the perceived evil of alcohol consumption and intoxication.

The harm principle is derived from the classic account of the appropriate boundaries between actions that are of concern to the individual alone and those that are of concern to others that was set out by John Stuart Mill (1859 [1985]: 68) in his essay *On Liberty*. Here, Mill stated:

> [T]he sole end for which mankind are warranted, individually or collectively, in interfering with the liberty of action of any of their number is self-protection. That the only purpose for which power can be rightfully exercised over any member of a civilised community, against his will, is to prevent harm to others. His own good, either physical or moral, is not a sufficient warrant.

According to Mill, in a *civilised* community, individuals cannot be protected from themselves, only from other people. Mill understood that individual liberty can be preserved only if people are given freedom of choice that extends to actions that others deem self-harming. Hence, from a Millian perspective, if an individual wishes to take heroin we may try to persuade them of the error of their ways, we may choose to exclude them from our company, but we cannot forcibly stop them from using their drug of choice.[2]

To cross this dividing line between the individual and the collective is to assume that we know what is best for others better than they themselves do. But the ends that people pursue in life must be a matter for each individual, not for other people, to determine. For example, many heroin users, such as the acclaimed novelist William S. Burroughs (1953 [1977]), have argued that the benefits of heroin use outweigh the costs. Few people would agree with Burroughs's assessment, but that does not mean that it does not accurately reflect his own preferences or that he should be prevented from pursuing those preferences. It is wrong to impose our own preferences on others who may not share our assessment

---

2   It is worth noting that in reality activities like drug use require more than one willing participant; people willing to manufacture, distribute and sell the commodity in question are also required. Hence, drug use requires a critical mass of people before it can take place and therefore one lone individual who wished to engage in such activities would be unable to do so unless others were willing to facilitate his or her actions.

of the costs and benefits of different courses of action; to prevent other people from choosing their own ends is to deny their capacity for autonomous choice and ultimately to deny their very humanity.

Furthermore, once the principle that autonomous individuals may be prevented from freely choosing actions that harm no one but themselves has been transgressed, the fact that there is no objective measure of what actions are harmful and therefore should be prohibited means that practically any intervention can be justified. Milton Friedman (1992: 59), for example, has argued that the writings of Karl Marx have led to the deaths of more people than the use of alcohol, tobacco and other recreational drugs combined. On this basis it might be contended that Marx's books should be banned, but in reality this simply demonstrates the problems that arise when the harm principle is extended beyond direct harm caused to others by specific actions.

Policy lessons of this collection

The chapters in this collection illuminate a number of generic lessons and implications for policymakers and all those with an interest in the creation of effective public policy in some of the most challenging areas.

Prohibition places markets into the hands of criminal enterprises

Wherever the manufacture, distribution and supply of goods and services are prohibited organised crime syndicates will be alert to the substantial profits that can be made from their illegal provision. As Thornton and Bowmaker describe in Chapter 3, prohibition drives a 'wedge' between the cost of production and the final selling price, ensuring that those prepared to take the risk of supplying illegal goods and services can reap exceptional profits.

The US prohibition of alcohol, for example, enabled a number of criminal organisations that had previously profited from illegal gambling and prostitution to expand into the supply of alcohol and illegal drinking premises and make previously unprecedented profits. As a consequence, many criminals, such as the infamous Chicago gangster Al Capone, amassed substantial tax-free fortunes. After prohibition was repealed in 1933, organised crime moved into the supply of those recreational drugs that remained illegal, where once again huge fortunes could be made: in 1989 *Forbes* magazine listed the Colombian drug baron Pablo Escobar as the seventh-wealthiest man in the world and estimated that his Medellin drug cartel had an annual income of $80 billion.

In all the cases of prohibition discussed in this book – from gambling to prostitution and from medicinal to recreational drugs – there is extensive criminal involvement in the supply of illegal goods and services. Indeed, even where goods and services are not prohibited but are subject to punitive taxation, criminal organisations will seek to exploit the wedge between cost of production and final selling price, as in the case of the growth of tobacco smuggling and the sale of counterfeit cigarettes in the UK as taxes on tobacco products have risen in recent years. Organised criminal enterprises are one of the principal beneficiaries of prohibition.

Just because the manufacture, distribution and sale of a product have been prohibited it does not necessarily follow that its manufacture, distribution and sale will cease. On the contrary, it is more likely that its manufacture, distribution and sale will move from the legal to the illegal sector. The costs of illegal supply are borne by the whole of society, as criminality becomes more profitable and therefore more attractive, innocent bystanders are caught in the (sometimes literal) crossfire between competing gangs and (as discussed below) police resources are devoted to combating organised crime.

Prohibition increases the risks of already risky activities

By shifting the supply of goods and services into the black market under the control of criminal organisations, prohibition greatly increases the risks of already risky activities. In Chapter 3, Thornton and Bowmaker note that a large firm like McDonald's would be quickly bankrupted if it sold a large number of contaminated products, but such constraints do not exist in black markets. Prohibition of recreational drugs greatly increases the dangers of drug use as producers may have little incentive to ensure the safety of their product and users must purchase drugs without adequate knowledge of their purity or exact contents – which can lead to accidental overdoses and poisonings.

Chapter 9 describes how street prostitutes who work covertly to avoid detection by law enforcement agencies – perhaps because their clients in particular fear discovery – are at considerably higher risk of violence than those prostitutes who are able to work in legal brothels where physical attacks are extremely rare. Likewise, outlawing boxing is likely to lead to an increase in illegal fights without proper safety precautions and access to swift medical treatment.

Prohibition criminalises people who would not otherwise be criminals

Prohibition involves the creation of consensual crimes – that is, the criminalisation of acts voluntarily undertaken by consenting adults. It forces people who wish to undertake such acts outside the law and by so doing criminalises people who would otherwise be law-abiding.

The social costs of this phenomenon can be best illustrated by the impact of recreational drug prohibition in the United States. A quarter of the 2.2 million people held in US prisons are incarcerated solely for non-violent drug-related crimes. Many of these prisoners are young people whose prospects of a 'straight' career are significantly reduced by the stigma and experience of incarceration. The burden of the US drug laws falls particularly heavily on black men, who represent a small minority of drug users but a large majority of those convicted of drug-related crimes. The enormous social cost of this phenomenon can be illustrated by the fact that the rate of imprisonment for black males in the USA in 2004 was 4,419 per 100,000, a far higher rate of imprisonment than that for black males in South Africa in 1993 at the height of the violent struggle against the apartheid regime, when the incarceration rate was 851 per 100,000 (Cole, 2005).

Prohibition diverts law enforcement resources away from conduct that harms third parties

The enforcement of any prohibition involves a substantial direct financial cost. To detect, arrest, prosecute and finally punish those engaging in prohibited activities requires substantial resources for the police, the courts and other government agencies. To give an indication, the annual budget of the US Drug Enforcement Administration in 2006 was $2.4 billion.[3] This does not include the separate costs of state police, customs, coastguard and court time also spent enforcing the US 'War on Drugs'.

Prohibition, then, fuels the growth of government bureaucracies that must be funded from general taxation. As a result of the prohibition of recreational drugs, for example, taxes are higher than they would otherwise be and a large proportion of the taxes that are allocated to law enforcement are allocated to the pursuit of (what might be termed) consensual crimes rather than crimes with direct third-party victims, such as murder or burglary. As Thornton and Bowmaker show in Chapter 3, prohibition imposes an *opportunity cost* on society of the goods and services that could have been provided if the money used for enforcement had been spent elsewhere.

The government bureaucracies that are created to enforce prohibitions become a vested interest that can effectively lobby against decriminalisation and campaign for further prohibitions. Failing bureaucracies rarely advocate their own closure, but rather lobby for additional resources and often stricter and more far-reaching controls so that they can 'get the job done'. Law enforcement and similar agencies in many countries are among the primary sources of misinformation about the supposed dangers of illegal drugs and other activities in their

---

3   According to the DEA's own website: www.usdoj.gov/dea/agency/staffing.htm.

efforts to justify their existence and/or acquire additional resources. For example, the 'drug facts' published by the US Office of National Drug Control Policy state that marijuana 'meets the criteria for an addictive drug', an assertion clearly contrary to the medical evidence.[4]

Prohibition increases public ignorance

An important justification of prohibition is that many people do not fully appreciate the likely consequences of their actions and for this reason, where ignorance is widespread, government should prohibit certain activities to protect the public. As Martin Ricketts and Geoffrey E. Wood make clear in their overview of the economics of prohibition in Chapter 2, however, by its very nature prohibition tends to increase public ignorance. It may be argued, for example, that would-be boxers do not possess the necessary information to assess the risks of boxing. If boxing is criminalised, however, fighters are even less likely to be able to access reliable information about its possible dangers.

Concerns about public ignorance might logically lead to a role for government as a provider of reliable information rather than to the prohibition of voluntary activities between consenting adults. Indeed, as Alberto Mingardi describes in Chapter 6, arguments for restricting the advertisement of pharmaceuticals on the grounds that the public do not have the necessary expertise to judge the efficacy of different drugs are particularly perverse given that advertising is potentially a rich source of precisely the kind of knowledge that patients are said to lack.

Organised interest groups are crucial to the introduction of prohibitions

The chapters in this collection show that prohibitions frequently result from the ability of organised interest groups to capture the policy process

---

4   ONDCP website: www.whitehousedrugpolicy.gov/drugfact/marijuana/index.html#go11.

and impose their preferences on the rest of the population. As discussed by K. Austin Kerr in the final chapter of this collection, the Anti-Salon League played a crucial role in the campaign for the amendment of the United States constitution to prohibit the manufacture, distribution and sale of alcohol in the early twentieth century.

Other chapters show the centrality of professional associations of clinicians to campaigns for the abolition of boxing (Chapter 4); the significance of an 'unholy alliance' (or perhaps more accurately 'part-holy alliance') of religious anti-gambling organisations and providers of existing gambling services which has succeeded in persuading a number of governments to restrict the expansion of new gambling opportunities (Chapter 10); the importance of the protectionist interests of the brewing industry in preventing the legalisation of other recreational drugs (Chapter 3); and the critical contribution of feminist groups to campaigns for the prohibition of pornography and prostitution (Chapters 7 and 9). These groups may represent a minority interest and a minority of public opinion, but their organisation, concentration and visibility mean that they are able to use the political process to impose their preferences on the majority who are not organised, and who are dispersed throughout society and less visible to policymakers.

Prohibition almost never works and is almost always counterproductive

The costs described above might be considered worthwhile if prohibition actually worked, but unfortunately empirical evidence suggests that prohibition almost never works and is almost always counterproductive.

The prohibition of recreational drugs is again a striking example. In the USA, cannabis has been de facto prohibited since 1937, while in Holland it has been de facto legal since 1970 and today it may be freely bought and sold in licensed 'coffee shops'. In 1997, of the US population aged twelve years and over, 32.9 per cent had used cannabis in their lifetime. In Holland, by contrast, the proportion was only 15.6 per cent. Although the difference is less marked when older population cohorts are separated and analysed, the evidence is nevertheless clear that cannabis use is greater in the USA where it is illegal than in Holland where it is legal (MacCoun and Reuter, 2001: 253).

The 36-year War on Drugs waged by the US government appears to have had no significant impact on drug use. During this time the price of drugs has fallen while their purity has risen. In 1980 the average street price for a single wrap of heroin (the amount required to get 'high') was $3.90, while by 1999 the cost had fallen to a mere 80 cents. The street price of cocaine has similarly declined from approximately $375 per gram in 1981 to $100 per gram in 1995. The average purity of heroin sold on the streets was 3.6 per cent in 1980, while by 1999 average purity had risen to 38.2 per cent (Cole 2005; MacCoun and Reuter, 2001: 31). Prohibition provides incentives to suppliers of drugs to increase their potency as penalties for supply are often based on the physical amount supplied, so dealing in a more concentrated form of the drug may lead to less severe punishment if caught (Thornton, 1998).

Legislation to ban the ownership of handguns and other firearms has been similarly ineffective in combating violent crime. In Chapter 5, Mauser shows that while the murder rate in England was fairly constant between 1974 and 1997, after handguns were banned in 1997 it rose dramatically from 11.2 murders per million people in 1997 to 15.5 per million in 2001.

Mauser presents similar evidence from the Republic of Ireland and Jamaica, two countries that banned all firearms in the 1970s. Ireland banned firearms in 1971, a year in which there were ten murders in that country. Since 1995 there have never been less than 38 murders per year, and in 2005 there were a total of 54 murders. Jamaica banned firearms in 1974 when its murder rate already stood at a shocking 10 per 100,000 people. Since then the murder rate has continued to rise inexorably, not falling below 31 per 100,000 people since 1995. Mauser shows that there is no evidence that the introduction of gun control legislation reduces the murder rate or the overall rate of violent crime.

Similarly, there is no evidence that strict government controls on medicinal drugs enhance patient safety in comparison with other regimes. As Alexander Tabarrok describes in Chapter 8, the proportion of drugs withdrawn after they have reached the market – the crucial measure of the efficacy of pre-introduction safety measures – is the same in the USA, where the Food and Drug Administration imposes some of the strictest controls in the world, as it is in other countries that have more 'lax' standards. Patients in countries such as the UK and Spain have access to more drugs and are able to benefit from the introduction of new drugs more quickly without compromising their safety than their counterparts in the USA.

In Chapter 11, Mark Cherry illuminates a failure of prohibition that rarely receives the attention of the public and policymakers. The present prohibition of the sale of human organs for transplant throughout the world has led to a severe shortage. The resulting long waiting times for transplants prolong human suffering and mean that many patients die before receiving a replacement organ. In particular, by offering financial incentives to living donors of kidneys it would be possible to greatly increase the supply of kidneys for transplant and thereby improve the prospects of a strong genetic match between donor and recipient – at present the low supply of kidneys for transplant means that many transplants are undertaken despite a relatively poor genetic match, thus leading to high rejection rates. Furthermore, an open market in organs for transplant will prevent the medical and ethical problems created by the existence of black markets in organs.

Why should prohibitions almost always fail? A number of reasons can be identified. First, prohibition almost always leads to offsetting behaviour. Hence, just as the seventeenth- and eighteenth-century window taxes led to houses with bricked-in windows in British streets, so punitive taxes on tobacco lead to cigarette smuggling and counterfeiting, prohibition of recreational drugs leads to vast networks of illegal manufacture, distribution and sale, and the outlawing of prostitution leads to the provision of 'massage' and 'escort' services in grey markets. Just because government passes legislation to make something happen, it does not necessarily follow that it will.[5]

Second, for prohibition to be effective requires a level of government spending and interference in people's day-to-day lives which is unacceptable in a free society. As described above, the War on Drugs presently costs the US government billions of pounds every year and has seen millions of US citizens incarcerated, yet the street price of drugs continues to fall and the purity of illegal drugs continues to rise. It is hard to imagine the price (in every sense of the term) that would have to be paid in order to make a significant impact on the illegal supply of recreational drugs. Prohibition may be achievable in a totalitarian state prepared to devote substantial resources to law enforcement, even at the risk of impoverishing its citizens, but it cannot be made to work in a free society where people are accustomed to a high level of prosperity.

Third, prohibition very often fails because it addresses the *symptoms* rather than the *causes* of social problems. For example, gun control is not a solution to violent crime or a high murder rate because violent criminals are perfectly capable of illegally acquiring firearms or finding other means of killing people, for example with knives or fists. The reduction of violent crime requires a much more sophisticated public policy approach than simply seeking to prevent criminals from accessing one particular type of weapon.

Fourth, for reasons that are not well understood, prohibition very often appears to promote the very behaviour it is intended to eliminate. Filley (1999) has shown, for example, that attempts to prohibit smoking by US teenagers by restricting the sale of cigarettes to minors had exactly the opposite effect to that intended: in towns where additional restrictions on the sale of cigarettes were introduced, smoking among teenagers rose compared to its incidence in control towns where no new measures

5   Veljanovksi (2006) provides an excellent discussion of offsetting and other adaptive behaviour.

were introduced. Filley notes that similar results have been produced by interventions aimed at reducing teenage drinking and by attempts to reduce serious road traffic accidents by manipulating speed limits (ibid.). Exactly why prohibition should have this opposite perverse effect is not entirely clear, but it is probably a combination of the 'forbidden fruit effect' – whereby activities that are forbidden become more attractive, especially to young people – combined with offsetting behaviour.

Prohibition, public policy and responsibility

The policy implications of the analyses of prohibition contained in this collection are relatively straightforward. Prohibition imposes significant costs on individuals and society as a whole and produces few benefits in return. Prohibition places markets into the hands of criminal enterprises. It criminalises people who would not otherwise come into conflict with the law. It makes risky behaviour even more risky. Prohibition increases public ignorance and very probably encourages the behaviour it seeks to prevent. Given the substantial costs and minimal benefits of prohibition it is clear that prohibition is bad public policy.

On the basis of the evidence presented in this collection, it would seem reasonable to propose that all actions without direct third-party victims should be legalised. In most cases legalisation would be a straightforward matter of repealing the relevant legislation. The legalisation of recreational drugs would probably necessitate the creation of a regulatory regime similar to that which presently governs the sale of alcohol in most countries to prevent sale to minors and to provide health information to consumers.

In many countries at present special interest groups are engaged in campaigns advocating the prohibition of a number of goods, services and activities, notably tobacco, prostitution and boxing. In the UK, there have been a number of new restrictions on the sale and use of tobacco products introduced in recent years that would seem to be a precursor to an outright ban. This collection shows that such legislation would be a serious mistake. It would provide an enormous boost to organised crime, criminalise law-abiding smokers, make smoking an even more dangerous activity than it is already and possibly lead to an increase in the number of smokers.

To propose that the manufacture, distribution and sale of a particular good or service should be legalised is not to endorse that good or service or to advocate its consumption. Rather, it is to state that what consenting adults choose to do with their own bodies is a matter of individual conscience. It is possible to simultaneously believe that people should not consume a particular good or service and that that good or service should be legal; one simply believes that abstinence should be the result of individual choice, not government diktat. Indeed, given the ineffectiveness of most states in enforcing prohibitions, it is perfectly feasible that the consumption of a good or service will be lower within a society in which it is legal than within one in which it is illegal. As noted above, this is presently the case for cannabis use in Holland and the USA.

In summary, this collection discusses many controversial activities – such as prostitution, pornography, recreational drug use, gambling, drinking, boxing and the sale of human organs for transplant – that are often deemed morally wrong. The attempt to impose our own moral values on others is a mistake, however, and the costs of this mistake usually fall upon those we are trying to protect or help. An alternative approach is to allow adult men and women the freedom to choose and to require them to take responsibility for the consequences that follow. We may find that when people are given responsibility, they act responsibly. This is the basis of a free society.

References

Burroughs, W. S. (1953 [1977]), *Junky*, London: Penguin.

Cole, J. (2005), *End Prohibition Now!*, Medford, MA: Law Enforcement Against Prohibition.

Dicey, A. V. (1914 [1981]) *Lectures on the Relation between the Law and Public Opinion in England during the Nineteenth Century*, New York: Transaction.

Filley, D. (1999), 'Forbidden fruit: when prohibition increases the harm it is supposed to reduce', *Independent Review*, 3(3): 441–51.

Friedman, M. (1992), 'The drug war as a socialist enterprise', in A. S. Trebach and K. B. Zeese (eds), *Friedman and Szasz on Liberty and Drugs*, Washington, DC: Drug Policy Foundation Press.

Locke, J. (1698 [1993]), *Two Treatises of Government*, Cambridge: Cambridge University Press.

MacCoun, R. J. and P. Reuter (2001), *Drug War Heresies*, Cambridge: Cambridge University Press.

McGee, R. W. (1993), 'If Dwarf Tossing is outlawed, only outlaws will toss dwarfs: is dwarf tossing a victimless crime?', *American Journal of Jurisprudence*, 38: 335–58.

Mill, J. S. (1859 [1985]), *On Liberty*, London: Penguin Classics.

Nozick, R. (1974), *Anarchy, State, and Utopia*, Oxford: Blackwell.

Thornton, M. (1998) 'The potency of illegal drugs', *Journal of Drug Issues*, 28(3): 725–40.

Veljanovski, C. (2006), *The Economics of Law*, London: Institute of Economic Affairs.

2 PROHIBITIONS AND ECONOMICS: AN OVERVIEW

Martin Ricketts and Geoffrey E. Wood

Introduction

Why do we have prohibitions? Economics does not find them easy to justify. There are two reasons for this. The first is that economics rests on individualistic premises. 'Individuals are the best judges of their own welfare' is an important judgement which underlies most of economics. For example, it underpins the famous demonstration of the gains from international trade which David Ricardo gave in his *Principles of Political Economy and Taxation* in 1817. Individuals trade according to what they see as their own advantage. More recently, it underpins what is called 'welfare economics'. This branch of economics, which broadly speaking derives from the work of the nineteenth-century economist Vilfredo Pareto, is concerned to analyse policies according to how they affect the welfare of individuals, each of whom is presumed to know what is good for them. This body of analysis has led to a large number of conclusions concerning the 'efficiency' or otherwise of market equilibria. Efficiency, in this context, is defined as the inability to make one person better off without harming another person *in his or her own estimation*. Further, the private value of anything is simply the maximum that the relevant person is prepared to pay for it, or alternatively the minimum that they would require to induce them to forgo it.[1]

The second reason why prohibitions and economics are not seen consorting together in public very often is that the discipline is primarily

---

1   There are interesting consequences that have entertained economists for many years deriving from the fact that these two possible measures of value are not necessarily the same. This does not, however, immediately affect our argument.

(though admittedly not universally) utilitarian. Strictly speaking it does not permit the direct comparison of one person's utility with another, but policy analysis in economics is conducted in terms of a 'cost–benefit' calculus in which the 'best' situation requires the marginal social cost of any activity to equal its marginal social benefit. In other words, policy analysis tries to lead us to the situation where the cost from a small increase in some activity has at last risen to just equal the benefit from that activity. This would mean that the activity stopped increasing when it was just about to add more to costs than to benefits. There may be instances where 'too much' of an activity occurs – too much traffic on a particular stretch of road, too much noise, too much pollution and so forth – but it would be a rare circumstance in which the 'answer' required banning all traffic, aircraft movements or pollution emissions. That *no* emission of a particular pollutant might be better than any positive level can reasonably be considered as a possibility, but economists would not start out expecting that conclusion, but rather the one that less of it but still some amount was desirable.

Why, then, do we observe prohibitions? One answer might be that the political process does not lend itself to the nice calculation of marginal cost and benefit. Another is that, in their collective political decision-making, people do not naturally think as 'marginalists'. Something is either 'legal' or it is 'illegal' and politics is about deciding which is which.[2] In a common-law system where, in principle, all is permitted that is not forbidden, the whole business of legislation could be argued to be 'skewed' towards prohibiting things. In contrast, a system in which all was forbidden that had not been explicitly permitted would result in legislation entirely concerned with removing prohibitions. There is a sense in which it is only under the former system that 'explaining' a prohibition is an interesting problem since under the latter system it is, by assumption, simply the status quo.

---

2   There is a strong tendency on the part of both the judiciary and legislators to see things in these simplistic terms. There are in fact many alternatives to this approach towards achieving behavioural change. See, for example, Veljanovski (2006) and Becker (1976: ch. 4).

In the rest of this chapter we will be considering prohibitions under a number of different headings in order to clarify both the circumstances in which prohibitions might receive some support from economic theory and those in which they are objectionable.

The apparently 'prohibition-free' world implied by our opening remarks derives from a number of important assumptions – in particular, the sanctity of individual preferences and the security and zero-cost exchangeability of a complete set of property rights in all scarce goods and scarce resources. Even under such 'idealised' circumstances, however, the existence of some 'prohibitions' is implied – those prohibitions that buttress the claims of property and support the operation of market processes. These prohibitions are discussed below.

Prohibitions are also frequently defended by those who question either the individualism of economic theory, or the feasibility of establishing tradable rights to all resources, or both. We will discuss this set of issues under the subheadings of preferences, paternalism, pollution and policing.

Market process

The oldest and most universal prohibitions against killing, stealing, bearing false witness, coveting other people's possessions and so forth are concerned with the governance of one person's dealings with another. No one can have property in his or her person or in a physical asset if others do not assent – at least to the extent of not challenging the property claim using force. Thus, the market system is itself dependent upon the institutions of property and the rules of fair dealing. The more that people are prepared to 'love their neighbours as themselves' and to treat others as they themselves would wish to be treated, the fewer resources will be devoted to war and theft and the more to forging mutually advantageous agreements. Further, while laws would exist, the costs of litigation would be low simply because it would seldom be resorted to. In addition, modern 'institutional' economists have emphasised that the inculcation of a sense of 'guilt' in a group of people concerning infringements of property or failure to abide by agreements is highly efficient because it leads to compliance and rule-governed behaviour even in the absence of monitoring and policing mechanisms.

Markets may be said, therefore, to depend upon widespread acceptance of the 'rules of the game' and (by implication) prohibitions on infringing them. These prohibitions are entirely about methods of proceeding – such as banning the use of force or fraud. They are not about banning the particular ends that transactors might have in mind in their market activities. Most modern prohibitions, however, are about stopping certain activities (even if undertaken voluntarily). The era of 'prohibition' in the United States, for example, was specifically about the attempt to outlaw trade in alcohol during the 1920s.

Preferences

Prohibitions in the areas of drugs, alcohol or gambling are sometimes rationalised on the basis of the 'addictive' properties of these activities. Economists analyse consumer behaviour on the assumption that preferences are 'well behaved' – by which they mean that a person's willingness to pay for more of any good (what economists would call the individual's 'marginal willingness') declines as his or her consumption of it increases. This assumption accords with the common observation that people generally buy a whole range of goods and services. If the marginal willingness to pay for a good actually *increased* as consumption levels rose then any consumer willing to pay more than the prevailing price for the first unit would find their willingness to pay for succeeding units remained higher than the market price and consumption would rise until the person's budget was exhausted on that one good.[3] Although a determined libertarian might still argue that such 'badly behaved' preferences are still a person's preferences and should not be used to justify

---

3 Economists call such preferences non-convex – if the preferences satisfy that mathematical property then they lead to specialisation in consumption.

prohibitions and coercive state intervention, a more common view is that these preferences are in some sense distorted – a kind of infection from which the person requires protection in order to pursue their 'true' interests.

Unless one takes the libertarian position, for alcoholics and others susceptible to addiction it is undoubtedly true that zero consumption (a privately imposed prohibition) is the best solution.[4] Where some people can undertake the same activities without such ill effects, however, state-imposed prohibitions on these activities impose costs on one set of people in the interests of another. The conventional approach of the economist would then be to ask whether the 'gainers' from a prohibition could potentially compensate the 'losers' – always assuming that everyone actually knew where they stood. In a world in which no one knew whether or not they would be susceptible to various addictions we would have to imagine a situation in which each person was assumed to know the probability of being afflicted in this way and to use their 'true' preferences to evaluate the expected costs and benefits of a state-enforced prohibition. Severely adverse consequences and a high level of risk aversion, for example, might favour a prohibition, especially if the net benefits of the addictive good to the non-addicted were small.

It will be objected by the libertarian that it is always open to someone not to risk consuming potentially addictive goods and that people for whom the expected certainty-equivalent value of using them is negative will avoid them. Those who are not risk averse or who think the probability of addiction is very low might choose to take the risk. There is thus no reason why a state-enforced prohibition is justified – any more than (say) prohibiting the climbing of mountains. A public prohibition in a world of full information and 'private' addictive goods cannot improve

---

4   Some economists have argued to the contrary, suggesting that addiction can be a rational choice. People get addicted not only to drugs and so forth, but also to, for example, music, work and eating. Thus it can be maintained that much behaviour would have to be excluded from a theory of rational choice if that theory excluded addiction. See Becker and Murphy (1988).

on individual choice. The case for a prohibition must ultimately involve a degree of paternalism (an assertion that people do not understand where their own 'true' interests lie – even before succumbing to addiction); an implicit claim that people are not well informed about consequences or probabilities; or an assertion that the costs of addiction are not truly 'private'. These matters are discussed in the following sections.[5]

Even where people *do* understand their long-run interests, however, and are well informed about the possible adverse consequences of an addictive private good, a case can be made for a prohibition. Just as a person who requires a painful operation in a dire emergency might instruct his surgeons to ignore any pain-induced appeals to desist out of a rational fear of his or her own human weakness, so people might support prohibitions in order to supplement their own too-feeble reserves of self-control. Something similar seems to have been involved in the somewhat subdued public opposition to the prohibition of smoking in pubs. Many non-smokers were opposed to this infringement of the right of any Englishman to smoke himself to death in public if he so wished. But in contrast, many of the mortuary-bound smokers seem to have welcomed the chance to kick the habit at last, free of the influence of peer pressure and the temptation of the pub's cigarette vending machine.

Paternalism

To favour some external buttress to unaided individual willpower is not paternalism. Paternalism implies substituting an outside set of choices for those made by the individual. For example, performing a painful operation forcibly against a person's expressed preference to die rather than undergo such an ordeal would be paternalistic. Many prohibitions are justified on grounds of paternalism, and it is here that the conflict

---

5   We do not discuss here the reasons given at the time for the introduction of prohibition in the USA. The interested reader will find information on these in Chapter 12 in the present collection. It is worth remarking that the distinguished economist Irving Fisher favoured this particular prohibition.

with standard economic thinking is most obvious. Regulations prohibiting child labour or restricting hours of work, for example, are not based upon the addictive nature of work but on the premise that certain people cannot unaided be expected to judge correctly their own welfare. In the case of children, the protection implied may be from the influence of their parents or from other adults prepared harmfully to take advantage of a child's relative ignorance, inexperience or the lack of ability to act on their own decisions, however wise these decisions may be. In the case of adults, the justification for such 'protection' is more likely to emphasise supposed market imperfections that derive from the use of market power on the buyer's side of the market.

Prohibitions introduced in the name of safety are often founded on paternalistic motives. Regulations prohibit particular 'unsafe' technologies and require the use of 'safe' ones. Individual choice and market processes are assumed to lead to undesirably high levels of risk-taking. Those of us who become dizzy merely watching old black-and-white footage of workers eating lunch sitting apparently unsecured on girders suspended high over a New York street during the construction of the Empire State Building are apt to conclude that there might be some truth in this. But people with vertigo are probably not the best qualified to assess the risks for people who are free of this affliction.

Where prohibitions are defended on the grounds that they protect people against the consequences of their ignorance, the natural response is to argue that the alternative to prohibitions is to promulgate information, dispel ignorance and thus allow the market to price risk more accurately. Some aspects of conventional economic theory have given rise to apparently powerful 'public good' arguments in favour of some state involvement in information collection and dissemination. The argument essentially is that no individual would collect and disseminate such information because they would get no benefit from doing so, or at least insufficient to compensate them for their efforts, since once the information is available to one it is available to all. These arguments should be approached with caution.

It would obviously not be correct to assume that agencies of the state are always better informed than private individuals – especially when knowledge of local circumstances and specialised activities is involved. Some types of information concerning risk, however, might plausibly remain uncollected and unpublished without some public intervention, and free market liberal economists have given support to the state's gathering and disseminating this type of information. For our purposes here, however, the important point is to note that, once more, standard economics recommends addressing and treating a posited 'market failure' in the provision of information. It does not recommend prohibitions. Something else is required before any form of 'market failure' can be used to justify such a draconian policy.

One reason why policy does not always stop at providing information is, once again, paternalism. A policy of giving people information will not work, even if the information is pertinent and accurate, if they cannot interpret it. Psychologists might doubt, for example, that individual consumers could consistently interpret information on the differences in the probability of death or serious injury per mile travelled or per journey undertaken for different transport modes and different companies. They might question the ability of consumers to make use of information about life expectancy and health to induce 'appropriate' savings decisions and might expect people to adopt a rate of time preference that is 'too high' and which leads to an unduly short time horizon. In other words, individuals might in their current decisions pay too little heed to the future consequences of their decisions, in the sense that once they were in the future they might wish that they had taken a different decision in the past. Paternalism can thus infiltrate all aspects of a person's choices. It can dismiss the person's preferences as 'irrational'; it can deny that the person has adequate knowledge and understanding of the constraints that he or she faces; and it can question the ability of a person to calculate the 'best' course of action in the face of great complexity.[6]

---

6   This last instance is sometimes referred to as the problem of 'bounded rationality'.

As we have pointed out, all these paternalistic arguments run counter to the standard and widely accepted assumptions of economics, but they constitute an important part of the usual case for prohibitions. If making decisions is itself extremely costly and if the state has information that reveals the irrationality of acting in a particular way for almost any set of 'well behaved' preferences – why not prohibit the activity? Why not ground an airline or prohibit the use of a drug rather than simply rely on publishing information about accident rates or allergic reactions and so forth?

To state the question in this way is, of course, to suggest the answer. How often can we really rely on the state having such conclusive information? How likely is it that there is no one who, for various personal reasons, finds it perfectly rational to fly on a dangerous airline or to take a chance (perhaps their last chance) with an experimental drug? Whatever the information available to the state there will always be plenty that it does not have, and much local information that they consider very relevant to their own predicament will be available to particular people. Any prohibition introduced to protect one class of people from making a 'mistake' and acting against their interests will simultaneously prevent another class from taking advantage of their greater local knowledge to improve their own welfare. In the nature of things it is impossible to know in advance whether the gains outweigh the losses, for that requires comparing the value of information that is known to information that is (at the time of introducing the prohibition) unknown. In other words, all such prohibitions imply either a pretence to universal knowledge or a gamble that all the information unknown to the state would not, were it to be revealed, show the prohibition to be irrational. As regards the objection that no policy can take account of knowledge that is unavailable, it is important to realise that 'unavailable' does not mean non-existent. Rather it means the class of tacit knowledge and local knowledge that is costly, or by definition impossible, to convey to the state. To make policy decisions on the basis that all such knowledge is unimportant because unavailable is precisely the mistake made by defenders of state power and state planning in the debates of the mid-twentieth century.

In the case of 'private' goods or 'bads', therefore, prohibitions can be explained on economic grounds only with some difficulty. Severely addictive goods present problems and might conceivably justify a prohibition on paternalistic grounds. Justifications based upon the protection of people from their own ignorance are much less secure because the information available to governments can be communicated at reasonably low cost to others, and a prohibition prevents an individual valuing and using the local information at his or her disposal.

Pollution

Many prohibitions are introduced to cope not with failures of private choice over private goods but with problems of public 'bads'. Conventional economics recognises that all affected agents should be party to an agreement if economic efficiency is to be achieved. In the case of 'private' goods agreements simply concern a willing buyer and a willing seller and there are no 'external' costs that spill over and affect others. If, however, there are agents 'external' to a contract who are adversely affected and who remain uncompensated, the offending activity will be carried on to an extent that is inefficient when the wellbeing of all those affected is taken into account.

An interesting and from time to time topical example of this problem emerges from the existence of the National Health Service (NHS). Consider the following two examples. It has been claimed that illnesses and injuries caused by alcohol abuse (somehow defined) cost the NHS some £3 billion per annum.[7] More recently, in January 2007, the British Medical Association (BMA) said that the gaming industry should pay £10 million per annum to the Responsibility in Gambling Trust to deal

---

7   BBC News website, 'Alcohol illness "may cripple NHS"', 28 February 2002, http://news.bbc.co.uk/1/hi/uk/1846589.stm.

with something they term 'problem gambling'.[8] These figures are not only imprecise but the methods by which they have been derived would allow for other quite different numbers to be produced. Nevertheless, the difficulty they raise is a genuine one. While such difficulties are a flaw in the NHS (people may be more inclined to self-harm if they believe the NHS will cover the costs), liberalisation could be expensive without NHS reform to require all or most of the cost of treating self-inflicted illnesses to fall on the patient or his or her estate.

Two kinds of response have been proposed to this problem of external cost. The cost can be 'internalised' by imposing taxes or other methods of charging a price so as to represent the marginal damage inflicted by an activity.[9] This requires the state to have a great deal of knowledge of the external costs incurred, and also the administrative resources to set up the mechanisms necessary to confront polluters with the external costs of their actions. Alternatively, the cost can be 'internalised' by ensuring that adversely affected people are drawn into the process of contracting. By introducing 'property' in peace and quiet, unpolluted air, road space, segments of the electromagnetic spectrum, flowing watercourses and so forth, costly aspects of an activity can no longer be offloaded on to others without compensation (i.e. without eliciting their agreement). This requires that property rights can be defined and enforced and that the costs of negotiating agreements (transactions costs) are sufficiently low to let the transactions take place. The 'taxing' tradition is associated with A. C. Pigou (1924), the 'property rights' one with Ronald Coase (1960).

Once more we note that prohibitions do not arise easily out of either tradition. If an activity completely disappears it will either be because it has been 'priced out of the market' – no one is prepared to pay for the government-estimated social damage inflicted – or because the assent of all the parties cannot be achieved, and the level of 'damages' imposed by the courts for the contravention of property rights is expected to be too

---

8   BMA website, www.bma.org.uk/ap.nsf/Content/Gamblingbrief.
9   The NHS reform just described is an example of such internalisation.

onerous to warrant proceeding. By using a 'price' to suppress an activity the government does not have to pretend to know all the circumstances in which it might or might not be worth paying. Similarly, by introducing tradable property rights, valuations are revealed through the process of negotiation and exchange rather than being estimated centrally on the basis of highly incomplete information.

Prohibitions have been introduced in environmental policy, however, and sometimes a consensus emerges that the prohibition has been successful and socially optimal. A good example of such a consensus is the Clean Air Act (1956) in the UK, which prohibited the burning of coal in domestic hearths in certain 'smokeless zones', and thereby transformed for the better the environment in London and other cities. Death rates from respiratory diseases fell sharply as particulate matter in the air was reduced and 'smog' no longer formed. Another 'success story' followed the phased banning of chlorofluorocarbons (CFCs) – chemicals used widely as aerosol propellants and in refrigerators – in the Montreal Protocol of 1987. These chemicals when exposed to the air reacted readily with stratospheric ozone and thus gave rise to 'ozone depletion' with the associated danger of exposing the population to greater levels of radiation from the sun. Recent research has indicated that the policy has been successful in halting and to some extent reversing this process.

A 'Pigou-based' policy in these areas would have recommended a tax on particulate emissions from domestic hearths equal to the marginal external damage inflicted and a similar tax on the use of CFCs. The alternative of establishing clearer rights to air quality and relying on tort law to control emissions (the 'Coasian approach') would have foundered on the problem of transactions costs – including bargaining costs and the costs of litigation and enforcement. These costs would of course be even more prohibitive in the context of a 'global' problem such as stratospheric ozone depletion where intergovernmental negotiation to control CFCs seems to have been the only practicable option. The complete phasing out of certain harmful activities by direct intervention in processes of production or consumption can therefore occasionally be justified. For such prohibitions to work, however, there must be suitable initial conditions.

In the case of both coal fires and CFCs there existed known close substitutes. Householders in the UK were expected to burn coke or other 'smokeless' fuels and manufacturers of refrigerators to use other known chemicals to fulfil the same functions as CFCs. Although not costless, the use of substitutes imposed only minor additional burdens on households or manufacturers, while the social benefits of both prohibitions were believed to be substantial and widely understood. While it is still true that a tax might have carried some theoretical advantages – some activities might have been entirely suppressed under a prohibition that otherwise would have been prepared to compensate for the external costs imposed on others – such advantages could have been gained only by requiring the measurement of household emissions and the introduction of a tax-levying bureaucracy.

If it is known that social efficiency requires a very large percentage cut in emissions, the administrative costs of implementing a Pigouvian tax might outweigh any benefits that in the absence of such costs it might have over a complete prohibition. Prohibitions also require enforcement, of course, but the technology of enforcement is important. Once the emission of smoke was prohibited, for example, it was a relatively easy job to police the ban. Smoke was easily visible and was, in itself, a contravention of the prohibition. Checking whether meters had been installed and taxes paid would have added a whole raft of additional complexity and public expense.

It is thus occasionally possible to construct a Coasian argument for a prohibition. Such an argument will always imply an assertion of knowledge on the part of the government, but that is true of virtually any intervention. Just as Coase rationalises 'the firm' as the substitution of 'internal organisation' for 'market contract', so state action can be seen in a similar light. Where the use of decentralised market processes such as price signals and individual negotiations is very costly, a more 'managed' and interventionist process of resource allocation can be justified. It is well known that entrepreneurs wishing to introduce new ideas and to expedite change find they have to forge vertically integrated enterprises to enforce their will rather than negotiate endlessly with uncomprehending suppliers. A government recognising the social advantages available from a proposed change and wishing to move rapidly might similarly prefer direct instructions ('do not emit smoke, burn smokeless fuel') to market incentives.

The dangers implicit in the argument sketched above are, however, substantial. Competitive forces punish entrepreneurs who overestimate their organisational capacities, whereas any self-correcting mechanisms in the case of state action are far weaker. Further, the very idea that the government might have access to information sufficient to warrant direct intervention in the form of prohibitions is considered by many people to be improbable. Far from having access to better information than other organisations, governments have long been recognised as being subject, as Adam Smith (1776 [1925]: vol. II, p. 184) expressed it, to 'innumerable delusions'. The delusion that they are well informed is probably one of the most endemic problems of all governments. But to rule out the possibility that a government might gain access to information of crucial importance to the future welfare of the population, information that might require action in the form of prohibitions, would be to deny entirely one of the traditional justifications for the existence of the state. The sovereign, as Thomas Hobbes (1651 [1968]: 239) put it, has the role of using his 'prospective glasses' on behalf of a short-sighted population 'to see a farre off the miseries that hang over them'. Like two stags, the 'public choice' approach to government action is locked in a head-to-head tussle with the 'public interest' approach, with neither having an unchallenged advantage.

Policing and enforcement

Any attempt to modify human behaviour will require enforcement. Prohibitions are not, therefore, unique in this respect. The use of taxes, for example, can be undermined by evasion, just as prohibitions can result in non-compliance or 'civil disobedience'. Prohibitions seem historically to have given rise to particularly intractable problems with respect to enforcement, however. The most obvious examples are prohibitions in the areas of alcohol and drugs. Where matters of 'private' behaviour are concerned, prohibitions simply increase the 'price' at which the prohibited activity can be purchased to compensate for the perceived risks of criminal detection, prosecution and punishment. Whereas the proceeds of a tax would be received by the government, the proceeds of the higher prices induced by prohibition are received (net of fines) by criminals, with all the accompanying social disadvantages that this implies.[10] Where addictive substances are involved, the dynamics of the situation are notably adverse, since rising prices will reduce the quantity demanded only through the operation of income effects (impoverishing the addict) and not at all through substitution effects. Only the most draconian policies to assist the detection of criminals and the most brutal punishment of offenders are likely substantially to suppress a prohibited 'private' good.

Prohibitions are enforced by agents of the state. This greatly reduces total policing effort. Only a very weak 'private' interest on the part of individual animal lovers or environmentalists (perhaps mediated through charitable organisations) would in the presence of prohibitions be mobilised, for example, to police a ban on shooting elephants or tigers. One of the great advantages of Coasian responses to problems of pollution or the depletion of 'the commons' is that by creating privately assigned property rights, an incentive is created for all the holders of these rights to protect and enforce them by reporting infringements and by using all the resources of the civil law of property, tort and contract.

---

10   It may be maintained that the prohibition creates the criminals. But there have to be qualifications to this. Prohibition of alcohol, for example, encouraged those who were already infringing some laws to go into the alcohol supplying business, as well as criminalising previously consensual and mutually beneficial activity.

Conclusion

The argument of this paper can be summarised in the form of a simple application of a well-known result in 'Law and Economics' (Calabresi and Melamed, 1972). Where transactions costs are low, a court of law adjudicating on a civil dispute should simply grant an injunction (thereby confirming a property right) and allow private bargaining to resolve the dispute. If transactions costs to the litigators are high and information costs to the court are low, the preferred action is to rely on a liability rule to protect entitlements and impose compensatory damages, assuming that the complaint is upheld and a property right has been infringed. By extension, where a public harm is pervasive and transactions costs render the civil courts powerless to adjudicate, the use of Pigouvian tax mechanisms to put a price on the social damage inflicted by an activity is suggested. Complete prohibition of an activity is likely to be efficient only in the rare circumstances where transactions costs are high, information costs to the government are low, the efficient level of the activity is zero or close to zero, and policing costs are also low.

Nevertheless, prohibiting exchange (the establishment of inalienable property rights) can be efficient in certain circumstances. For example, the sale of land to a polluter will greatly reduce the value of many other people's property. As Calabresi and Melamed (ibid.: 1111) express it, 'Where there are so many injured Marshalls [read 'people'] that the price required [to induce injured parties to allow the activity] under the liability rule is likely to be high enough so that no one would be willing to pay it, then setting up the machinery for collective valuation will be wasteful. Barring the sale to polluters will be the most efficient result ...'[11] Low policing costs might derive from the fact that the number of potential polluters is small and each is known to the government. Alterna-

---

11 An anonymous referee has pointed out that liability rules will also be relevant to the analysis of the provision of 'self-harming' goods and not just to the case of activities causing external harm. If suppliers of harmful drugs are held legally liable, transactions costs arguments of the type rehearsed here could be deployed to make the case for a ban. Conversely, attempts at liberalisation might be frustrated by liability rules.

tively, low policing costs might derive from high public acceptance (the prohibition imposes a relatively small cost on each person in exchange for a significant perceived benefit). Policing costs fall further if the ability to observe non-compliance enables 'peer pressure' to be used to assist the prohibition.

References

Becker, G. S. (1976), *The Economic Approach to Human Behaviour*, Chicago, IL: University of Chicago Press.

Becker, G. S. and K. M. Murphy (1988), 'A theory of rational addiction', *Journal of Political Economy*, 96(4): 675–700.

Calabresi, G. and A. D. Melamed (1972), 'Property rules, liability rules and inalienability: one view of the cathedral', *Harvard Law Review*, 85(6): 1089–128.

Coase, R. (1960), 'The problem of social cost', *Journal of Law and Economics*, 3: 1–44.

Hobbes, T. (1651 [1968]), *Leviathan*, ed. C. B. Macpherson, London: Pelican Classics.

Pigou, A. C. (1924), *The Economics of Welfare*, London: Macmillan.

Smith, A. (1776 [1925]), *An Inquiry into the Nature and Causes of the Wealth of Nations*, ed. E. Cannan, London: Methuen.

Veljanovski, C. (2006), *The Economics of Law*, London: Institute of Economic Affairs.

3 RECREATIONAL DRUGS
Mark Thornton and Simon W. Bowmaker

Introduction

On the whole, economists have tended to be against prohibition of recreational drugs, dating back to the days of the ban on alcohol in the USA. Tullock and McKenzie (1985: 7) state that:

> In the early part of this century, many well-intentioned Americans objected to the consumption of alcoholic beverages. They succeeded in getting the Constitution amended to prohibit the sale of alcohol. By the 1930s most of them had given up because they discovered how difficult it was to enforce the law. If they had consulted economists, I'm sure they would have been told that the law would be very difficult and expensive to enforce. With this advice they might have decided not to undertake the program of moral elevation. The same considerations should, of course, be taken into account now with respect to other drugs.

There have been exceptions, however. Irving Fisher, one of the USA's greatest ever mathematical economists, was a leading proponent of alcohol prohibition. As late as 1927, Fisher claimed he could not find one economist to speak out against prohibition at a meeting of the American Economic Association, and in *The Noble Experiment*, published in 1930, Fisher clearly remained a strong believer in the virtues of alcohol prohibition:

> Summing up, it may be said that Prohibition has already accomplished incalculable good, hygienically, economically and socially. Real personal liberty, the liberty to give and enjoy the full use of our faculties, is increased by Prohibition. All that the wets

can possibly accomplish is laxity of enforcement or nullification: in other words, enormously to increase the very disrespect for the law which they profess to deplore. Hence the only satisfactory solution lies in fuller enforcement of the law. (Fisher, 1930: 454–5)

More recently, Thornton (1995, 2004) reports that in relation to illicit drugs the majority of economists (in the USA at least) are relatively anti-prohibition. He reports the findings of a survey he conducted in 1995 of 117 randomly selected professional economists based on membership of the American Economic Association. Of those who offered an opinion, 58 per cent were in favour of drug policy in the USA being steered towards decriminalisation of drugs. Only 16 per cent favoured complete legalisation, while 71 per cent of those who gave a response other than keeping the status quo favoured either legalisation or decriminalisation. Less than 2 per cent supported stronger prohibition other than longer prison sentences and increased enforcement budgets.

In a separate survey conducted in 2004, Thornton solicited the views of US economists actively engaged in drug policy research. Three general conclusions emerged. First, most argued that the current policy of prohibition in the USA is fairly ineffective, very ineffective or even harmful. Second, most agreed that the current policy stance ought to be shifted. Third, most believed that this shift ought to be in the direction of liberalisation. A source of disagreement, however, centred on the degree of liberalisation.

In light of the above, the principal purpose of this chapter is to provide an analysis of the costs and benefits of prohibition and an evaluation of the likely outcomes of drug legalisation. To set the scene, we begin with an overview of the history of recreational drug prohibition.

A brief history of recreational drug prohibition

Drugs such as cannabis (marijuana), cocaine and opium have been consumed ceremonially, medicinally and recreationally for thousands of years.¹ Prior to widespread prohibition the biggest political development with drugs was the British government's encouragement of opium use in China under the auspices of the British East India Company. In the eighteenth century the company controlled the opium-producing areas in India and had a dominant position in the trade of Indian opium into China. The profits helped subsidise British control of India and kept exports to China balanced with imports.

In the late 1830s the British government started the First Opium War by sending a naval expedition that easily defeated Chinese forces, opened up Chinese ports to British trade and won monetary compensation and Hong Kong as a British colony from China. The Second Opium War began in 1856 when Britain, France, Russia and the USA attacked China in order to gain increased access to Chinese markets and to legalise opium in China. The Emperor was forced to pay the British government £20,000, which was, according to Abadinsky (2001: 29), 'more than enough to offset the balance of trade which was the real cause of the war'.

While these events took place on the other side of the world they would have effects across the globe. The East India Company also brought opium back to Britain, while Chinese immigrants brought the habit of opium use to the USA. This would provoke local regulations and restrictions in the USA and UK during the second half of the nineteenth century and the early twentieth century. The Chinese opium trade was also the focus of the International Opium Commission, which convened in Shanghai, China, in 1909. The USA initiated the Commission to push its prohibitionist agenda, which would become the hallmark of future international drug conferences.

The growth of global prohibition

As late as 1894 the Royal Commission on Opium and the Indian Hemp

---

1   For a more detailed introduction to the history of drug use and laws, see Abadinsky (2001: ch. 2).

Commission reported that regular use of opium and marijuana was not harmful, and Brecher (1972) reports that drug use in the USA was not associated with the socially destructive outcomes that have often been experienced in the second half of the twentieth century. The global prohibition of drugs grew on a framework of international agreements that were primarily instigated by the USA.[2] Musto (1973 [1987]) dubbed the cause of narcotic prohibition 'the American disease' and showed that this instinct to prohibit is a faulty ideological notion within the dominant ideological group.[3]

The first Opium Conference met in The Hague, Netherlands, in 1911. The meeting was contentious in that the USA pushed for strong prohibitory measures even though it had no such domestic laws of its own, while other nations sought to protect their interests in the opium trade or opium production. The second Opium Conference at The Hague – on the eve of World War I – produced a patchwork agreement referred to as the International Opium Convention, which committed the signatory nations to pass and enforce laws that would reduce abuse of narcotic drugs. This would become the foundation of global narcotics prohibition because it was incorporated into the Versailles Treaty as Article 295 and thus committed all the signatory nations of the World War I peace document to implement all of its anti-narcotic measures.

In 1914 the USA passed the Harrison Narcotics Act, which avoided constitutional restrictions on the police powers of the central government by regulating narcotics via its taxation power. All doctors were required to register and to keep detailed records of narcotics prescriptions and to pay a $1 annual tax. This 'tax' soon developed into a de facto prohibition as addicts and doctors were arrested for engaging in addiction maintenance, drug addiction clinics were closed and the black market developed.

2   For a short overview of the UN Drug Control Conventions and institutions see the United Nation's *World Drug Report* (1997: 168–80).
3   For a good overview of the history and development of American drug policy legislation, see Musto (1987).

In 1914 the UK enacted emergency legislation known as the Defence of the Realm Act at the outbreak of World War I. This legislation gave the British government the power to regulate people's 'morality' by proclamation rather than via parliamentary legislation. In 1916 the Defence of the Realm Act (Ordinance 40b) established strict controls over the sale and possession of cocaine and opium and mandatory closing times for pubs. In 1920 the Dangerous Drugs Act brought the UK into compliance with the Hague International Opium Convention by placing severe restrictions on cocaine, heroin, morphine and opium. In the early 1920s the UK followed the USA's lead by criminalising doctors who prescribed addiction maintenance for their patients.

The Harrison Narcotics Act was clearly a violation of the 'spirit' of the US Constitution, while in the UK drug prohibition was an emergency wartime measure. In neither case was it the result of widespread public outcry against drugs and in neither case was it subjected to detailed public debate. Rather, narcotics prohibition was mandated globally by the hastily conceived conference at The Hague on the eve of World War I and by a minor article in the tragically conceived Versailles Treaty.

While the USA continued to press a puritanical line on heroin, however, the UK reversed course in the mid-1920s to re-establish medically supervised addiction maintenance programmes based on the Rolleston Committee report, and ushered in the 'British System' of addiction treatment which was made law in 1932 and lasted until the 1960s.[4]

The USA passed the infamous Constitutional Amendment to prohibit alcohol consumption that went into effect in 1920. Promoted as the most important social reform in history, it was actually a colossal failure in terms of consumption, health, crime, violence and corruption (Thornton, 1991b). When the Great Depression finally hit, Americans

---

4   For a good overview of British drug policy see Turner (1991), who shows the 'pragmatic incoherence' of the British system and that its social and medical aspects were actually built on the pre-existing private sector charitable systems such as that of the Salvation Army.

realised that alcohol prohibition was also a public finance disaster and repealed it, beginning in 1933 (Thornton and Weise, 2001).

The UK added cannabis to its Dangerous Drugs Act in 1928, while the USA passed the Marijuana Tax Act in 1937. The Tax Act was designed to circumvent constitutional scrutiny by placing a $100 tax per ounce of marijuana (approximately $1,400 or £750 in 2005) and was therefore a very lightly veiled prohibition. At the time, marijuana use was not a major issue, nor was there any extensive public debate in either country.

After World War II the USA continued to pass more punitive anti-drug legislation. The Boggs Act of 1951 increased penalties for drug violations, and in 1956 the Narcotics Control Act increased penalties to draconian levels. In 1961 the UN consolidated all the previous international agreements under the United Nations Single Convention, which obligated member nations to bring their local laws into compliance with its regulations on over one hundred drugs. While it appeared to bring order at the international level, the USA turned more to drug treatment (Narcotic Addict Rehabilitation Act of 1966), while the UK began dismantling the British System by eliminating the use of heroin, cocaine and dipipanone for the treatment of addiction and substituting methadone clinics under the Dangerous Drugs Act of 1967.

The War on Drugs was launched with the USA's Comprehensive Drug Abuse Prevention and Control Act of 1970, the UK's Misuse of Drugs Act of 1971 and the UN's 1971 Convention on Psychotropic Substances. The US legislation was a multi-pronged attack, but notably removed constitutional restrictions on federal drug law enforcement, while in the UK the Home Secretary was given direct authority to add new drugs and to upgrade drugs to higher penalty levels. The new UN Convention expanded the list of restricted drugs to include synthetic drugs, including amphetamines, barbiturates and hallucinogens. More recently, in the UK the declassification of marijuana from a Class B drug to a Class C drug took effect in 2004 and represented the first major change to UK drug policy since the 1971 Act. Under the new law, possession of marijuana remains illegal but will ordinarily not be an arrestable offence.

Drug policy has continued to evolve and to recycle failed policies. This gradual ratcheting up of prohibition over the twentieth century has been fuelled by optimism unguided by reason or memory. The UN even committed itself in 1998 to a drug-free world by 2008. While the USA is sticking with prohibition, there are indications that policy may have begun to ratchet downward at the UN, in the UK and in many other countries, particularly in Europe, away from prohibition in the direction of the 'Dutch Experience', where harm reduction policies are given greater emphasis. The Netherlands has nominal prohibition against all drugs but it is targeted primarily against the largest dealers of the most dangerous drugs. Consumers are not prosecuted and the problems of drug abuse are addressed socially and medically, not criminally. The results in terms of drug use, drug abuse, health, crime and violence have been relatively good (Engelsman, 1991).

The costs and benefits of prohibition

A cost–benefit analysis of past events is difficult because not everything has a tangible monetary value, such as a human life, and even when economists make a good-faith effort to provide such numbers, they will naturally be viewed with scepticism.

Analysing the future is even more difficult because of inherent uncertainty, and there have been gigantic miscalculations, such as the Tennessee Tombigbee Waterway project in the USA, which famously underestimated costs and overestimated benefits, as did the Channel Tunnel scheme in Europe. The 'Big Ditch' in Boston, another transportation project, is now $12 billion (£6.5 billion), or nearly 500 per cent, over budget.

A traditional cost–benefit analysis of prohibition versus legalisation would go as follows: prohibition raises the price of good X by 100 per cent and would reduce consumption by 50 per cent. If consumption is 50 per cent lower, then all health and social problems associated with good X will be improved by 50 per cent. Next multiply the number of lives saved by one monetary amount and the number of lives helped by another monetary amount. Then compare these combined figures with the amount spent on prohibition. This process is not unreasonable when applied to small changes within the market economy, such as an increase in the sugar tariff. With prohibition, however, you cannot assume *ceteris paribus* conditions, because with prohibition everything about the recreational drug market changes radically. Fortunately the economist can ask what the *opportunity cost* is – what do we give up when we allocate these resources to prohibition?

The high indirect costs of prohibition

The opportunity cost could be any government service or tax cut that we sacrifice for drug prohibition. If we begin with the status quo and allocate some of the law enforcement budget to enforcing drug prohibitions, what will happen to crime? With fewer police officers safeguarding property and tracking non-drug criminals, the commission of crimes will be easier and more crimes will be committed. If you increase the law enforcement budget, you will apprehend a larger number of criminals, but that would overextend prison resources (and the court system) and prisoners would have to be given early releases from their sentences. If non-drug criminals are released early, then the cost of crime decreases and that would, *ceteris paribus*, result in an even higher rate of crime. You could also expand prison capacity, but that not only increases the direct cost of prohibition, it also increases the opportunity cost because the labour force is reduced and once in prison drug offenders and their families face large permanent decreases in their future economic outcomes. One of the primary goals of prohibition is strong independent families, but the result is just the opposite.[5]

Another important opportunity cost of prohibition can be gleaned from the black market because with prohibition we lose all the legal

---

5   See Benson et al. (2001) for a discussion of and evidence on most of these issues.

and competitive safeguards that an open market provides. McDonald's would be crippled or bankrupt if it sold even a small number of deadly hamburgers. Toyota does not sell cars to minors and it certainly would not sell cocaine or heroin to minors. These constraints do not exist in black markets, and unlike pharmaceutical companies, coffee manufacturers and distilleries, consumers of illegal recreational drugs have little idea of the strength or potency of the products they are buying. In fact the more prohibition has been enforced the more potent and dangerous drugs have become and the more dangerous substitutes have come on to the black market (Thornton, 1998). Any reduction in the quantity of illegal recreational drugs is easily offset by the higher potency and the significant increase in health risks. Some consumers may simply switch to legal substitutes such as whisky, prescription painkillers and sniffing volatile solvents.[6] The overall increase in health risk is an opportunity cost that is counterproductive to a primary goal of prohibition, which is to reduce health risks in society. The spread of AIDS via 'dirty' hypodermic needles would also fit into this category.

Political corruption is another cost of prohibition. Prohibition drives up the cost of illegal recreational drugs, with more enforcement resulting in higher prices. The 'wedge' that prohibition drives between the cost of production and the final selling price provides an incentive for illegal drug sellers to bribe law enforcement officers, judges and politicians for protection against capture, prosecution and incarceration. This was a major problem during the alcohol prohibition in the USA, as it is now with recreational drug distribution around the world, especially in countries that produce drugs, such as Afghanistan, Bolivia, Colombia, Lebanon and Mexico (see Marshall, 1991; Lupsha, 1992; Andreas, 1998). Such corruption can make legal and political systems dysfunctional and greatly weaken the economy.[7]

---

6   The UK averages more than one death per week, mostly of teenagers, from volatile solvents. The average home will contain two dozen or more of these solvents in products ranging from butane lighters, to paint thinners, to nail polish removers.

7   See Thornton (1991a) for a more detailed treatment of this issue.

This type of analysis could easily be extended to violence, addiction, organised crime, the enticement of youth into drugs, decay of the inner city and other related issues. The point is that prohibition creates profit opportunities that create 'unintended consequences' that are directly counterproductive to the goals of prohibition. In addition, prohibition prevents local governments from applying routine sanctions and regulations such as taxes, location restrictions and limits on the hours of operation. In summary, these negative effects mean that the cost of prohibition exceeds government expenditures on prohibition.

Prohibition does have benefits

Economics teaches that public policy is economically driven. Policies certainly are linked with ideologies but at some level a policy must provide some groups, classes or 'interests' with benefits, or they will not be implemented or survive in the long run. One important corollary of this view is that the survival of a public policy does not depend on the policy producing net social benefits for its survival. Thus, a sugar tariff can survive if it produces concentrated benefits for domestic sugar producers which are less than the costs imposed on the multitude of sugar consumers.

Prohibition does not eliminate the demand for recreational drugs. People who want recreational drugs have access to illegal drugs as well as legal recreational drugs and inferior substitutes such as sniffing volatile solvents. Therefore one cannot sustain a claim that consumers are beneficiaries of prohibition. A non-naive and straightforward view of the beneficiaries of prohibition (and other policies) was put forth by Bruce Yandle in his 1983 article 'Bootleggers and Baptists: the education of a regulatory economist'.[8] His model provides the explanation that it is the unlikely combination of Baptists (who oppose drinking alcohol on Sundays) and bootleggers (who sell alcohol illegally) which explains the

---

8   Yandle (1998) applies the Baptists and Bootlegger model to environmental regulation.

persistence of Sunday pub closing laws in the American South. We need only add brewers to Yandle's Baptists and bootleggers. This is not to say that all brewers support drug prohibition, or that some Baptists do not support prohibition – it is only to give three likely examples of groups that benefit from prohibition.

Baptists – generally considered – benefit from prohibition because they believe the consumption of recreational drugs is harmful and immoral. Their ideology holds that these drugs are objectively sinful and that any use of the drugs is inherently evil. Because the goods are evil, it is not good enough to personally abstain; the ideology demands that society must be cleansed of their use. Prohibition satisfies this demand and provides utility to people who believe in this point of view. This applies broadly, even to atheists who support prohibition based on the naive view that it is good for society. Pro-prohibitionist citizens support prohibitionist candidates.

The term bootleggers originally applied to those who smuggled illegal alcohol (i.e. moonshine), but it also applies to those in the recreational drug distribution business, and even those who supply other illegal products such as 'bootleg' DVDs. In contrast to Baptists and their ideological and subjective utility, bootleggers are in the recreational drug business and benefit monetarily from prohibition. Recreational drug bootleggers make up a vast global network of individuals ranging from the Colombian cocaine kingpins to the teenagers who sell drugs on city streets. How these individuals influence public policy is unclear, but we do know that they bribe law enforcement and public officials at all levels of government, especially at the level of 'organised' crime. To this we can add the influence of the criminal justice system and any organisations that benefit from greater expenditures on prohibition. This category of beneficiaries is probably of secondary importance to that of the Baptists.

Brewers and those industries that sell substitutes for illegal recreational drugs form the third example of the beneficiaries of prohibition. This would include the makers of beer, wine and distilled spirits as well as the makers of tobacco products. At the margin, prohibition will raise the prices of illegal recreational drugs and divert more sales to legal recreational drugs such as whisky and cigarettes. As with the bootlegger, the brewer's incentive is monetary, rather than ideological or subjective. We can add the pharmaceutical drug industry because prohibition drives demand from illegal recreational drugs to pharmaceutical drugs such as OxyContin, Vicodin, Valium and Ritalin. This broad category of interests is probably the least important of the three examples.

When we examine the costs and benefits of prohibition from the economic point of view, we get a much clearer picture than that provided by a traditional cost–benefit analysis. The analysis of the opportunity cost of prohibition demonstrates that we give up valuable safeguards that exist in the economy. As a result we experience more crime and corruption, and much more dangerous products, all of which are contrary to the goals of prohibition. The economic benefits are also problematic because the beneficiaries are not consumers or society as a whole, but rather the black marketeers and their legal market competitors. The Baptists get great subjective satisfaction from prohibition, but that satisfaction is illusory.

Potential outcomes of legalisation

For the remainder of the chapter, we examine the likely outcomes of an economy shifting drug policy away from prohibition towards some form of legalisation. Four alternative policies are evaluated: government monopoly, government regulation, the sin tax and the free market. In turn, each of these policies represents a spectrum of possible policy choices.

Government monopoly

One measure that is often considered a replacement policy for prohibition is to establish a government monopoly for the distribution of drugs, particularly narcotic drugs such as heroin. This approach would place the production and distribution of drugs in the hands of the state and thus provides direct control over most aspects of the marketplace. Several US states monopolise the distribution and sale of liquor, and a few also do so for wine (Benjamin and Anderson, 1996; Benson et al., 2003). Two other examples of these government monopolies are the 'market' for human organ transplants and state lotteries.

One consequence of this policy approach is that government can directly control the product. It can establish rules for production, distribution and consumption and therefore mandate the composition of the product (for example, potency), price, quantity limits and hours of operation. With human organ transplants the government prohibits the sale of organs and determines who gets those available. With state lotteries the government regulates what products can be sold, their price and the method of sale. Some state liquor monopolies control the wholesale distribution, choosing products and setting wholesale prices, while others monopolise retailing as well, thus determining the number, location, operating hours and practices of retail outlets, along with prices and which products are sold.

Government monopolies can also establish regulations concerning who is allowed to purchase and consume the product. In the area of drugs, government-run liquor stores restrict the sale of their products to adults, although the liquor is often resold by adults to minors or obtained from government stores by minors by theft or deception. Methadone clinics have a monopoly on the distribution of narcotics, but they generally provide the drug only to registered addicts. The methadone is often provided at no charge, but the addicts are required to consume the product on the premises in order to prevent resale.

The results of government monopoly vary depending on whether it is contracted out or publicly run and whether it distributes its product at high prices or gives the product away for free to predetermined consumers. State-run liquor monopolies and state lotteries generally provide diminished access, high prices, limited product selection and high levels of tax revenue to the government. Revenues typically range from 30 to 50 per cent of sales, but the high prices tend to encourage smuggling. Most importantly, restricting access by this means does little to distinguish (and punish) bad behaviour from good behaviour (Whitman, 2003).

Government regulation

Economic analysis of regulation often focuses on price regulations. While price regulations might be applied in a legalised drug market, it is much more likely that other aspects of the market would be regulated. In fact, while price constraints are often a part of government-imposed regulations in markets, regulations actually deal with many other aspects of most markets (Benson, 2003). One need only examine the markets for prescription drugs, or various alcohol markets.

Thus, there have been many reformers who have suggested that illicit drugs be made legally available but only through a regulated process whereby buyers and sellers meet certain government requirements. Kleiman (1992) argues that alcohol drinkers and marijuana smokers should pay a high tax, have a revocable licence and a limit on the amount they consume. Under his scheme, cocaine users would be registered and could receive a limited amount of cocaine from regulated distributors either at a high price or under therapeutic supervision. Tobacco users would also be registered, sellers would be licensed, quantities would be limited and heavier taxes would be imposed. Heroin prohibition would be rigidly enforced, but addicts would be registered and placed in maintenance and treatment programmes. The cost of administering Kleiman's approach would be extremely high, of course, and violations would probably be rampant, but there are alternative approaches as well.[9]

The prescription-licence approach has many variations both inside

9   See Kleiman (1992) and Thornton (1994) for a critique.

and outside of drug markets. Within 'prescription' drugs markets consumers are generally registered, licensed or given a prescription for narcotic drugs from a medical doctor or drug treatment therapist. Drugs can then be purchased from a licensed pharmacy or maintenance programme facility in limited quantities. Permission to consume could be obtained along a spectrum that runs from only for legitimate medical needs, to addiction maintenance and treatment, to any adult who the doctor determines is knowledgeable and healthy enough to consume such drugs. Drug prices can range from the highly taxed to free at government-run maintenance programmes.

Benjamin and Anderson (1996) point out that the form of alcohol control (taxation and regulation) among states in the USA is clearly a function of the cost of inducing compliance. Most states along the Canadian border where smuggling is easy employ a very different approach to alcohol control to most interior or Southern states. Similarly, alcohol control differs in the traditional 'moonshine' states in the Appalachian region, where social norms support illegal production, compared with other states.

One good example of the legalisation and regulation of an illegal market is the casino gambling industry in many US states. Here casinos are licensed, regulated and taxed. Generally, the requirements and taxes are considered normal rather than strict or lax, and the results have been quite positive.

Sin taxes

Another alternative to prohibition is to allow drugs to be sold in the market, but to impose a special tax on the product above the normal sales tax, called an excise tax. This sin tax approach is common on alcohol and tobacco products, and is also used in the case of gasoline and a variety of other products.

One potential advantage of a sin tax approach is that it is relatively politically attractive. It provides politicians with revenues, while imposing the tax allows them to continue to condemn the product. Although many of its advocates contend that the resulting revenues can and should be earmarked for enforcement, treatment or some other specific purpose, legislators will probably reduce revenues directed at such purposes from other sources as the earmarked sin tax revenues rise. Spending on the desired activity will not rise in the way that advocates intend it to.

Other shortcomings of the sin tax approach also require recognition. For instance, technically most excise taxes are paid by the seller and involve high compliance costs. In essence, enforcement costs are shifted, at least to a degree, from the public sector under prohibition, to sellers. Naturally, sellers have incentives to avoid such costs, so if they are high (and/or if the tax is so high that it dramatically reduces their sales and revenues), illegal sales will continue, much as under prohibition.

Excise tax also tends to be 'regressive' – it takes a larger percentage of income from low-income households who purchase the taxed product than from high-income households. In the political arena this may be seen as a benefit of the sin tax, in that it presumably reduces consumption more effectively among low-income groups. On the other hand, such taxes create relatively strong incentives for buyers, and particularly low-income individuals who want to consume the good, to turn to black market sources. Most sin tax advocates assume that raising taxes simply raises prices and results in reduced consumption. They fail to see that as prices rise consumers have incentives to look for substitutes and producers have incentives to supply them. One substitute for highly taxed goods is the same good sold in an illegal market.

A major problem with the sin tax approach is the difficulty in setting the tax rate. Low tax rates would have little effect on consumption, while high tax rates can spur black markets to develop in order to allow consumers to avoid the taxes. The underground production, smuggling, crime and corruption associated with prohibition therefore also occur with significant sin taxes. Becker et al. (2006) are among the minority of sin tax advocates in that they recognise that illegal markets will persist under this approach, thus necessitating continued spending on enforcement. They suggest that setting the optimal level of expected punishment for black market activities will eliminate that market.

Finally, another drawback of a sin tax approach which corresponds to a prohibition approach is that, like prohibition, taxes are targeted against consumption in general, not the external harm that some consumption may produce. For example, the tax on red wine in the USA does have the effect of reducing the consumption of red wine over the entire economy, but this reduces the health and other benefits of red wine, and yet does little to target specifically the potentially harmful effects of wine consumption, such as automobile accidents (Mast et al. 2000).

Free market

Under a free market approach, the supply of and demand for a drug would be determined solely on the basis of market forces. Competitive conditions would result in relatively low prices and diversified offerings of competitive products, while consumer sovereignty would dictate that the products that best satisfied consumers in terms of price, quality and so on would dominate the market.

We would also expect a large number of suppliers to enter the market and for most suppliers to leave the underground economy. Although it is impossible to project what a mature market would look like in terms of the precise number of firms and products, it is safe to say that most consumption would be served by commercial production, rather than by home production. Looking at other mature industries such as soft drinks, cigarettes, toothpaste, beer and over-the-counter drugs, we find that a small number of firms supply the majority of the products sold in the marketplace.

The supporters of prohibition rest much of their case on the increase in consumption that would be experienced with legalisation, but neglect to consider that legalisation would remove the costs of prohibition.

Indeed, some prohibitionists believe that all the problems related to drugs and drug prohibition, including crime and corruption, will simply get worse as a function of the (greatly) increased consumption of drugs, despite considerable evidence to the contrary.

The advocates of legalisation are often quick to emphasise all the costs of prohibition but often downplay or dismiss the increased consumption expected under legalisation. Prohibitionists suggest that once prohibition is lifted, consumption of drugs will skyrocket because of a lack of legal restriction, a significant decrease in price and the use of commercial advertising promoting their use. They feel that lower prices would increase consumption among current consumers, but more importantly legalisation would increase the number of consumers who currently abstain only because of the legal threats or the perceived morality of the law.

Overall, however, in a free market scenario, many abstainers would not consume the drugs, particularly hard ones such as heroin and cocaine, even if they were legal, because they consider the consumption of those drugs to be immoral, dangerous or repugnant. Those who refrain only because of the legal threat would probably consume the drugs responsibly for fear of running foul of other legal threats, such as driving-under-the-influence laws or the loss of their job or reputation.

In fact, legalisation reformers sometimes suggest that there will be little or no increase in consumption because illegal drugs are readily available and competitively priced against their legal counterparts. Potential purchasers must consider, however, more than just price and availability. Buying illegal drugs could mean going to prison, losing one's job or overdosing. The possibility that these threats diminish the actual number of drug consumers cannot be completely discounted.

Some individuals may be affected by the 'forbidden fruit' effect, which actually increases their demand for illegal products. By making a good illegal you draw attention to it and encourage its use as a way of rebelling against society or unjust laws. If prohibition creates this forbidden fruit effect and increases sales in a black market, then demand could decrease as a result of legalisation. There is some evidence for the existence of this effect discussed in the Introduction to this collection, but nothing that would suggest its magnitude in the case of drugs.

The actual increase in consumption would probably be somewhere between the two opposing positions; positive but not ominous. Moving from prohibition to a completely free market would probably lead to an increased consumption of drugs. First, current consumers would face a lower price and increased quality. Second, new consumers would enter the market owing to the lifting of criminal sanctions and the improved safety of the products. Third, there would be a move from drugs that are currently legal and highly taxed, such as alcohol and tobacco, into newly legalised drugs that are not. Fourth, legal products would tend to be sold in lower-potency forms so that the quantity of product as measured by weight or volume sold would increase. Fifth, there would be a surge in demand for the legitimate medicinal uses of marijuana, cocaine and heroin, which are currently prohibited or restricted.

The drug policy debate often neglects the distinction between free markets governed by the rules of private property, contract and tort, and 'free-for-all' markets without any enforceable rules of the game. The fact is that rules against fraud, duress, imposition of intentional or accidental harms and trespass or other involuntary takings do exist in all modern economies. Furthermore, even when these rules are not instituted by the state, various kinds of 'privately imposed' regulations would virtually guarantee that the production, distribution and consumption of drugs such as marijuana, cocaine and heroin would be significantly different compared with black market conditions. With legalisation, market behaviour will look more like Budweiser, Marlboro and Coca-Cola, and less like Al Capone, *Miami Vice* and *The Sopranos*.

Conclusion

Following a brief history of recreational drug prohibition, this chapter has examined the costs and benefits of prohibition and provided an analysis of the major forms of legalisation that are available to policy-makers throughout the world. On balance, it appears that there are many unintended, negative consequences of prohibition, including crime and corruption. Further, there is evidence that prohibition may also cause or exacerbate the various risks associated with using recreational drugs. While it has been established that prohibition is harmful in numerous respects, the analysis has also shown that many of the alternatives are not perfect either. Government monopoly, government regulation, sin taxes and the free market have all been described and assessed with the help of well-developed economic models. As each of these policies has been used in a variety of different industries, this chapter has drawn upon a wealth of historical experience to further understand their implications. Given that the reader will most likely face the prospect of changes to drug policy in his or her lifetime, this analysis should provide valuable information.

References

Abadinsky, H. (2001), *Drugs: An Introduction*, Blemont, CA: Wadsworth/Thomsom Learning.

Andreas, P. (1998), 'The political economy of narco-corruption in Mexico', *Current History*, 97(618): 160–65.

Becker, G. S., M. Grossman and K. M. Murphy (2006), 'The market for illegal goods: the case of drugs', *Journal of Political Economy*, 114(1): 38–60.

Benjamin, D. K. and T. L. Anderson (1996), 'Taxation, enforcement costs, and the incentives to privatize', in T. L. Anderson and P. J. Hill (eds), *The Privatization Process: A Worldwide Perspective*, Lanham, MD: Rowman & Littlefield.

Benson, B. L. (2003), 'Regulatory disequilibrium and inefficiency: the case of interstate trucking', *Review of Austrian Economics*, 15(2–3): 229–55.

Benson, B. L., I. S. Laburn and D. W. Rasmussen (2001), 'The impact of drug enforcement on crime: an investigation of the opportunity cost of police resources', *Journal of Drug Issues*, 31(4): 989–1006.

Benson, B. L., D. W. Rasmussen and P. R. Zimmerman (2003), 'Implicit taxes collected by state liquor monopolies', *Public Choice*, 115(3–4): 313–31.

Brecher, E. M. and the editors of *Consumer Reports* (1972), *Licit and Illicit Drugs*, Boston, MA: Little, Brown.

Engelsman, E. L. (1991), 'Drug policy in the Netherlands from a public health perspective', in M. B. Krauss and E. P. Lazear (eds), *Searching for Alternatives: Drug-Control Policy in the United States*, Stanford, CA: Hoover Institution Press.

Fisher, I. (1930), *The Noble Experiment*, New York: Alcohol Information Committee.

Kleiman, M. A. R. (1992), *Against Excess: Drug Policy for Results*, New York: Basic Books.

Lupsha, P. (1992), 'Drug lords and narco-corruption: the players change but the game continues', *Crime, Law and Social Change*, 16(1): 41–58.

Marshall, J. (1991), *Drug Wars: Corruption, Counterinsurgency and Covert Operations in the Third World*, Forestville, CA: Cohan and Cohen Publishers.

Mast, B. D., B. L. Benson and D. W. Rasmussen (2000), 'Entrepreneurial police and drug enforcement policy', *Public Choice*, 104(3–4): 285–308.

Musto, D. F. (1973 [1987]), *The American Disease: Origins of Narcotic Control*, Oxford: Oxford University Press.

Musto, D. F. (1987), 'The history of legislative control over opium, cocaine, and their derivatives', in R. Hamowy (ed.), *Dealing with Drugs: Consequences of Government Control*, Lexington, MA: D. C. Heath and Co.

Thornton, M. (1991a), *The Economics of Prohibition*, Salt Lake City, UT: University of Utah Press.

Thornton, M. (1991b), 'Alcohol prohibition was a failure', *Policy Analysis*, 157, Washington, DC: Cato Institute.

Thornton, M. (1994) 'Review of Against Excess: drug policy for results', *Review of Austrian Economics*, 7(1): 147–50.

Thornton, M. (1995), 'Economists on illegal drugs', *Atlantic Economic Journal*, 23(2): 73.

Thornton, M. (1998), 'The potency of illegal drugs', *Journal of Drug Issues*, 28(3): 725–40.

Thornton, M. (2004), 'Prohibition vs. legalization: do economists reach a conclusion on drug policy?', *Econ Journal Watch*, 1(1): 82–105.

Thornton, M. and C. Weise (2001), 'The Great Depression tax revolts revisited', *Journal of Libertarian Studies*, 15(3): 95–105.

Thornton, M., B. L. Benson and S. W. Bowmaker (2005), 'Economics of drug liberalization', in S. W. Bowmaker (ed.), *Economics Uncut: A Complete Guide to Life, Death and Misadventure*, Cheltenham: Edward Elgar.

Tullock, G. and R. B. McKenzie (1985), *The New World of Economics: Explorations into the Human Experience*, 4th edn, Homewood, IL: Richard D. Irwin, Inc.

Turner, D. (1991), 'Pragmatic incoherence: the changing face of British drug policy', in M. B. Krauss and E. P. Lazear (eds), *Searching for Alternatives: Drug-Control Policy in the United States*, Stanford, CA: Hoover Institution Press.

United Nations International Drug Control Programme (1997), *World Drug Report*, New York: Oxford University Press.

Whitman, D. G. (2003), *Strange Brew: Alcohol and Government Monopoly*, Oakland, CA: Independent Institute.

Yandle, B. (1983), 'Bootleggers and Baptists: the education of a regulatory economist', *Regulation*, 7(3): 12.

Yandle, B. (1998), 'Kyoto, bootleggers and Baptists', PERC Policy Series, Bozeman, MT: Political Economy Research Center.

4 BOXING[1]
Ralf M. Bader

Introduction

Boxing is a dirty and much-denounced industry. It involves violence, drugs, corruption and even death. Very often cries are rallied to regulate this industry and standardise the rules, to clean up the business and unionise the boxers. Many even demand an outright ban. Indeed, boxing has constantly been under threat of being banned or heavily regulated. Professional boxing has already been prohibited in a number of countries, including Sweden (since 1970[2]), Norway (since 1981), North Korea and Cuba, and government regulations are extensive in most places. The American, British, Canadian and World medical associations have all called for the abolition of boxing.

In Britain, the British Medical Association (BMA) has been campaigning for a ban on all forms of boxing for a number of decades.[3] It has sponsored legislation in Parliament to try to get the sport abolished and has issued several publications to the same end. The Boxing Bill has been on the agenda since 1962 and still continues to be discussed in the House of Lords and the House of Commons. In 1995, a Bill to abolish boxing for profit was defeated in the House of Lords by only two votes. The BMA has narrowly lost this round, but the fight continues. They have not yet thrown in the towel and we can be sure

---

1 I would like to thank John Meadowcroft, Andrew Buchan and an anonymous referee for helpful comments on an earlier draft of this paper.
2 The ban on boxing in Sweden was lifted in 2007. The relegalisation is not complete, however, in that professional fighters must now adhere to amateur rules.
3 See BMA (2006).

that they will try again and again until their goal has been achieved.

At the same time, professional boxing is an important entertainment industry. Through it many people make their livelihood and large masses of people are entertained. It is a multimillion-dollar business; every year over $500 million in revenue is derived from boxing, mainly from advertising and income through pay-per-view television. Boxing is a highly popular sport. Many people follow professional boxing and amateur boxing is widely practised.

In this chapter, I would like to assess this debate, focusing on two issues, namely the risks of boxing and the ethical status of boxing. It will be argued that boxing should not be banned, even though it may well be a dangerous, imprudent and immoral thing to do. There is no justification for using the coercive power of the state to interfere in people's lives and prevent them from voluntarily deciding to fight for money. The arguments made by the proponents of prohibition are generally incoherent, insofar as they fail to identify any characteristic that differentiates boxing from other dangerous activities to which they do not object. Moreover, the critics of boxing fail to provide any substantive ethical arguments that could support their normative judgements.

The dangers of boxing

Boxing is seen as a violent sport that leads to many injuries and even deaths. Proponents of prohibition usually point to this fact and somehow think that it is sufficient to motivate a ban on boxing. They list the number of deaths and the possible risks of brain damage involved, and thence somehow conclude that boxing should be banned. Let us set aside for the moment the difficult question of how one can derive normative conclusions from these descriptive facts and simply assess the empirical evidence.

It is far from obvious that the evidence is actually in favour of the critics of boxing. This is because the damages resulting from boxing are relatively small compared with certain other sports that hardly anyone would consider banning. We just have to look at the brutality of shinty or rugby to see that boxing is not exceptionally violent. Particularly telling are the statistics on death rates. When compared with the dangers of horse racing and skydiving, we can see that boxing is, relatively speaking, not very risky. Between 1945 and 1995 there have been 361 boxers whose deaths have been recorded worldwide. This is indeed a tragic result, but when it is compared with the death rates of other sports, we have to conclude that boxing is relatively innocuous, as can be seen from the statistics in Table 1.

Table 1 **Average annual fatality rates in the US per 1,000 participants between 1945 and 1979[4]**

Horse racing	12.8
Skydiving	12.3
Hang gliding	5.6
Mountaineering	5.1
Scuba diving	1.1
Motorcycle racing	0.7
College football	0.3
Boxing	0.13

According to figures provided by the Office of Population Censuses and Surveys, there were three deaths in England and Wales from boxing between 1986 and 1992. In the same period, there were 77 deaths in motor sports, 69 deaths in air sports, 54 deaths in mountaineering, 40 deaths in ball games and 28 deaths in horse riding.

The Sports Council investigated sports accidents based on the general household surveys from 1987 to 1989. A standardised 'risk factor' was calculated for each sport by comparing the number of sports accidents with the number of occasions in which individuals participated in each sport. Sports were then placed in one of four categories, ranging from high to negligible risk. Based on this analysis, boxing was placed in the negligible-risk category along with golf and snooker.[5]

4　See McCunney and Russo (1984).

5　These statistics are not meant to suggest that boxing is harmless. There clearly are many

While it is true that boxing was once a brutal sport, many things have changed. It is in the interests of boxers and promoters to reduce the risk of serious injuries. This leads to self-regulation. Boxing is continually evolving and becoming more professional. Improvements in the rules and the equipment reduce the risks of injury. Medical treatment improves, making the detection, treatment and prevention of health problems much easier. Boxing is now a professional sport, which means that boxers are well trained and well prepared. As a result of these changes, boxers are being protected more and more.

Of particular importance to the reduction in risks are changes in the rules of boxing. The rules evolve. Partly they are self-imposed, partly externally imposed. At the beginning, the changes were mostly self-imposed by the boxers. In Britain in 1743 the first set of formal boxing rules was developed by James Broughton, often referred to as the 'father of British boxing'. These were followed in 1839 by the London Prize Ring Rules. In 1867 the Queensberry Rules were published, but gained hold only slowly. Up to 1892 it was still the case that most fighting took place according to London Prize Rules. The Queensberry Rules form the basis of modern boxing rules. Most importantly, they include the introduction of boxing gloves, which greatly reduce the risk of serious injury.[6]

Regulation by the state can often lead to adverse consequences since government officials often lack incentives to adequately enforce the regulation; a government official may be able to gain financially from boxing only by engaging in corrupt practices, whereas promoters and boxers have most to gain from a sport widely perceived as free from corruption. For good regulation to be effective, it must be well enforced, but good enforcement requires the existence of adequate incentive structures. Even if the legally imposed rules are good and are identical to

---

risks associated with boxing, in particular in the form of cumulative brain damage. Rather, these statistics are supposed to show that there are many highly dangerous activities to which nobody objects and which no one would consider prohibiting.

6　For a discussion of the historical development of measures to improve the safety of boxers, see Jordan (1993).

those that would have been selected by a market procedure, there can be serious problems resulting from poor enforcement of these rules. Where the incentives for good enforcement by the state are lacking, the boxer faces increased risks. For example, the division of fighters into different weight categories matters a lot and helps to reduce the risk of injury. These rules must, however, be properly enforced if this risk reduction is to take place. If it is done privately, then the incentive structure will be right to ensure that people stick to the rules. But at the moment this is done rather inadequately by government bodies. The danger of this bad enforcement can be seen in cases of uneven fights, resulting from match-fixing and corruption. Fixed fights are particularly dangerous since the two fighters are not equal. Indeed, a number of deaths have resulted from uneven fights. For example, in the fight between Arturo Gatti and Joey Gamache in 2000, Gamache sustained severe damage and has been advised by his doctors not to fight again. This is due to incompetent government officials from the notorious New York State Athletic Commission who did not adequately enforce the weight limits, letting Gatti enter the fight even though he weighed 15 pounds more than Gamache.[7]

Like any private industry, the boxing industry is self-regulating to the extent to which it is not externally regulated but left on its own. The discipline of the market encourages good behaviour. As in any other industry, boxers and promoters are trying to sell a product. As with any other product, they need to find a selling point to get a competitive advantage over others. When boxing falls into disrepute, profits will fall. This can currently be seen to be happening in the USA, where the bad name of boxing has damaged the industry. A good indication of the dissatisfaction with the current state of boxing is the flourishing of 'ultimate fighting'. Consumers want to see fair fights for the simple reason that it is just no fun to see an uneven fight, like that between McNeeley and Tyson in 1995, where McNeely got knocked out after 90

---

7   See *Boxing Monthly*, 12(4), August 2000.

seconds.[8] Fixed fights are bad for boxers since they are dangerous and they are bad for promoters since they are bad for business. Entrepreneurs in the boxing industry will come up with new ideas to bring boxing back into fashion, as can be observed in the recent trend of trying to promote 'clean boxing'. There simply is no need to regulate the business in this respect since such regulation will be too late anyway and will mostly do the wrong things. Rather than relying on the government to fix matters, we should enquire whether the government might not be the cause of the problem, since corruption is likely to take place when government officials are in charge.

Reducing the risks to boxers and encouraging clean boxing is simply a matter of putting into place the right incentive structure, so that adequate contractual arrangements can then develop. Boxers and promoters have the right incentives, not politicians and bureaucrats. Why should we suppose that promoters are unable to promote clean fights when they directly profit from them, while believing that bureaucrats and politicians in Washington, London or wherever they may be are disinterested, benevolent and rational? Moreover, it is the boxers and promoters who have local and specialised knowledge that allows them to innovate and behave in an entrepreneurial manner. They know where the risks and opportunities are. The incentives to act and the knowledge required for action both lie in the hands of the boxers and promoters, while politicians and bureaucrats lack both the adequate incentives and the relevant knowledge. Instead of appealing to politicians to change things for the better, we should be expecting that most interventions on their part are likely to make matters worse.

Interventions in the boxing industry are subject to the usual problems of intervention. As public choice theory reminds us, there is no reason to expect politicians to act in the best interests of the boxers, given the lack of incentives to do so. Politicians, like most other people, often behave in self-interested ways. There are even adverse incentives

---

8   For an account of the background to this fight, as well as to similar events, see Jack New-field's contribution entitled 'The shame of boxing' in *The Nation*, 12 November 2001.

that are likely to lead them to act in bad ways, resulting from lobbying by special interest groups and the general short-sightedness of politicians. In the USA, the regulation of boxing is at the moment organised by state commissions and, as journalist and documentary film-maker Jack Newfield once said, it is clear that 'they do not have the interests of the boxers at heart'.[9] Surely it is better to rely on those who do have a personal interest, namely the boxers and the promoters.

Additionally, there is the problem of unexpected consequences arising from interventions. As Ludwig von Mises argued (1926), the logic of intervention is likely to ensure that interventions end up undermining the aim they were initially intended to fulfil, and also to bring about negative side effects. We cannot isolate a particular issue since the social and economic system is a highly complex system in which everything is interrelated. At most, there is the possibility of a short-term success, but this will be followed by long-term problems, as well as problems in adjacent areas. For example, a general ban on boxing might well have disadvantageous social side effects resulting from the outlawing of local boxing clubs that play an important stabilising and socialising role in societies.

Even if we were to prohibit boxing, it would still take place. A prohibition would simply cause it to move somewhere else, to different countries, or simply to go underground, as has been the case in countries like Norway, where certain martial arts were banned. In particular, relatively moderate forms of fighting, such as professional boxing, would suffer from regulations, whereas more brutal forms of professional fighting would be likely to flourish under prohibition. This would leave the boxers with less choice and increase the relative pay-off of choosing to get involved in the more violent forms of fighting. As a result, boxers will be even more dependent and more easily exploited. The higher the bargaining power of the organisers of fights, the more likely it is that they can get boxers to agree to conditions that are less beneficial to

9   Interview, Wisconsin Public Radio, 3 March 2002.

them. The boxers will no longer be able to resort to legal measures and the court system. Accordingly, it is much better to leave boxing in the open, where interactions are based on voluntary contractual agreements that are legally enforceable.

The proponents of prohibition usually respond to the argument that boxing will go underground by saying that this is irrelevant since boxing is immoral and hence should be prohibited independently of whether or not the prohibition will bring about the end of fighting. This reply is fine if we do indeed want to ban boxing on the basis of moral considerations, in which case it should still be banned even though the ban is likely to produce negative unintended consequences. If we want to ban it for consequential reasons, however, then this reasoning no longer holds. If we are appalled by the violence of boxing and try to stop it, to protect the boxers, then we should not attempt to ban boxing, since such an intervention is likely to turn out to be counterproductive. Banning is likely to make things worse (in terms of the wellbeing of the boxers) and the unintended consequences hence undermine the rationale for banning.[10]

Accordingly, we can see that boxing is, relatively speaking, fairly innocuous. The risks involved in boxing are lower than those of many other sports that hardly anyone would consider banning. Moreover, if we want further risk reductions in boxing, then we need more professionalism, not less, and we need more money going into the industry, not less. We need the right incentive structure for encouraging improvements. This incentive structure is provided by the market. The discipline of the market is the best thing to rely upon, rather than the goodwill of legislators and administrators.

Is boxing immoral?

The editor of the *Journal of the American Medical Association*, G. D.

---

10 The same holds for milder forms of intervention and regulation. They will also have unintended consequences, but the smaller the intervention, the smaller the consequences tend to be.

Lundberg (1983: 250), said that boxing was an 'obscenity [that] should not be sanctioned by any civilized society'. This is a common claim. Many people complain that boxing is 'barbaric', 'repugnant' and 'immoral'. No coherent and detailed explanation is given, however, as to why it should be banned. These normative judgements are just left hanging in the air and no support or justification is provided. Describing boxing in derogatory terms is not enough. Giving statistics regarding the dangers of boxing and telling stories about personal tragedies of boxers is not enough. We need to be given an *argument* that supports the ban for boxing. What is it about boxing that is obscene? What is wrong with obscenity? What gives society or the state the right to use force or the threat of force to intervene in people's lives and prevent them from engaging in this 'obscenity'? What makes it the case that they should intervene?

There are two questions that need to be considered. First, we need to ask whether we should allow people to put themselves into risky situations, in which it is likely that harm will occur to them. Here, the answer clearly seems to be 'yes'. If we do not let people choose the risks involved in boxing, we would have to prevent them from participating in a large number of activities. Not just other risky sports would have to be prohibited, but risky activities in general. Moreover, the boxers are aware of the risks and voluntarily decide to box. It is their choice and they are responsible for the consequences; it is they who have to pay the price for their decisions.[11]

Some very difficult ethical questions arise regarding the limits of choice. Are there any limitations as to what we can do to ourselves or agree to be done unto ourselves? Are we justified in letting other people inflict physical harm on us? It is usually assumed that there are limits to what we can legitimately choose, and it might then be suggested that boxing should be banned since it falls outside these limits. A possible analogy could be drawn between boxing and suicide. Since we do not

---

11 The usual problems arise in countries in which there is a national healthcare system, insofar as people living risky lives impose these costs on other people. This is not a problem resulting from boxing, however, but from the misguided collectivised healthcare system.

allow someone to commit suicide, even though it is a voluntary choice undertaken in full knowledge of the consequences, it could be argued that there should be similar limits with respect to boxing. First of all, however, it is not at all clear that suicide should indeed be prohibited. We can perfectly well accept that people should not commit suicide, but then argue that no one has the right to interfere in their lives and stop them from doing so. Even on the assumption that suicide should indeed be prohibited, the analogy breaks down. This is because there is an important disanalogy in that in the case of suicide someone is intentionally harming himself, whereas in the case of boxing someone is intentionally and knowingly entering a situation in which he faces the risk of bodily harm. Thus, we do not have a case of self-harm, but simply a case of risky behaviour, and we allow people to drive cars, drink alcohol and go skydiving even though the risks in many cases are higher than the risks associated with boxing.

It is a duty that we owe to ourselves not to expose ourselves to too much risk and not to harm ourselves, and it is consequently not a duty that can be legitimately enforced. The state is justified only in enforcing duties that have correlative rights attached to them, since the non-fulfilment of such a duty would constitute a rights violation. Any duty that lacks a correlative right, however, cannot be enforced by the state, and any attempt at enforcing such a duty would constitute a violation of the agent's autonomy. Since duties to the self do not have correlative rights, given that we do not have rights against ourselves, they are not enforceable. Prohibiting boxing is not justified since violations of this duty do not involve any rights violations that the state should prevent. If I damage myself then this is my problem and no rights have been violated that would justify interference.[12]

---

12 As usual, these statements must be qualified insofar as an agent who has voluntarily taken upon himself obligations that conflict with his decision to box can be stopped from boxing. That is, if I make a contractual agreement in which I declare that I will never box, then it is legitimate to prevent me from boxing. This in no way establishes, however, any general conclusions about the legitimacy of boxing.

Second, we need to consider whether we should allow people to intentionally inflict harm upon others, given that they have agreed to it. Boxing is seen to be immoral because it involves violence for the sake of violence. The aim of a fight is to hurt the opponent. It is not merely an unintended consequence that people get hurt, but the very *telos* of the activity. Injuries are not merely accidents but the intended results. Dr Bill O'Neill, the boxing spokesman of the British Medical Association, said that boxing 'is the only sport where the intention is to inflict serious injury on your opponent, and we feel that we must have a total ban on boxing'.[13] Similarly, Lord Taylor of Gryfe said that boxing 'is the only sport in which the infliction of bodily harm is the purpose of the exercise'.[14] This can thus be seen to be the only argument against boxing that remains.

It is true that the intention of harming one's opponent distinguishes boxing from some other sports. In order to be consistent, however, the proponent of prohibition must be arguing for a total ban on boxing, not only for a ban on professional boxing. Moreover, he must also argue for a ban on all activities that are sufficiently similar to boxing in the relevant respects, i.e. at least a ban on all martial arts where there is the intention of hurting the opponent. This condition is often not fulfilled, and proponents of the prohibition of boxing generally do not discuss martial arts and often claim that amateur boxing should not be banned. This attitude is unacceptable; martial arts and amateur boxing equally involve an intention to hurt the other person, and if it is this aspect of boxing that we are objecting to, then these sports should also be banned. When looking at the discussions regarding boxing, it often seems that people are objecting to the commercialisation of boxing. They seem to be opposed to the idea of someone fighting for money. No arguments are given to support these prejudices, however. The only arguments that are provided refer to the dangers of boxing and the intention to harm, but these arguments are not then thought through to their logical

13 BBC, 3 May 1998.
14 House of Lords, vol. 567, col. 1015, 6 December 1995.

conclusions, and other sports that clearly do fulfil these criteria are generally not objected to.

Even when we simply focus on those critics who do not arbitrarily discriminate between professional and amateur boxing, such as the BMA, we can nonetheless see that their position is problematic. It does not suffer from internal inconsistency, but suffers from a lack of arguments in support of their premises. In particular, there is the dubious premise that we should ban activities that aim at hurting other people. This is an ethical judgement, claiming that this kind of behaviour is immoral and unacceptable and deserves to be prohibited. Usually, however, no arguments are proposed in its favour. The proponents of prohibition do not provide any ethical arguments to support their case. Instead, they just claim that boxing is 'immoral', 'evil' and should accordingly be prohibited. It appears, however, that there is no requirement or justification for a prohibition on ethical grounds since the boxers voluntarily consent, which entails that harming no longer constitutes a rights violation.

Even though there may be good ethical arguments for condemning boxing, it does not follow from this that there should be a prohibition on boxing. The duty that we have of not intentionally harming other people, given that they have voluntarily agreed to it, is not an enforceable duty. In Kantian terminology it is a duty of virtue, not a duty of right.[15] In this respect it is like the duty of charity; charity is something that should be done but not something that can or should be enforced. Thus, even though boxing might be immoral in the sense that we have a duty not to do it, it is nonetheless not a publicly enforceable duty. Normally, intentionally harming someone constitutes a rights violation and the state, as well as any private individual, is justified in interfering in order to prevent this rights violation or punish the offender. Once consent has been given, however, no rights violation takes place any more and no interference is justified. Accordingly, when it comes to the question of whether boxing should be banned by means of the coercive power of

---

15   See Kant (1996), especially pp. 119–220.

the state, it seems pretty clear that this should not be the case on ethical grounds. People should, at most, voluntarily refrain from boxing, but they should not be forced to do so. Any attempt to force them would be illegitimate and resistance to it would be justified.

The proponents of prohibition must establish not only that boxing is contrary to moral considerations, but that the government has a right and a duty to ban it. Boxing might well be a dangerous, foolish, imprudent and immoral thing to do, but this does not provide the state with the right to interfere with people's lives and prevent them from participating in these forms of activities.

Conclusion

The boxing industry can take care of itself. Incentives and knowledge point in the direction of improvement. As self-imposed rules evolve, and as techniques improve because of increasing professionalism, the risks will go down. Any proponent of prohibition has to explain what makes boxing different and why we should ban boxing, but not other sports. Empirical evidence shows that boxing is less dangerous than many other sports that are deemed unexceptionable. The only relevant difference is that boxers intend to do harm to others. Bodily damage is not just an unintended side consequence, but the very aim of boxing. As has been shown, however, this in no way justifies coercive interference by the state since boxing is a voluntary activity that does not involve any infringements of rights.

Most criticisms of boxing are plain incoherent, inconsistent and hypocritical. Critics fail to identify any salient features that differentiate professional boxing. The characteristics that are usually deemed objectionable are shared by many other sports and are often exhibited by them to a greater extent. Thus, if the critic is to be consistent, then he has to call for banning much more than just boxing, namely for a ban on most dangerous and risky activities, thereby ending up with an absurdly paternalistic and interventionist position.

Alternatively, he can take up a sensible position by accepting that professional boxing should not be prohibited and then try to convince people to voluntarily refrain from boxing. He can try to change the profession from within, improve the conditions of boxers and awareness of the risks involved in boxing, rather than use the coercive machinery of the state to impose his preferences and paternalistic attitudes on other people. In this respect the BMA deserves much praise for its efforts in increasing the awareness of the dangers of boxing, but it should not forget that good intentions do not justify the use of the coercive power of the state to interfere in people's lives and restrict their freedom of choice.

References

BMA (British Medical Association) (2006), 'Boxing debate', http:// bma.org.uk/ap.nsf/content/boxingpu.

Jordan, B. D. (1993), 'Medical aspects of boxing: a historical perspective', in B. D. Jordan (ed.), *Medical Aspects of Boxing*, Boca Raton, FL: CRC Press.

Kant, I. (1996), 'The metaphysics of morals', in M. J. Gregor (ed.), *Practical Philosophy*, Cambridge: Cambridge University Press.

Lundberg, G. D. (1983), 'Boxing should be banned in civilized countries', *Journal of the American Medical Association*, 249: 254–7.

McCunney, R. J. and P. K. Russo (1984), 'Brain injuries in boxing', *Physician and Sportsmedicine*, 12: 52–67.

Von Mises, L. (1926), 'Interventionismus', *Archiv für Sozialwissenschaft und Sozialpolitik*, 56: 610–53.

5 FIREARMS[1]

Gary A. Mauser

Introduction

Human ingenuity is impressive, and no less so when it comes to finding ways to kill. How effective can it be to limit the availability of one of these tools, firearms, in reducing the incidence of criminal violence, murder or suicide?[2] The introduction of stricter firearms regulations is almost always justified as a reaction to a recent rise in violent crime, although fears of political unrest may be equally important, if less often discussed publicly.[3] Politicians promise that restrictive gun laws will make society safer, but proof has been lacking. Such laws must be demonstrated to cut violent crime, homicide and suicide; otherwise these claims are hollow promises. It's time to ask whether stringent gun laws actually work, because regardless of how restrictive such laws are, and the trend is to be ever more restrictive, these kinds of laws impose

1   An earlier version of this chapter was published by the Fraser Institute (Mauser, 2003). The chapter has been expanded to include discussions of Scotland, the Republic of Ireland and Jamaica. I would like to thank Peter Allen and C. B. Kates for their critical comments on earlier drafts. The chapter has benefited from their contributions. Despite their gracious help, I remain responsible for any and all errors or omissions that may remain.

2   As startling as it may appear, many powerful tools for murder (even mass murder) are readily available in highly regulated societies. For example, petrol, propane and knives are easy to obtain. As recent events in the UK have shown, even amateurish terrorists are familiar with the first two and knives are involved in more murders in the UK than guns. Given the ubiquity of ropes, tall buildings and motor vehicles, it is not difficult for suicidal individuals to find adequate substitutes for firearms. See Kates and Mauser (2007) for an analysis of the effectiveness of gun laws in reducing overall murder or suicide rates in Europe.

3   Historical analyses of private cabinet papers reveal that British firearms laws have reflected government concerns about the potential for public disorder and revolution as well as criminal violence (Malcolm, 2002: 142).

high costs on citizens by stimulating the growth of governmental bureaucracy.

Firearms pose an intractable problem for government: on the one hand, allowing individuals to own firearms risks relinquishing power, which might facilitate criminal violence, or more ominously encourage local regions to claim independence from the central government, or even lead to revolution. English history, for example, is replete with examples of local barons or dukes rebelling against the king, often encouraged by foreign powers. On the other hand, a government might wish under some conditions to allow 'responsible' civilians to have firearms as a means of extending its power. The police might reluctantly admit that they cannot protect everyone, so individuals could be encouraged to take greater steps to protect themselves and their local communities. While perhaps difficult to imagine today, historically England has relied upon armed civilians to help maintain law and order. More recently, the Home Guard was created to play a vital role during World War II.

Empirical support for firearms laws has proved to be elusive in the USA as well as the UK. In 2004 the US National Academy of Sciences released its evaluation from a review of 253 journal articles, 99 books, 43 government publications and some empirical research of its own. It could not identify any gun law that had reduced violent crime, suicide or gun accidents (Wellford et al., 2004). The US Centers for Disease Control reached a similar conclusion in 2003 in their independent review of research on firearms laws (Hahn et al., 2003). The recent mass shootings at Virginia Tech vividly illustrate the failure of restrictive gun laws to protect the public. Virginia Tech, like almost all schools, is a 'gun free zone'. Obviously, gun bans do not keep murderers from obtaining or using guns.[4]

Historical ignorance allows some to credit stringent gun control for the generally low homicide rates in the United Kingdom and western

---

4   Strict gun laws are effective, however, in keeping guns out of the hands of responsible citizens who might be better able to defend themselves and others with firearms.

Europe. This claim cannot be accurate because murder in Europe was generally lower before the gun controls were introduced (Barnet and Kates, 1996: 1239). Stringent gun controls were not adopted in either the United Kingdom or western Europe until after World War I. Consistent with the outcomes of the American studies mentioned above, these strict controls did not stem the general trend of ever-growing violent crime throughout the post-World War II industrialised world (Malcolm, 2002: 209, 219).[5]

The divergence between firearm laws in the UK and the USA increased during the 1980s and 1990s. In the late 1990s the UK moved from stringent controls to a complete ban on handguns and many types of long guns. Without suggesting that this caused violence, the ban's ineffectiveness was such that by the year 2000 violent crime had increased so much that England had the developed world's highest rate of violent crime, far surpassing even the USA (van Kesteren et al., 2001). During these same two decades, more than 25 states in the USA passed laws allowing responsible citizens to carry concealed handguns. There are now 40 states, covering more than 60 per cent of the population, where qualified citizens can get such a handgun permit (O'Hanlon, 2006). As a result, the number of Americans who are allowed to carry concealed handguns on the street has grown to 3.5 million (Kates, 2005: 64).

This chapter examines the claim that restrictive gun laws are effective in protecting public safety. If this approach to violent crime, widely adopted by the UK and other countries in the British Commonwealth, is more effective than the gun laws in operation in the USA, then, other factors being equal, the crime rates in those countries with restrictive gun laws should fall faster than the corresponding crime rates in the USA. If, on the other hand, the British-style gun laws do not live up to the promises made for them – that is, they are not as effective in

---

5   The most frequently proposed explanations for the increasing crime rate in Europe since World War II are demographic changes, organised crime and the international drug trade. Clearly, the increasingly integrated nature of Europe facilitates illegal activity as well as legitimate businesses. See van Duyne and Levi (2005), and Malcolm (2002).

reducing violent crime as the American approach – then one would not expect to see differences in the trends, or conceivably crime rates in the USA would fall even faster. The uniqueness of the criminal justice system in the United States makes that country a singularly valuable point of reference.[6]

A variety of Commonwealth and English-speaking countries have adopted British-style gun laws. Surely, if this approach is effective in dealing with criminal violence, stringent restrictive gun laws will have actually reduced violent crime in at least some places where they have been introduced.

Two sets of countries will be compared with the USA in this chapter. First, I will look at countries that introduced laws restricting general access to firearms in the 1990s (i.e. the United Kingdom, Australia and Canada). Next, I will compare the crime trends in two countries that attempted near-comprehensive firearms bans in the 1970s (Jamaica and the Republic of Ireland). In each of these countries, I compare the trends in violent crime, particularly homicide trends, with corresponding crime rates in the United States over the same time period.

It is important to remember that the goal claimed for stringent firearm laws is to reduce total criminal violence, not just gun violence. As Mr Kates and I have argued in another paper, the determinants of murder and suicide are basic social, economic and cultural factors, not the prevalence of any particular deadly mechanism (Kates and Mauser, 2007). Thus it follows that to evaluate the effectiveness of firearms legislation, one must measure the increase or decrease in criminal violence as a whole, not whether gun laws cause a drop – or an increase – in just firearms crime. If gun crime declines, but crimes with other weapons increase, so that the number of violent crimes does not decline, then these gun laws must be seen as failing (Malcolm, 2002).

The crucial test is whether gun laws improve public safety. There is no social benefit in restricting the availability of guns if total murder and

---

6   For a more thorough discussion of the differences among a wide variety of countries, including the United States, see Kopel (1992).

suicide rates remain unchanged. It is difficult to claim that public safety is better if there is no decrease in the number of lives lost. The evidence, as I will show, indicates that all that is accomplished (at best) by the removal of one particular means is that people manage to kill themselves or others by some other means.

In assessing the impact of legislation on crime rates, it is necessary to examine changes over time. A direct comparison of national averages is irrelevant. It is an entirely different question whether the Canadian average for a particular crime rate is higher (or lower) than that of the United States or England. Such patterns reflect the historical and cultural differences among nations, not the effectiveness of recent firearm legislation.[7] Evaluating legislation is analogous to evaluating a new diet. If we want to determine whether our new diet is effective, we must ask whether our weight changes after the diet is introduced. While it may be reassuring, it is logically irrelevant to our diet's efficacy that other people are fatter than we are.

Of course, even if crime rates decline (or increase) after the introduction of a new firearm law, this does not prove that the legislation caused the change. There may be alternative explanations that are more persuasive, such as the continuation of long-term trends. The question of causality is never fully answered even in complex econometric analyses or in experiments conducted under strict laboratory conditions. All that anyone can do is to attempt to eliminate most of the alternative explanations. By examining the trends in a diverse set of countries, I argue that alternative factors can be discounted to some extent. In none of the cases covered in this chapter do total homicide rates drop as a consequence of the introduction of more restrictive firearm laws.

Comparative studies rely upon police statistics rather than victim

---

7   Arguably, one of the reasons why violent crime rates tend to be higher historically in the USA and Jamaica than in Canada is that slavery played a smaller role in Canada than in either of the other two countries. Slavery had been abolished in Canada by 1810 by Lieutenant Governor John Graves Simcoe. For more information about slavery in Canada, see Craton (1974).

surveys. There are several reasons for this, even though there are well-known limitations to police data.[8] The first is that police statistics are the only data that are consistently available for the range of countries that I am considering over the full 30 years. Second, not only are victim surveys often unavailable for some countries,[9] but also the most important index of criminal violence is homicide, for which victim surveys are not possible. Third, despite their high reputation, victim interviews are of strikingly uneven quality both across nations and within nations across time.[10]

The first countries I shall examine are the United Kingdom, Australia and Canada. Each of these countries introduced draconian general laws in the 1990s that severely restricted access to firearms by citizens in an effort to improve public safety. These countries are large Western democracies with modern, functioning police forces, customs bureaucracies and with high levels of education. If any countries could be expected to control firearm misuse through the legal system, these countries would qualify. In subsequent sections of this chapter, the experiences of both the Republic of Ireland and Jamaica will be considered.

The United Kingdom[11]

Firearms policy in the United Kingdom has been driven by sensationalised coverage of firearm murders for almost twenty years. First, the Hungerford incident in August 1987 shocked Britain, and almost ten

8   Police statistics have been criticised because they are subject to changes in the public's willingness to report crimes, and, equally important, to variations in police recording practices.

9   Excellent victim surveys exist in Australia, Canada and the United States, as well as in England and Wales, but not in Scotland, the Republic of Ireland or Jamaica. See Nicholas et al. (2005).

10   Recent criticisms of the British Crime Survey's practice of placing arbitrary limits upon numbers of violent crimes that can be reported indicates the problem inherent in any survey approach (Barrett, 2007).

11   The crime trends of the Channel Islands and other nearby islands associated with the UK will not be examined here.

years later, in 1996, murders in Dunblane, Scotland, captured media attention (Malcolm, 2002: 201–3). In both cases, the media were outraged that licensed target shooters were able to own handguns, not that the police failed to follow established rules that should have prevented granting these killers a firearms permit, nor that no one attempted to stop these murders during the extended time over which they were committed.

The Firearms (Amendment) Act of 1988 was brought in by the Conservative government following the Hungerford incident, and the Firearms (Amendment No. 2) Act of 1997, which banned all handguns, was introduced by the Labour government following the shootings in Dunblane in 1996 (Greenwood, 2001: 8; Munday and Stevenson, 1996). Unfortunately, these draconian firearms regulations have not curbed violent crime.

England and Wales

In assessing the impact of this legislation, the principal jurisdiction of the UK is England and Wales. For historical reasons, police statistics are reported for England and Wales as if they formed a single unit.

Police statistics show that England and Wales are enduring a serious crime wave. In contrast to North America, where the homicide rate has been falling for over twenty years, the homicide rate in England and Wales has been growing over the same time period (see Figure 1). In the 1990s alone, the homicide rate jumped 50 per cent, going from 1.1 per 100,000 in 1990 to 1.6 per 100,000 in 2000, and has remained at this higher rate, averaging 1.7 per 100,000 since 2001 (Home Office, 2001).

As for violent crime in general, police statistics show a huge increase since the handgun ban, and since 1996 violent crime has been more serious than in the United States. The rate of violent crime jumped from 400 per 100,000 in 1988 to almost 1,400 per 100,000 in 2000 (ibid.; Nicholas et al., 2005; Walker et al., 2006). An unknown

Figure 1   Trends in homicide rates in England and Wales and the USA

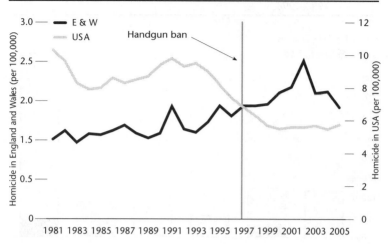

Source: FBI and Home Office

proportion of the recent increase may be attributed to changes in the recording rules in 1998 and 1999. In contrast, not only are violent crime rates lower in the USA, there they are continuing to decline (FBI, 2003, 2006).

The Home Office has also tightened up the enforcement of regulations to such an extent that the legitimate sport-shooting community has been virtually destroyed. For example, the number of shotgun permits issued has fallen almost 30 per cent since 1988 (Greenwood, 2001). The British Home Office admits that only one firearm in ten used in homicide was legally held (Home Office, 2001) (see Figure 2). But there is little pressure from within bureaucratic and governmental circles to discontinue the policy of disarming responsible citizens who hold their firearms for target shooting or for taking game for the table, after some centuries of being allowed to do so by the law. The costs to taxpayers of the firearms bureaucracy are unknown.

Clearly, there is no evidence that firearm laws have caused homicide

Figure 2   Legal status of homicide firearms, England and Wales
1992–1998

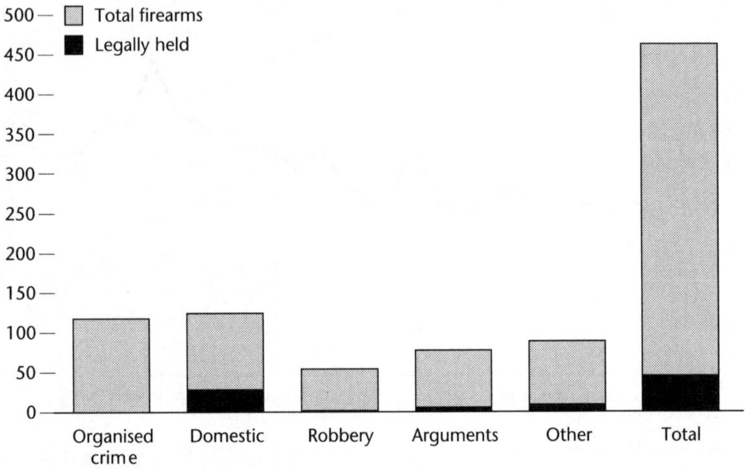

Source: Home Office, Criminal Statistics, England and Wales, 2001, Table 3d

or violent crime to fall. The firearm laws may even have increased criminal violence by disarming the general public.[12]

Scotland

It is important to examine the violent crime trends in Scotland as well, because it has almost 9 per cent of the total population of the United Kingdom. Firearms laws in Scotland are essentially the same as in England, despite differences between the English and Scottish legal systems (Peele, 1995: 417).

As can be seen in Figure 3, the homicide trend in Scotland resembles

---

12   It is not necessary to argue that disarming the citizenry caused the increase in violent crime, although it might have contributed. All that is required is that the cost of the British firearms bureaucracy has diverted scarce resources away from more effective crime-fighting approaches.

Figure 3   **Homicide trend in Scotland**
            Frequency of homicide incidents

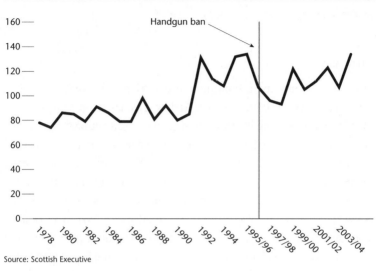

Source: Scottish Executive

that in England and Wales. The restrictive firearms laws have failed to slow down murderers; homicides continue to increase. For the ten years prior to 1997, there were 104 homicides per year; 1997 was an exceptionally quiet year, with only 90 homicides, but homicides have continued to increase. Since the handgun ban, there have been 110 homicides each year up to 2003, and for the years 2001–03 there were an average of 114 homicides per year (Scottish Executive, 2004a, 2006).[13]

Violent crime is also increasing. This is evident in both police statistics and victim surveys. Violent crime has increased from 14,500 incidents in 1994 to over 15,000 in 2001, 2002 and 2003. Over the same time period, rape and attempted rape also increased from under 6,000 per year to over 6,500 per year (Scottish Executive, 2004b). A recent victim

---

13 Note that the increase in the frequency of homicide represents a real growth in the Scottish homicide rate because the population of Scotland decreased by approximately 1 per cent between 1992 and 2003.

survey, conducted as part of a United Nations-sponsored survey of crime victims in 21 countries, identified Scotland as one of the most violent places in Europe (Tweedie, 2005).

Australia

Publicity surrounding a multiple murder triggered recent changes in Australian firearms policy. In Port Arthur, Tasmania, on 28 April 1996, Martin Bryant, a mentally deranged man, went on a rampage, murdering anyone he encountered, killing 35 people. The media afterwards focused almost exclusively on the killer's use of military-style semi-automatic firearms (Bellamy, 2003). Confusion remains over many of the details of this incident, including how Bryant came to have the firearms he used and whether or not the police response was adequate. No Royal Commission has ever examined the incident, despite the public perception that an open inquiry was required. The media focus on the firearms diverted public concern from police procedures.

Following garish media coverage of the Tasmanian killings, in 1997 the Australian government brought in sweeping changes to firearms legislation. The new controls on firearms introduced included the prohibition and confiscation of over 600,000 firearms, mostly semi-automatic or pump-action firearms, from their licensed owners, as well as new licensing and registration regulations (Lawson, 1999; Reuter and Mouzos, 2002).[14]

These stringent firearms regulations do not appear to have made the streets of Australia safer. In the years following their introduction, homicides involving firearms declined but murders with other weapons increased, so that the total homicide rate remained basically flat from 1995 through to 2001 (Mouzos, 2001). A subsequent report found that, despite the declining firearms homicides, there was an increase in multiple-victim incidents (Mouzos, 2003). The homicide rate reached a

---

14 For further information on the firearms legislation, see Lawson (1999) and Mouzos (1999, 2000).

Figure 4   **Homicide trend in Australia**

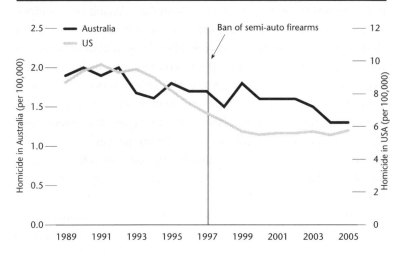

Source: FBI and Australian Bureau of Statistics

peak in 1991 and then began to decrease. The rate of decline prior to the 1996 firearms laws is indistinguishable from the rate afterwards.[15] Logically, this suggests that the firearms legislation had no effect upon the gradually declining homicide rate.

The plummeting homicide rate in the USA during the 1990s contrasts strongly with the slow decline in Australia (see Figure 4). In the USA, the homicide rate dropped 32 per cent between 1995 and 2001, while it fell by only 10 per cent in Australia. At the same time Australia banned and confiscated legally owned firearms, the number of states in the USA that allow their residents to carry concealed handguns increased from 28 to 40 out of the total of 50 states.

The divergence between Australia and the USA is even more apparent when one considers violent crime. While violent crime is decreasing in the USA, it continued to increase in Australia for four years following 1997, although it has recently started to decline. In 2003, the violent crime rate had decreased by 22 per cent in the USA since 1997, while it had increased by over 14 per cent in Australia.[15] Assault rates jumped from 623 per 100,000 in 1996 to 815 per 100,000 in 2002, easing just slightly to 798 per 100,000 in 2003. Robbery jumped from under 90 per 100,000 prior to 1997 up to 137 per 100,000 in 2001, before returning to pre-1997 levels in 2004 (ABS, 2005; AIC, 2001; Mouzos and Carcach, 2001). Despite the recent decline in violent crime in Australia, it is illogical to credit the 1997 firearms law for this drop given that violent crime did not begin to decline until four years after the gun law.

The destruction of the confiscated firearms cost Australian taxpayers an estimated $A500 million and has had no visible impact on violent crime (Lawson, 1999). The costs of the confiscation do not include the costs of bureaucracy, which, as has been shown in Canada, can be considerable. The proposed solution to the failure of the 1997 gun regulations is to pass even more restrictions on handguns. This is all the more remarkable because in Australia, as in Great Britain and Canada, few firearms used in homicide are legally held; in 1999/2000 only 12 out of 65 (18 per cent) were identified as being misused by their legal owner (Mouzos, 2001).

Canada

As in other countries, recent changes in firearms policy were precipitated by a media frenzy over a multiple murder. On 6 December 1989, Marc Lepine, born Gamil Gharbi, went to the University of Montreal campus, where he killed fourteen women and wounded another thirteen students, including four men, before he finally shot himself (Jones, 1998). Even though Gharbi encountered almost one hundred students and at least three teachers, no one tried to stop the murderer.

---

15 Violent crime is defined differently in the two countries, so they cannot be compared directly. The primary differences lie in how assault and particularly sexual assault are defined. In addition, in 2004 Australia withheld reporting on crimes of assault owing to a concern over the definitional variance across reporting states.

Figure 5   **Trends in homicide rates in Canada and the USA**

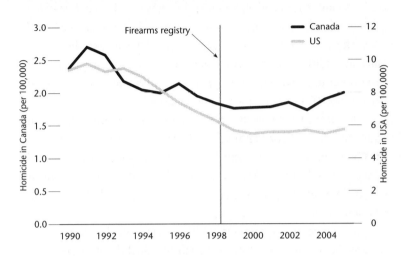

Source: Statistics Canada and the FBI

An investigation by the Montreal coroner severely criticised the police for their inadequate response and stated that the type of weapon used was not a significant factor in the murders (MacDonald, 1990: A1). Nevertheless, Canada twice introduced sweeping changes to its firearms laws, first in 1991, under the Conservative government, and then again in 1995 under the Liberals. These changes included prohibiting over half of all registered handguns in 1995, licensing firearm owners and requiring the registration of long arms (i.e. rifles and shotguns) in 1998.[16]

The Canadian homicide rate has remained essentially stable since the mid-1990s after declining during the early 1990s. In 2000 it began to increase again. Over this same time period, firearm murders have also declined, although this has been compensated by increases in

---

16   Handguns have been required to be registered in Canada since 1934. See www.cfc-cafc. gc.ca/pol-leg/hist/firearms/default_e.asp.

murders involving knives and clubs. The homicide rate plummeted in the USA while the Canadian homicide rate has remained flat (see Figure 5). Between 1991 and 1997, the homicide rates in both Canada and the USA fell by 32 per cent. Since 1997, the homicide rate in the USA has fallen an additional 19 per cent, from 6.8 per 100,000 in 1991 to 5.5 per 100,000 in 2004, while the Canadian rate has remained stable at 1.8–1.9 per 100,000 (Dauvergne, 2005; Gannon, 2006).

The contrast between the rate of criminal violence in the United States and that in Canada is much more dramatic. Over the past decade, the Canadian violent crime rate has stayed basically stable while in the United States during the same time period the rate of violent crime has decreased from 600 per 100,000 to 500 per 100,000 (FBI, 2003, 2006; Gannon, 2006).[17]

The Canadian experiment with firearms regulation is moving towards farce. Although it was originally claimed that this experiment would cost only $CAN2 million, the Auditor General reported in 2001 that the costs of the firearm registry were out of control and would be more than $CAN1 *billion* (Fraser, 2002a).[18] Unfortunately, her mandate was limited so she could not examine the entire sprawling programme. The final costs are unknown but, if the costs of enforcement are included, estimates now reach $CAN3 billion. It is important to recognise that the introduction of any expensive programme, such as universal firearms registration, typically causes expenditures for other policing priorities to be reduced. In Canada, the police budget was effectively frozen in the 1990s – that is, after factoring in inflation, there has been no real increase in the budget.

Though the stated goal of firearms registration is to disarm legally unqualified persons, the ministry discontinued background investigations in order to speed up the protracted process (Breitkreuz, 2004). This was one of the reasons why the Royal Canadian Mounted Police

---

17 See Gannon (2001) for a thorough discussion of the differences in measurement of crime rates in the USA and Canada.
18 This estimate was confirmed in a more thorough audit four years later (Fraser, 2006).

announced it does not trust the information in the registry (Fraser, 2002b).

An even more serious problem is that the security of the firearms registry has come under question after a series of large-scale robberies from gun collectors and gun shops in southern Ontario. These robberies appear to have been specifically directed by criminals who had access to inside information about the locations of gun collections (Bonokoski, 2006: 10; Tibbits, 2006: A10).

The countries considered to this point merely attempted to restrict certain types of firearms or to register firearms. A critical reader may well ask whether a more thorough firearms ban would have been more effective. The next two countries to be discussed enable the effectiveness of firearms bans to be evaluated. In the 1970s, both the Republic of Ireland and Jamaica passed legislation in order to prohibit virtually all firearms. These countries did not simply regulate firearms, or ban a particular type of dangerous firearm, but instead attempted a comprehensive ban of nearly all firearms. Each did so in a desperate effort to break a spiral of violence. Each of these countries has serious problems with organised crime or terrorists which a gun ban does not address.

The Republic of Ireland

Concerned by the rapid rise of sectarian violence in Northern Ireland, on 2 August 1972 the Irish Republic issued a Firearms Temporary Custody Order under the extraordinary powers it had given itself in the 1964 Firearms Act, Clause 4. It required no debate in Parliament; it became law as soon as the Minister for Justice issued the Order.[19] Virtually all firearms were required to be surrendered to the authorities within three days.

Even though the Irish Republic was not hit as hard as its northern neighbour, the threat was perceived as very real and the Irish government claimed that the risk of the Irish Republican Army (IRA) stealing

---

19   This legislation included all handguns, including airguns, and all rifles over .22 caliber. Thus shotguns and .22 rifles were excluded.

Figure 6   **Murder trend in the Republic of Ireland**
Number of murder incidents

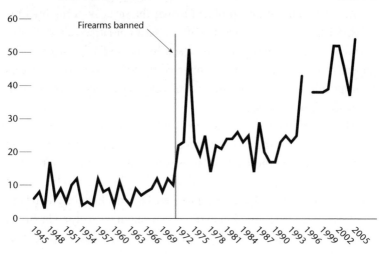

Source: Garda Stochana Annual Reports (no data available for 1996)

firearms from private homes justified the Custody Order.[20] Despite the firearms ban, the number of murders in the Republic of Ireland doubled with the introduction of the Custody Order. Prior to 1972, there were on average no more than 13 murders per year; but in 1972 the number jumped to 28 murders and the average remained at this level for the next twenty years, when it started to rise again to its present level of about 45 murders per year (Brewer et al., 1997; Garda Stochana, 2006).[21] Even more troubling, the murder of police officers rose dramatically as well.

20   The recent 30-year period of violence, colloquially called 'The Troubles', began with civil rights marches in 1968, but rapidly escalated into extreme violence. Murders in Northern Ireland jumped from 5 per year up to 1968, to 123 in 1971, and then to 376 in 1972.

21   Murder statistics for the Republic of Ireland are given as raw frequencies rather than rates per 100,000 population. In this way we can avoid any possible error introduced from over- (or under-) estimating annual population increases. The Republic of Ireland has grown but slowly over the past 30 years; the population has increased by only 3 per cent over the past fifteen years.

When Officer Fallon was murdered in 1970, with an illegal pistol, it was the first murder of a police officer for 28 years; but in the 29 years that followed, another thirteen officers were murdered, all with illegally held firearms. With a substantially static population, these figures represent dramatic rate increases. Apart from allowing small-calibre hunting rifles (calibres up to .270) in 1993, the Firearm Custody Order continued to be enforced right up until 2004 (Bernard, 2005).[22]

Clearly, the evidence linking the doubling of the murder rate to the introduction of the Custody Order is only circumstantial. Nevertheless, it can clearly be seen from Figure 6 that government efforts, including the draconian Firearms Custody Order and its extension for 32 years, certainly did not bring the murder rate down.

Other violent crimes have also increased over the past thirty or so years. For example, the number of robberies (including thefts) jumped from under 500 per year in the early 1970s to over 2,000 per year in the early 1980s, and even hit 3,500 in 1995. There were over 4,000 robberies in 2005, the most recent year for which statistics are available.

In hindsight, it appears difficult to believe that banning and confiscating firearms from target shooters, hunters and farmers could ever have been imagined to be a successful strategy to combat an organised group of terrorists such as the IRA. Nevertheless, the Irish government and police steadfastly pursued it for 32 years, regardless of its questionable legality, until forced to abandon it by legal action.[23]

---

22 I am indebted to Mr Derek Bernard for supplying the information about the murder of Officer Fallon and the detailed nature of the Irish firearms laws. Personal communication, Derek Bernard, 27 October 2005.

23 This legislation has recently been overturned in an Irish court. At the time of writing, the Custody Order and associated firearms ban has gone, only to be replaced by massive obstructionism and delay, defended usually on the grounds that 'a new Firearms Law is on the way and no new authorisations will be issued until it comes out' (private correspondence from John Sheehan).

Jamaica

In the early 1970s, Jamaica was shocked by a horrifying increase in drug-related violence involving guns. The murder rate jumped from between 6 and 7 deaths per 100,000 population in the late 1960s to 8 per 100,000 in 1970 and then to over 11 per 100,000 by 1973. In response, the Jamaican government decided to introduce the Gun Court Act in 1974. The Gun Court was a drastic institution that eliminated many safeguards in the British legal tradition such as open hearings and trial by jury (although these were retained for capital cases). The standard, mandatory sentence for almost any firearm offence, even the illegal possession of a single cartridge, was life imprisonment. Those charged would be imprisoned without bail until tried, often for two years or more.[24]

The results of the Jamaica Gun Court were not encouraging, even though the number of murders dropped the year the Gun Court was introduced. In 1973, before the Gun Court, 227 people were murdered and in 1974 this number fell to 195. Unfortunately, the number increased in 1975 to 266, and it increased again to 367 in 1976. Despite the continuation of draconian controls on firearms, the number of people murdered has continued to increase. In 2001, the most recent year for which statistics are available, 1,139 people were murdered in Jamaica.

The raw figures do not tell the full story because of population changes. Consequently, murder rates per 100,000 people in the general population have been calculated (Francis, 2001).[25] As may be seen in Figure 7, the murder rate jumped more than 50 per cent from 9 per 100,000 to over 16 per 100,000 from the early 1970s to the mid-1970s, and has continued to climb. Nor did the gun ban reduce gang shootings. A few years after the introduction of the Gun Court, the murder rate reached a deplorable figure of over 40 deaths per 100,000, but it

---

24   In 1982 and 1983, these conditions were relaxed somewhat, but they nevertheless remain draconian to the present day.

25   I am indebted to Professor Emeritus Alexander Francis of the University of the Western Indies for access to his extensive time-series of crime statistics in Jamaica.

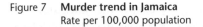

Figure 7   **Murder trend in Jamaica**
Rate per 100,000 population

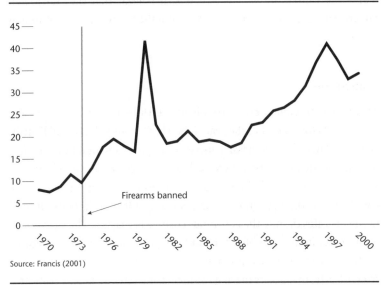

Firearms banned

Source: Francis (2001)

soon fell back down to between 18 and 19 per 100,000 for the rest of the 1980s. The murder rate began climbing again in the 1990s until it surpassed even the previous high in 2001, with 43 murders per 100,000.

It is difficult to argue that the Gun Court was successful. Perhaps more so than most, Jamaica is a special case. The two major political parties are both rumoured to have consistently employed criminal gangs to terrorise their opponents and, as a result of political corruption, these gangs have no trouble in smuggling whatever offensive weapons they desire. In a very real sense the gangs associated with whichever party happened to be in power were above the law. Let us remember that people accused of nothing more than the ownership of a single bullet lost their most basic legal rights and were punished with sentences harsher than those served for murder in other societies. As would be expected, there is no shortage of hypotheses about who or what is to blame. Each political party blames the other and both blame the United States. Nevertheless, it is clear that the crackdown on firearms did not manage to reduce either gun crime or criminal violence.

Conclusion

This review of violent crime trends in the United Kingdom, Australia and Canada found that in the years following the introduction of British-style gun laws, despite massive increases in governmental bureaucracy, total homicide rates either increased or remained stable. Similar trends were observed in total violent crime. Importantly, in not one of these countries did the new gun laws appear to result in a decrease in total homicide rates despite the enormous costs to taxpayers. The situation is even clearer in the Republic of Ireland and Jamaica, where violent crime, particularly murder, became much worse after the bans in both countries. Clearly, the factors driving the increasing rates of violent crime, for example organised crime or terrorism, were not curtailed by British-style gun laws.

The failure of British-style firearm laws to influence the total homicide rate in any of the jurisdictions examined here is suggestive but not conclusive. The causal link remains unproven. The British Home Office argues that crime would have increased even more rapidly had the gun laws not been imposed. That explanation is problematic, given the failure of British-style gun laws in other countries.

These trends contrast with the situation in the United States, where there was an impressive drop in the American homicide and violent crime rates. Three plausible explanations have been advanced for the plummeting criminal violence. First, it is driven by concealed-carry laws. Based on impressive analyses, Lott and Mustard conclude that adoption of these statutes has so deterred criminals from confrontation crime as to cause murder and violent crime to fall faster in states that adopted this policy than in the states that did not (Lott, 2000; Lott and Mustard,

1997).[26] Alternatively, two other American phenomena might be driving crime rates: the dramatic increase in both the prison population and the number of executions in the United States. During this time period, the prison population in the USA tripled, jumping from roughly 100 prisoners per 100,000 in the late 1970s to over 300 per 100,000 people in the general population in the early 1990s (Beck and Harrison, 2005). In addition, executions in the USA soared from about five per year in the early 1980s to more than 27 per year in the early 1990s (Bonczar and Snell, 2004). None of these trends is reflected in Commonwealth countries (Langan and Farrington, 1998). Further research is required to identify more precisely which element of the US approach is the most important, or whether all three elements acting in concert were necessary to reduce criminal violence.

Whatever the reason, the upshot is that violent crime in the USA, and homicide in particular, has plummeted over the past fifteen years.[27] This chapter merely scratches the surface in attempting to understand the link between firearm laws and crime rates. But the study corroborates American research that has been unable to identify any gun law that had reduced violent crime, suicide or gun accidents (Hahn et al., 2003; Wellford et al., 2004). Much more research needs to be conducted before firm conclusions may be drawn. We may need to wait for other countries to experiment with aspects of the American approach to be able to determine which elements are the most effective in reducing crime: aggressive police activity, increasing prison populations, capital punishment or empowering citizens to defend themselves. Nevertheless, the failure of British-style gun laws in all the countries examined here

---

26 Several critics have now replicated Lott's work using additional or different data, additional control variables, or new or different statistical techniques they deem superior to those Lott used. Interestingly, the replications all confirm Lott's general conclusions; some even find that Lott *under*estimated the crime-reductive effects of allowing good citizens to carry concealed guns. See the seven articles printed in the 2001 special issue of the *Journal of Law and Economics* (44(2)); see also Plassman and Whitley (2003). Lott (2003) reiterates and extends his earlier findings.

27 These trends are easily seen in the Uniform Crime Reports (UCR) data on the website of the Federal Bureau of Investigation (www.fbi.gov/ucr/ucr.htm).

should give pause to anyone who imagines that efforts to impose international controls on firearms will be successful in reducing criminal or political violence.

References

ABS (Australian Bureau of Statistics) (2005), *Recorded Crime – Victims, Australia, 2005*, Canberra, ACT: Australian Bureau of Statistics, www.abs.gov.au/AUSSTATS/abs@.nsf/DetailsPage/4510.02005? OpenDocument.

AIC (Australian Institute of Criminology) (2001), *Australian Crime, Facts and Figures, 2000*, Canberra, ACT: Australian Institute of Criminology.

Baker, J. and S. McPhedran (2007), 'Gun laws and sudden death: did the Australian firearms legislation make a difference?', *British Journal of Criminology*, 47: 455–69.

Barnet, R. E. and D. B. Kates (1996), 'Under fire: the new consensus on the Second Amendment', *Emory Law Journal*, 45: 1139–259.

Barrett, D. (2007), 'Government figures "missing" two million violent crimes', *Independent* (online edition), 26 June, http://news. independent.co.uk/uk/crime/article2710596.ece.

Beck, A. and P. Harrison (2005), 'Correctional populations in the United States, 1997', and 'Prisoners in 2004', in *Key Facts at a Glance*, Bureau of Justice Statistics, www.ojp.usdoj.gov/bjs/glance/ tables/incrttab.htm.

Bellamy, P. (2003), *Martin Bryant, www.crimelibrary.com/serial/bryant*.

Bernard, D. (2005), Personal communication, 27 October.

Bonczar, T. and T. L. Snell (2004), *Capital Punishment, 2003*, Bureau of Justice Statistics Bulletin, NJC 206627, November.

Bonokoski, M. (2006), 'In the wake of firearms thefts, it's possible the gun registry is not as secure as touted', *Toronto Sun*, 10 March.

Breitkreuz, G. (2004) 'CFC statistics: firearm licence refusals & revocations, by reason, by province as of February 1, 2004', Member

of Parliament, Saskatchewan, Canada, www.garrybreitkreuz.com/
publications/RefusalsandRevocationsbyReason2004–02–01.xls.

Brewer, J. D., B. Lockhart and P. Rogers (1997), *Crime in Ireland,
1945–95: 'Here there be dragons'*, Oxford: Clarendon Press.

Craton, M. (1974), *Sinews of Empire: A Short History of British Slavery*,
Garden City, NY: Anchor Books.

Dauvergne, M. (2005), 'Homicide in Canada, 2004', *Juristat*, 25(6),
Ottawa, Ontario: Statistics Canada.

FBI (Federal Bureau of Investigation) (2003), *Uniform Crime Reports,
Table 1: Index of Crime, United States, 1982–2001*, Digital document
available at www.fbi.gov/ucr/01cius.html.

FBI (Federal Bureau of Investigation) (2006), *FBI Uniform Crime Reports,
Preliminary Annual Reports, Preliminary Annual Uniform Crime
Report, 2005*, Tables 1 and 3, www.fbi.gov/ucr/2005preliminary/
index.htm.

Francis, A. (2001), 'Crime in Jamaica: a preliminary analysis', Paper
presented at the 2nd International Conference on Crime and
Criminal Justice in the Caribbean, Department of Government,
UWI, Mona, Kingston, 14–17 February.

Fraser, S. (2002a), 'Department of Justice – costs of implementing
the Firearms Program', in *2002 Report of the Auditor General of
Canada*, Ottawa, Ontario, www.oag-bvg.gc.ca/domino/reports.nsf/
html/20021210ce.html.

Fraser, S. (2002b), 'Royal Canadian Mounted Police – Canadian
Firearms Program', in *2002 Report of the Auditor General of Canada*,
Ottawa, Ontario, www.oag-bvg.gc.ca/domino/reports.nsf/
html/20021211ce.html#ch11hd3c.

Fraser, S. (2006), 'Canadian Firearms Program', in *2006 Report of the
Auditor General of Canada*, Ottawa, Ontario, www.oag-bvg.gc.ca/
domino/reports.nsf/html/06menu_e.html.

Gannon, M. (2001), 'Crime comparisons between Canada and the
United States', *Juristat*, 21(11).

Gannon, M. (2006), 'Crime statistics in Canada, 2005', *Juristat*, 26(4).

Garda Stochana (2000–2006), *An Garda Stochana Annual Reports 1999–2005*, www.garda.ie/angarda/statistics/.

Greenwood, C. (2001), 'Labour's gun plan', *Shooting Times and Country Magazine*, April.

Hahn, R. A., O. O. Bilukha, A. Crosby, M. Thompson Fullilove, A. Liberman, E. K. Moscicki, S. Snyder, F. Tuma and S. P. Briss (2003), *First Reports Evaluating the Effectiveness of Strategies for Preventing Violence: Firearms Laws. Findings from the Task Force on Community Preventive Services*, Atlanta, GA: Centers for Disease Control, www. cdc.gov/mmwr/preview/mmwrhtml/rr5214a2.htm.

Home Office (2001), *Criminal Statistics, England and Wales, 2000*, Norwich: HMSO.

Jones, A. (1998), 'Case study: the Montreal massacre', www.lbduk.org/dv_and_bias_in_the_media_Canada%20white%20ribbon.htm.

Kates, D. B. (2005), 'The limits of gun control: a criminological perspective', in T. D. Lytton (ed.), *Suing the Firearms Industry: A Legal Battle at the Crossroads of Gun Control and Mass Torts*, Ann Arbor, MI: University of Michigan Press.

Kates, D. B. and G. A. Mauser (2007), 'Would banning firearms reduce murder and suicide? A review of international and some domestic evidence', *Harvard Journal of Law and Public Policy*, 30(2): 649–94.

Kopel, D. (1992), *The Samurai, the Mountie, and the Cowboy*, New York: Prometheus Books.

Langan, P. and D. Farrington (1998), *Crime and Justice in the United States and in England and Wales, 1981–96*, NJC 169294 (October), Washington, DC: Bureau of Justice Statistics, US Department of Justice.

Lawson, J. B. (1999), 'New national gun laws – are they cost effective?', *Institute of Public Affairs Review*, 51(4): 27–8.

Lott, J., Jr (2000), *More Guns, Less Crime*, 2nd edn, Chicago, IL: University of Chicago Press.

Lott, J., Jr (2003), *The Bias against Guns*, Washington, DC: Regnery.

Lott, J., Jr and D. B. Mustard (1997), 'Crime, deterrence, and right-to-carry concealed handguns', *Journal of Legal Studies*, 26(1): 1–68.

MacDonald, D. (1990), 'Killer Lepine had 60 shells left: report on Montreal massacre', *Edmonton Journal*, 15 May.

Malcolm, J. L. (2002), *Guns and Violence: The English Experience*, Cambridge, MA: Harvard University Press.

Mauser, G. A. (2003), 'The failed experiment: gun control and public safety in Canada, Australia, England and Wales', Public Policy Sources, no. 71, Vancouver, BC: Fraser Institute.

Mouzos, J. (1999), *Firearm-related Violence: The Impact of the Nationwide Agreement on Firearms*, Trends and Issues no. 116, Canberra, ACT: Australian Institute of Criminology.

Mouzos, J. (2000), *The Licensing and Registration Status of Firearms Used in Homicide. Trends and Issues*, Trends and Issues no. 151, Canberra, ACT: Australian Institute of Criminology.

Mouzos, J. (2001), *Homicide in Australia, 1999–2000*, Trends and Issues no. 187 (February), Canberra, ACT: Australian Institute of Criminology.

Mouzos, J. (2003), *Homicide in Australia, 2001–2002*, Research and Public Policy Issues 46, Canberra, ACT: Australian Institute of Criminology.

Mouzos, J. and C. Carcach (2001), *Weapon Involvement in Armed Robbery*, Research and Public Policy Issues 38, Canberra, ACT: Australian Institute of Criminology.

Munday, R.A.I. and J. A. Stevenson (1996), *Guns and Violence: The Debate before Lord Cullen*, Brightlingsea: Piedmont.

Nicholas, S., D. Povey, A. Walker and C. Kershaw (2005), *Crime in England and Wales, 2004/2005*, Home Office Statistical Bulletin, London: Home Office.

O'Hanlon, K. (2006), 'Concealed-weapons bill adopted', *Journal Star*, Lincoln, NE, 31 March, www.journalstar.com/articles/2006/03/31/legislature/doc442c57ae8eb55289989057.txt.

Peele, G. (1995), *Governing the UK*, 3rd edn, Oxford: Blackwell.

Plassman, F. and J. Whitley (2003), 'Confirming "more guns, less crime",' *Stanford Law Review*, 55: 1313.

Reuter, P. and J. Mouzos (2002), 'Australia: a massive buyback of low-risk guns', Paper presented to the American Society of Criminology, Chicago, IL.

Scottish Executive (2004a), *Homicide in Scotland, 2003 – Statistics Published*, Justice Department, Criminal Justice Division, 24 November, Edinburgh: Scottish Executive.

Scottish Executive (2004b), *Recorded Crime in Scotland, 2003*, Criminal Justice Series, CrJ2004/5.

Scottish Executive (2006), *Homicide in Scotland, 2004/2005*, Scottish Executive Statistical Bulletin, Criminal Justice Series, CrJ/2005/12, www.scotland.gov.uk/Publications/2004/11/20292/47178.

Tibbits, J. (2006), 'Gun registry called a breeze to hack by ex-webmaster', *Montreal Gazette*, 13 March.

Tweedie, K. (2005), 'Scotland tops list of world's most violent countries', *The Times*, 19 September, www.timesonline.co.uk/article/0,,2-1786945,00.html.

Van Duyne, P. C., and M. Levi (2005), *Drugs and Money: Managing the drug trade and crime-money in Europe*, London: Routledge.

Van Kesteren, J., P. Mayhew and P. Nieuwbeerta (2001), 'Criminal victimization in 17 industrialized countries: key findings from the 2000 International Crime Victimization Surveys', 23 February, The Hague: Ministry of Justice.

Walker, A., C. Kershaw and S. Nicholas (2006), *Crime in England and Wales 2005/06*, Home Office Statistical Bulletin, London: Home Office, www.homeoffice.gov.uk/rds/crimeew0506.html.

Wellford, C. F., J. V. Pepper and C. V. Petrie (eds) (2004), *Firearms and Violence: A Critical Review*, Washington, DC: National Academy of Sciences.

6 ADVERTISING
Alberto Mingardi[1]

Introduction

In 1959, one of the first books published by the Institute of Economic Affairs was a 216-page monograph on *Advertising in a Free Society*, written by Ralph Harris (1924–2006) and Arthur Seldon (1916–2005). The book is a lively testimony to the spirit of both men and to the ethos of the intellectual enterprise they had just started: it is a passionate defence of advertising against the most common misconceptions about it in the public discourse and the mistakes of mainstream economic analysis that underlie those very misconceptions.

Harris and Seldon's work is far from being outdated and still speaks to us, especially because of their emphasis on the bonds between the institutions of advertising and the institutions of a free economy. Harris and Seldon wrote:

> In earlier ages, when men were forced to supply their needs from the direct labour of their family, organized advertising played no part in the economy of strictly local communities. However defined, advertisements consist basically of *invitations* to buy or sell, to borrow or to lend, to work or to patronize worthy causes. Every advertisement is a call to action of some kind or another. It makes no sense unless addressed to people with freedom to decide

---

1   Part of this chapter was written as a section of a common reflection on advertising with Carlo Stagnaro. I am grateful to Oscar Giannino and Carlo Lottieri for their remarks and suggestions on an earlier version of the chapter and to Jacob Arfwedson for many discussions about the advertising of pharmaceuticals in particular. I am indebted to David Perazzoni for his technical assistance. This essay is dedicated to the memory of Ralph Harris – hero, master, friend.

for themselves the pattern of their work and lives. (Harris and
Seldon, 1959: 1, emphasis added)

Advertising is possible only in a society of individuals conceived and
respected as adults who can make conscious decisions over their own
choices. This intuition by Harris and Seldon will serve as a starting point
for reflecting on advertising today. If advertising as a business practice is
now less under attack than before,[2] it is partly because the advertising of
those goods commonly understood as 'dangerous' has been prohibited.
In particular, tobacco and pharmaceutical products (with few exceptions) cannot be advertised in the territory of the European Union.[3]

Far from being a peripheral problem, this fact indicates the persistence of paternalism and misconceptions about the nature of advertising.
This chapter argues for the freedom to advertise any kind of good, as
a corollary to the set of freedoms granted to an individual in a free
society.

In the course of this work, we will move from a brief review of the
apparently weightiest arguments in favour of the stringent regulation of
advertising practices to the arguments in support of freedom in advertising provided by scholars of the Austrian school of economics. We
will then take into consideration the specific case of pharmaceutical
products, the sale of which is considered at length in Chapter 8 of this
collection and which epitomises the kind of 'advertising paternalism'
referred to herein.

---

2   This may be related to the fact that scepticism over the contents of advertisements is now
    truly widespread in our society. A recent pool of 1,306 young Americans (aged eight to
    eighteen) showed that fewer than one in ten (6 per cent) agreed with the statement 'ad-
    vertisements tell the truth' and more than half (57 per cent) said they often notice tricks
    companies use to get them to buy something. About three-quarters (73 per cent) thought
    that companies try to get people to buy things they do not really need. See www.harrisin-
    teractive.com/news/allnewsbydate.asp?NewsID=1082.
3   Tobacco advertising is regulated by Directive 2003/33/EC of the European Parliament.
    The advertising of prescription drugs is regulated by Directive 92/28/EC.

Can advertising actually change people's behaviour?

To what extent can advertising actually exert a decisive influence on people's preferences? Different policy attitudes to regulating advertising are basically rooted in different answers to this very question.

It is not easy, in this respect, to assess the lingering impact of the argument of Vance Packard's *The Hidden Persuaders* (1957), which can be relied upon to surface in every discussion of this topic. Advertising is purported to be part of the endless host of manipulative tactics of which we are unaware, which Packard explored in his work. This literature, in its turn, has spawned a long catalogue of urban legends, ranging from alleged 'subliminal messages' from soft-drink makers at the entrance to cinemas, supposed to somehow 'compel' filmgoers to purchase an unwanted drink, to a number of other equally amusing examples.

There are at least a couple of problems with this approach, both of them significant. The first is philosophical. Such a view assumes a very limited notion of free will: if a person's will can be bent with such ease, how is it possible to believe that any individual can act freely? Thus, from a political perspective, such a notion is potentially destructive of any representative democratic government. If an individual is so vulnerable to commercial advertising as to be deeply influenced in choices of trivial relevance to his life, what is to be said of political advertising? Are electoral TV ads, posters and rallies bound to crush individual consciousness, to the point of turning each person into a puppet in the hands of all sorts of political hucksters?

Packard's theory can be easily falsified by even a cursory glance at our everyday experience. After all, whatever the flaws of modern democracy, we can observe repeated changes of governing majorities and swinging preferences in the voters. Politics cannot be reduced to mere political communication, and the current rulers, although enjoying easier access to a number of 'approval-shaping' devices, are often rejected by their electorate.

Moreover, the belief that commercial advertising is able to significantly orient consumers' choices tends not to be supported by the relevant research literature. Two noteworthy examples can be mentioned in view of their particular ethical implications, namely direct advertising to children and tobacco advertising.

With regard to the former, it is usually alleged that this kind of advertising could decisively determine the choices of younger viewers (particularly in the choice of toys and snacks), undermining the authority of parents and their ability to control such choices. The main offender is supposed to be television, the medium with which younger consumers are most intimately acquainted (obviously as children mature advertising in print and on the Internet become progressively more relevant).

It should be noted, however, that empirical studies have shown that children *as young as five* display well-defined preferences about TV programming – they choose to watch some shows instead of others, according to their personality, age, cognitive development and gender (Valkenburg and Janssen, 1999).

As in the case of adults, the relevant literature shows that children are not a passive advertisement audience, that they do not fall for everything that comes out of the TV screen, and are instead able to nurture opinions and preferences about the specific commercial they are watching. More specifically, a 1994 study shows that children as young as eleven display a large degree of *scepticism* about the contents of selected advertising campaigns (Bousch et al., 1994).

Children are a valuable and significant market: they directly purchase a sizeable amount of merchandise and they exert a significant degree of influence on their families' consumption choices. It is thus easy to see why they are targeted with intensive marketing campaigns with the aim of promoting the products intended for their consumption.

Nevertheless, advertising can have both intended and unintended consequences – commercials convey information that is not always consistent with the message or the image the product-maker meant to communicate. From the way an advert is made, from the highlights of the commercial and its look (wherefrom one can infer the amount of resources allocated to the campaign, if not its total cost), it is possible to glean a large amount of information. Very young consumers actively participate in this process and, contrary to the common prejudice, have been recognised as *advertising literate* (Preston, 1999: 368).

Furthermore, a report by the Institute of Psychology of Bonn University conceded that no study can show a direct and exclusive causal relationship in children between advertising and consumption because of the complexity of the variables involved (quoted in Bergler, 1999).[4]

In this respect, it is interesting to observe the effects of advertising on tobacco consumption. Cigarette producers had been in the dock for a long time before the implementation of the European Directive dated 26 May 2003, which banned all media advertising of tobacco products.[5] In many countries, the ban goes as far as to forbid billboard advertisements, and it has been suggested that tobacco producers should be banned from sponsoring sports events and athletes. The question arises, though, whether a clear link does (or did) exist between tobacco consumption and advertising.

Judging from the perpetual alarms raised about the number of 'young' smokers, it would appear that the ban on tobacco advertising did not have a remarkable impact on the decision to begin smoking. Antismoking activists typically wish to raise the bar farther and farther. For example, former Italian minister of health Girolamo Sirchia has blamed not only TV ads but also the mere fact that smokers are frequently portrayed in movies, TV serials and shows for inducing the young to smoke.[6]

Again, this viewpoint reflects a very limited view of individual will and responsibility, leading to the belief that the mere sight of another person behaving in a particular manner can compel an individual to emulate them. On this basis, one could hardly explain why

---

4   For a valuable survey of this issue, see Furnham (2000).
5   In its turn, this directive complemented a more intricate legislative process, which ostensibly peaked in 1998 with the issue of Directive 43, which famously barred cigarette makers from sports events sponsorship.
6   See www.ministerosalute.it, May 2002.

detective movies are not banned, since, by this rationale, they are likely to encourage crime!

Cigarette advertising has been singled out for inducing younger consumers to tobacco use, enticing them to begin smoking by virtue of the association of the most important tobacco brands either with events generally held to be glamorous and cool (notably motor sports) or with lively and alluring images.

Unfortunately for those who entertain this notion, the available evidence, as exhaustively reviewed by Hugh High in his IEA Hobart Paper *Does Advertising Increase Smoking?* (1999), does not support this apparently suggestive conclusion. As High illustrates, a survey of the major studies on this matter shows that it is impossible to substantiate the existence of a solid causal link between advertising and tobacco consumption (since, as a well-known maxim in social sciences goes, correlation does not imply causation).

Moreover, a US government study of one of the most recognisable and, arguably, most potentially influential brands is worthy of note. This study was of the R. J. Reynolds campaign centred on the fictional character of Joe Camel, whose influence on younger minds was supposedly very high. After a close review of available evidence, the US Federal Trade Commission concluded that there is no demonstrable link between the inclination to buy and smoke cigarettes among young people and the strong brand identity of Joe Camel.

It is not immediately obvious that the success of a brand is associated with the widening of its constituency: a 1995 survey showed that the youths more able to identify Joe Camel were those more likely to disapprove of cigarette smoking (Mizerski, 1995; High, 1999: 87–8).

Beyond any oversimplifications, therefore, the crucial finding of studies on this topic is, as High (1999: 94) summarises, that 'while tobacco advertising *may be* associated with tobacco consumption, it does not follow that tobacco advertising induces people, particularly youngsters, to smoke'.

This finding, along with evidence relating to the relationship between children and advertising, buttresses the conclusion that individual will cannot be 'manipulated' by the contents of commercials. Advertising does not control society; it simply conveys information. In so doing, it satisfies a real consumer demand – the availability of information is a way, or rather *the* way, to reduce uncertainty. To wear designer clothes enhances the social persona of the wearer; to purchase the drink of a renowned maker guarantees that the taste will be the same everywhere, guarding the consumer from unpleasant surprises (as well as, obviously, from enjoyable discoveries).

Advertising and the theory of entrepreneurial discovery

In the view of Austrian economist Israel M. Kirzner, the role of advertising is misconceived in the framework of mainstream economics (i.e. it is posited that public choices are more or less purposefully shaped) because advertising cannot easily be accommodated within neoclassical economic theory. In such analysis advertising is usually held to be a 'generally harmful and wasteful phenomenon, responsible for serious divergence of capitalist performance from the efficiency conditions in the perfect competition model' (Kirzner, 1997: 54).

Although some neoclassical economists do realise that advertising conveys information, Kirzner suggests that it is not by chance that others, as famously illustrated by John Kenneth Galbraith (for example, 1958: ch. 11), do not understand this practice, to the point of seeing it as evidence that in fact market relations are not characterised by the notion of 'consumer sovereignty'.

Kirzner's theory of entrepreneurial discovery, focusing on the alertness of the entrepreneur and his role as 'discoverer of the unknown' – in brief, on the creative content of his trade – offers a more convenient explanation of advertising:

> In order to serve the preferences of consumers, producers have
> to do far more than merely fabricate and make available the
> goods they believe consumers desire most urgently. They must

do more, even, than to make available the information they believe consumers need to acquire and appreciate the goods on offer. After all, the entrepreneurial discovery perspective shows that mere availability does not guarantee that those needing information will have it. Even if information is staring them in the face they may simply not notice it, and remain unaware that there is anything further to be known. It is therefore necessary for producers, intent on winning the profits from innovatively serving consumer preferences, also to *alert consumers* to the availability and the qualities of goods. Clearly there is a role for advertising beyond 'providing information in response to consumer demands'. (Kirzner, 1997: 55)

If we view the entrepreneur not as a mere producer of goods, information about which is somehow already available to consumers, but as an *innovator* – if, in other words, we have a *dynamic*, as opposed to *static*, notion of competition – advertising becomes necessary. In this case advertising is not mere 'information dissemination', but becomes an aggressive strategy aimed at depicting both a product and its features in the most enticing way.

The reason is obvious: the career of an entrepreneur is not characterised – if not in exceptional instances – by the exclusive attention to one market, however attractive. Everyone is a 'plural consumer', hardly interested in the satisfaction of a single need and characterised instead by diverse requirements, by different wants and desires and by constantly evolving preferences.

Even the most simple and trivial event of our life as consumers – the choice between product A and product B – cannot exist in an 'informational void', but needs a steady flow of fresh information, since the available offer changes continually. As Kirzner (ibid.: 56) adds: 'The notion of "serving the consumers" must be broadened to mean fulfilling consumer preferences, not as they were before the entrepreneur began his activities, but as they will be once the entrepreneur has made consumers aware of his product.'

This perspective undermines any denunciation of the entrepreneur's attempt to 'orient' consumer's preferences. Contemporary forms of advertising, aggressive in style and aiming to grab the attention of potential customers, can be properly appreciated on the basis of producers' need to inform consumers of the existence of hitherto unknown products. People's preferences may be modified as a result of exposure to advertising, but this is because the stock of information available to them is increased and this affects their available choices. It is not because individual will is directly modified by watching television.[7]

It is clear that in a complex, changing and uncertain world, consumers can only be imperfectly informed of the features of the available goods. Eliciting their interest becomes an increasingly sophisticated endeavour and entails ever-rising attention and expenditure. Since each of us is a 'plural consumer' and time is a scarce resource, the advertisement must convince us to turn our attention to a specific product – and this just to make sure that we become acquainted with its characteristics.

This notion of advertising could mislead us into believing that capitalists invest substantial resources in an attempt to goad consumers into *purchasing unwanted goods* or, in other words, that the necessary amount of advertising for a given product is inversely proportional to the genuine wish of consumers to enjoy it.

This approach assumes that producers deem it more efficient to invest resources in goods they know or anticipate the public does not want, and then proceed to invest substantial resources in sophisticated advertising campaigns, and that the whole process is somehow more

---

7   A very important point, as far as the economic feasibility of using advertising to attempt to modify individual preferences, is raised by Gordon Tullock (1967: 16): '... new products which require no shifts in preferences are more likely to be chosen by entrepreneurs than those that do require such shifts. If changing preferences is worthwhile, then small changes will be preferred to large, and changes in areas where preferences are not strongly held, to changes in strongly held preferences. In a strictly technical sense, this process of attempting to change preferences only when such a change seems fairly easy will rationalize the individual's preference schedule. Where there is some tension between parts of the individual's preference ordering, changes which reduce the tension would normally be fairly easy and, hence, we should expect entrepreneurs to prefer such changes'.

rational than to simply invest in goods that are known or expected to be desired by the consumers.

There is no compelling reason to accept such a view, which assumes that consumers' free will can be bent and shaped by corporations (while, as we have seen, there is no evidence that it can be in any way 'controlled' by advertising) and that corporations themselves feel confident enough of this presumed control to systematically invest, as it were, in cheating and swindling their customers.

Such a view also contrasts with a straightforward observation, easily confirmed by common experience, that innovative products often do actually *improve our lives*. The entrepreneurial process does in fact change our lives, but it does not orient them in a direction that consumers themselves do not deem beneficial. After all, if we actually faced a deceitful practice, the problem should not be found in advertising as an instrument for a fraud, but in the fraud itself. Otherwise, one might as well advocate a ban on cars, since they are often used as getaway vehicles after robberies.

In this respect, Robert B. Ekelund and David S. Saurman (1988: 161) have emphasised how the host of 'consumer protection' regulations are usually based on flawed assumptions: 'consumers are considered irrational and the subjects of manipulation of advertisers and producers. The term "consumer protection" itself implies that consumers are weak and defenseless in the marketplace and that they must be somehow protected from any fraud associated with advertising'.

But 'consumers are not irrational and will not consciously act in a manner that is detrimental to their own self-interest. Consumers will not *continuously* buy empty cereal boxes [be defrauded] just because they are advertised on Saturday morning TV' (ibid.: 162). After all, producers themselves are consumers, since they consume all that they do not themselves make. The vision of a world in which everybody is a victim of someone else is a truly appalling image.

In brief, consumers' will is not oriented by advertising campaigns; rather, advertising is the device producers use to *inform* consumers of the existence of new products. Consumers are free to be wary of the information they receive and, in fact, empirical evidence shows that this is what actually happens.

Are dangerous products different? The case of pharmaceuticals

We have explored, albeit briefly, the major misconceptions about the role played by advertising in a free society. Conceivably, however, it could be argued that some products should escape the above analysis, because of their particularly dangerous nature.

It is easy to argue that if something is particularly dangerous by standards apparently shared by a given society, anything that may increase its circulation should be limited. Most of the time, such a result is simply pursued by making some particular consumption good illegal. The typical case may be that of those recreational drugs that are outlawed in most Western countries.

On the other hand, there are goods that though legally purchasable cannot be advertised. In the territory of the European Union, this is the case with tobacco (already mentioned) and most pharmaceutical products.[8]

As far as cigarettes are concerned, the ban on advertising is the consequence of a long political campaign involving lobbying and the creation of widespread concern among the public about tobacco smoking. The ban is therefore the conclusion of a long process. Now that tobacco smoking is largely conceived as an activity better to be avoided in our societies, we have adopted a policy that should somehow be in tune with the necessity of limiting cigarette consumption. Its effects may be questionable, but it certainly reflects the common wisdom of society – and it illustrates the political effectiveness of anti-smoking groups.

As far as pharmaceuticals are concerned, they are supposed to be *by*

---

8   As noted above, advertising of pharmaceutical products is prohibited by European Directive 92/28.

their very nature different from any other class of goods, as they affect in a very direct and immediate way people's health. The exceptional status of legal drugs therefore reflects partly their nature (remedies that heal and substances that poison are close cousins) and partly the fact that in the welfare state they are often 'reimbursed' by government (i.e. are free of charge). Both their nature and the scarcity of government funds suggest that consumption of pharmaceuticals has to be limited.

If we stick with the first argument, we see that the potentially harmful nature of a legal drug is not that it is dangerous per se (the principle that can harm is indeed the same principle that can heal), but because of the misuse an individual can make of a medicine.

The most effective argument against the advertisement of legal drugs is an obvious illustration of what is usually called a 'vicious circle': it is assumed that the patient does not have the degree of technical knowledge needed to assess the effectiveness of a medical product and therefore it is resolved that he cannot have the right to gather *further* information. In other words, ignorance excuses *more* ignorance.

It is perfectly plain that as a rule the patient cannot avail himself of the same degree of knowledge as a medical practitioner. This is an obvious consequence of the *division of labour* underpinning any advanced society. The division of labour likewise entails a *division of knowledge*.[9] Since the economic, intellectual and time resources available to each individual are limited, the reliance on skilled individuals is enormously convenient and helpful, since it exempts us from the need to deepen or widen our expertise in different areas. Each of us is 'rationally ignorant' of most things: gaining expertise in most fields entails too high a cost when compared with the expected benefit. The division of labour provides an answer to this quandary – somebody else has already paid that cost.

To have functioning plumbing we do not need to improvise as plumbers. The same applies for that uniquely important service provided

---

9   For an illuminating analysis of the extension of the division of knowledge in complex societies, see the second part of North (2005).

by physicians, whom we rely on for the monitoring of our health and for the treatment of any harmful condition.

This does not imply, however, that physicians ought to enjoy a complete monopoly on relevant information concerning our health: not only because it is too precious a good to be entirely left to someone else, albeit skilled in his trade, as paralleled in the old saying that 'war is too important to be left to generals', but also because every legal monopoly is known inevitably to bring about several problems that are easily avoidable in a market order – in this instance, in the information market.

Let us delve into this matter one step at a time. The fact that health is a crucial part of our lives is not per se a valid rationale for limiting the amount of information relating to the safeguard of the special good it represents. Feeding is likewise a crucial part of our lives, but nobody fancies a monopoly on bread-making or to entrust bakers with the task of prescribing us – according to their best scientific judgement – the most appropriate quantity and quality of our daily bread intake.

In actual fact, in a society of 'plural consumers' it is likely that people are keen to gather detailed information about the available goods, the more so when these goods are relevant to important facets of their lives. Arguably, it is more rational to allocate time and energy to gather information about products on which our welfare depends than about goods of minor importance to our daily lives.

In a free market consumers do not live in a 'wilderness of ignorance'. Nonetheless, information is not free – to gather it, it is necessary to sacrifice valuable resources (including leisure). Hence, the value of any additional scrap of information, according to economic logic, becomes increasingly smaller.

Consumers weigh rationally the costs and the benefits of collecting information and the amount of information they have reflects this fact. Consumers may be viewed as generally possessing an amount of information that is sufficient for them to make reasonably informed choices over most goods and services given the cost of becoming better informed. If this is the process underpinning the interaction of information and advertising in a market, it is hard to see the reason that supposedly makes the case of medicinal products and people's health different.

Specifically, it is worthy of note that a 2004 survey conducted by Populus and the Stockholm Network showed that patients in European welfare states are in fact seeking greater information. For example, 84 per cent of the Italian respondents to the poll thought that providing patients with a greater amount of information about their ailments would lead to an improvement in the quality of healthcare. The demand for greater information is clearly a major concern for Italians, along with giving patients more control over public health spending (supported by 69 per cent), providing more healthcare facilities (64 per cent), increasing the availability of drugs and treatments (56 per cent) and enabling patients to spend more of their own income on healthcare (55 per cent) (Disney, 2004: 116).

A survey conducted in 2002 by PatientView asked some patient advocacy groups whether the European Union should allow pharmaceutical companies to supply direct information about prescription drugs. Thirty-three per cent of the respondents answered in the affirmative and a further 17 per cent agreed provided appropriate controls were put in place.[10]

Significantly – and at least in part understandably – patient organisations themselves are the most vocal in denouncing the absurdity of what might be called a *shamanic* view of health, which holds it to be achievable only through the involvement of a medical practitioner.

Such a view is to be contrasted with an individualist perspective, one based on the assumption that every individual possesses his own body and is responsible for its good health. Kohout (2004) has defined the European approach to the problem as a 'veterinary' one: 'Diagnosis and cure is an information-demanding process. The more information a patient has on his or her illness and available therapies, the more it's likely that the best solution will be found. True, for a lazy or a sloppy

---

10 'Should pharmaceutical companies provide the public with more information on prescription medicines?', PatientView Report, June 2002.

doctor it's not easy to work with a well-informed patient. The information can't do any harm. But incomplete or distorted information can do much harm – and this is precisely what the drug information ban leads to.'

From such a perspective it is difficult to concur with the widespread restrictions on the advertising of pharmaceuticals and the dissemination of information to patients, such as those in force today in Europe.

Advertising is located at the intersection of what Ronald Coase identified as 'the market for goods' and 'the market for ideas'. In a now classic article, the 1991 Nobel laureate for economics showed how the case for regulating either market is basically the same (Coase, 1974).[11] Nevertheless, as is well known, passionate advocates of freedom of speech have often opposed the freedom of the market. Specifically, they have often maintained that the lack of information on the part of consumers requires broader regulation.

The same argument could be advanced in the case of the 'market for ideas', for which even the most ardent supporters of socialism are in favour of absolute freedom. Yet, similarly, individuals cannot always master all the information needed to approach in a thoughtful manner a specific 'product'. Far from it: a long catalogue of errors and horrors in the history of the world, in the name of a number of ideas, reveals that views and words can foster terrible tragedies.

Still, the deep-seated prejudice in favour of freedom of speech rightly reminds us that censorship is worse than the free circulation of sometimes unsavoury ideas. Censorship deprives each individual of the capacity to adjudicate good and evil, surrendering it to an appointed authority.

The prevalence of censorship in the field of healthcare could be a deliberate exception, but it may also reflect the heritage of the past. Bioethics scholar Tristram Engelhardt has brilliantly described the formation in every society of a group of 'healers', a 'moral and intellectual

---

11   For a discussion of the subject of this paper, see the Coase interview by Thomas Hazlett
     for *Reason*, available on the Web at http://reason.com/9701/int.coase.shtml.

elite, i.e. a group of individuals who 1) own complex technical knowledge, and a special dedication 2) to help people who are threatened by illness, deformity, and premature death and 3) to preserve and increase professionals' skills' (Engelhardt, 1986: 309).

This is not the place to delve into the complex host of ethical questions raised by Engelhardt; still, it is worth quoting his characterisation of the patient as a 'stranger in a strange land', 'an individual in an unknown territory, who doesn't precisely know what is to be expected, and how [his] environment may be controlled' (ibid.: 312).

In this respect, information – particularly about more substantive matters than the use of a particular drug – plainly raises serious ethical issues: 'moral problems arise if you have a high concept of liberty. Those who especially care about safeguarding self-determination, probably desire complete information, even though that may possibly result in harm' (ibid.: 340).

Although in considering the appropriateness of full information about each and every kind of treatment we may enter a veritable minefield, the issue is far simpler when we examine the need to widen the range of sources of information relating to the availability of medical preparations. This is not meant to undermine the trust between the patient and the physician; rather, it entails adding a further source of information to those already available.

Even David A. Kessler, former chief of the US Food and Drug Administration, conceded having been mistaken in opposing, during his tenure, the widening of the number of conduits for direct information from the industry to patients. From an educational standpoint, in the view of Mr Kessler, this would have several benefits.[12] In addition, the International Alliance of Patients' Organisations has recently issued a policy statement on 'health literacy', signalling a worrying lack of knowledge on the part of patients.[13]

---

12   R. Misra, 'Ex-FDA chief recants on drug advertising', *Boston Globe*, 17 April 2002.
13   See The Patient's Network, *Promoting Patient-centred Healthcare around the World*, 18 June 2003.

While no particular legislative proposal is advanced in this chapter, it seems obvious that no knowledge is possible without access to information, and allowing direct information from drug manufacturers would give patients greater access to sources of information. The path to follow therefore consists in allowing the customer (i.e. the patient), whenever he so desires, to draw up an inventory of the available information, not as a substitute, but as a complement to that provided by the medical practitioner.

The laws in force, besides, do not seem to be compatible with Article 3 of the European Charter of Patients' Rights, which states: 'Every individual has the right to access to all kinds of information regarding their state of health, the health services and how to use them, and all that scientific research and technological innovation makes available.'[14]

Moreover, two important developments provide further arguments for reforming the European regulatory framework: the widening use of the Internet[15] and the emergence of a widespread pattern of corruption among physicians.

Internet access is increasingly common in the Old Continent. Whereas in March 2000 only 18 per cent of European families had access to the Internet, in December 2001 this figure had reached 38 per cent. In 2008 it is reasonable to estimate that at least 50 per cent of the whole European population above the age of fifteen makes use of the Internet at home, school or in the workplace.

At the same time, we have witnessed a veritable boom in health-related websites, often recommending 'alternative medicine' treatments or questionable preparations. In 2004 the *Journal of Medical Internet Research* conducted a survey of such websites, remarking that in 97 per cent of the instances surveyed there is a clear lack of some basic information necessary to ensure proper use of the recommended product (Walji et al., 2004).

---

14 See the European Charter of Patients' Rights at http://home.online.no/~wkeim/files/european_charter.htm.
15 For a thorough discussion of this issue, see Evans et al. (2004).

·

Seemingly absurd recommendations abound – for example, some websites claim that a well-known mood-altering drug, Prozac, can inhibit the craving for food, and can thus significantly contribute to a personal diet. But this suggestion conflicts with the recommended usage of this medical preparation. Regrettably, while these 'outlaw' websites' continued existence is not threatened, drug manufacturers, in this instance Eli Lilly, are not allowed to counter their claims by means of a proper information campaign.[16] Similar considerations also apply to the rampant spread of counterfeit medical products sold on the Web.

A second factor in support of further liberalisation is corruption in the medical profession. In a number of outrageous recent cases, medical practitioners have allegedly accepted 'gifts' and 'favours' from the pharmaceutical industry in exchange for prescribing to their patients the products of these munificent drug-makers.

These cases are significant not only in view of the resulting loss of trust in the medical profession, but also – and more importantly – because their 'institutional' cause is plain. The corruption of the physician by the industry is perfectly rational, as the latter is prevented from directly informing the patient about its products. Indeed, medical practitioners are usually the only link between producers and consumers of pharmaceuticals.

Liberalising information and breaking the monopoly on health currently enjoyed by the medical profession could have a moralising effect on the physicians themselves. In a free information market, the industry and the patients would be able to communicate directly, undermining the rationale for corruption.

There is one last, important counter-argument to the free dissemination of information: since most medical products are provided through socialised national health services, increasing their demand by virtue of advertising could bankrupt the already ailing finances of the welfare state. It is not by chance that individual European countries are free

---

16 For example, see http://helpuniversity.com/pharmacy/weight-loss/phentermine-prozac-for-weight-.html.

to lift the ban in the case of non-prescription and non-reimbursable drugs.[17] In fact, the major trend in Europe is not only to limit the amount of information to patients, but also to check health spending in general and drug spending in particular. While direct-to-consumer advertising could perhaps lead to greater government expenditure on drugs, this must put into context. Any resulting growth in health spending would result from the fundamental unsustainability of the welfare state rather than advertising per se. The remedy should thus be aimed at the disease, not its symptoms.

Conclusion

This chapter has shown that advertising does not change people's behaviour: it simply presents, in a way aimed to grab their attention, useful information about the products developed by entrepreneurs. It may add to the stock of information at our disposal, and by doing so affect our preferences. Advertising cannot, however, force people to act in a particular way.

Citizens deserve to be treated like adults, capable of distrusting information from dubious sources. Pluralism in sources of information – including adverts – is preferable to censorship. Furthermore, advertising is an essential tool for enterprises and also benefits consumers: it is the means by which potential customers become aware of the goods and services that a business can provide.

The claim that these benefits do not apply to healthcare products, based on the premise that human health has a different moral status to every other good provided in the market, reflects a *shamanic*, as opposed to an *individualistic*, view of the issue. The case of the ban on advertising tobacco products has shown us that there is only a limited correlation between the consumption of dangerous products and the attractiveness of advertising. Accordingly, pursuing a ban on advertising medicines

---

17　This is, for example, the case in Italy.

basically implies that patients are too ignorant to make a conscious and not completely advertising-driven choice.

This view reflects the belief that good bodily health must unavoidably be achieved through the mediation of third parties (the modern and scientific heirs of the ancient faith healers) and that successful healing must put aside individual opinion. Such a belief is incompatible with the fundamental principles of a free society.

Advertising is at the intersection of the 'market for goods' and the 'market for ideas', and thus it is unwise to promote any kind of ban on it – not even for dangerous goods such as pharmaceuticals. The reasoning behind such a policy entails too deep a distrust of individuals' competence to be accepted in a free society.

In conclusion, this discussion of the ban on the advertisement of medicines has exposed the ideology underpinning it, confirming what Harris and Seldon highlighted: '[advertising] makes no sense unless addressed to people with freedom to decide for themselves the pattern of their work and lives'. The freedom to produce and watch adverts is not the most exciting of our freedoms, but it is nevertheless fundamental to choice and competition in a free economy.

References

Bergler, D. (1999), 'The effects of commercial advertising on children', *International Journal of Advertising*, 18(4): 411–25.

Bousch, B., M. Friestad and G. Rose (1994), 'Adolescent scepticism towards TV advertising and knowledge of adviser tactics', *Journal of Consumer Research*, 21(1): 165–75.

Coase, R. (1974), 'The market for goods and the market for ideas', *American Economic Review*, 64(2): 384–91.

Disney, H. (ed.) (2004), *Impatient for Change*, London: Stockholm Network.

Ekelund, R. B., Jr. and D. S. Saurman (1988), *Advertising and the Market Process. A Modern Economic View*, San Francisco, CA: Pacific Research Institute for Public Policy.

Engelhardt, H. T. (1986), *The Foundations of Bioethics*, New York: Oxford University Press.

Evans, T., A. Mingardi and S. Pollard (2004), *Why Greater Freedom of Information in European Healthcare Could Save Lives and Money*, Brussels: Centre for the New Europe.

Furnham, A. (2000), *Children & Advertising. The Allegations and the Evidence*, London: Social Affairs Unit.

Galbraith, J. K. (1958), *The Affluent Society*, Boston, MA: Houghton Mifflin.

Harris, R. and A. Seldon (1959), *Advertising in a Free Society*, London: Institute of Economic Affairs.

High, H. (1999), *Does Advertising Increase Smoking? Economics, Free Speech and Advertising Bans*, London: Institute of Economic Affairs.

Kirzner, I. M. (1997), *How Markets Work: Disequilibrium, Entrepreneurship and Discovery*, London: Institute of Economic Affairs.

Kohout, K. (2004), 'Europe's veterinary health care', *TechCentralStation*, 9 December, *www.techcentralstation.be/120904.html*.

Mizerski, R. (1995), 'The relationship between cartoon trade character recognition and attitude toward product category in young children', *Journal of Marketing*, 59: 58–70.

North, D. C. (2005), *Understanding the Process of Economic Change*, Princeton, NJ: Princeton University Press.

Packard, V. (1957), *The Hidden Persuaders*, New York: D. McKay.

Preston, C. (1999), 'The unintended effects of advertising upon children', *International Journal of Advertising*, 18: 363–76.

Tullock, G. (1967), *Towards a Mathematics of Politics*, Ann Arbor, MI: University of Michigan Press.

Valkenburg, P. and S. Janssen (1999), 'What do children value in entertainment programmes', *Journal of Communications*, 49: 3–21.

Walji, M., S. Sagaram, D. Sagaram, F. Meric-Bernstam, C. Johnson, N. Mirza and E. V. Bernstam (2004), 'Efficacy of quality criteria to identify potentially harmful information: a cross-sectional survey of complementary and alternative medicine web sites', *Journal of Medical Internet Research*, 6, *www.jmir.org/2004/2/e21*.

7 PORNOGRAPHY[1]
Nadine Strossen

Introduction

The general concept of 'prohibition' might well have negative connotations, especially for the many Americans who associate it specifically with our country's catastrophic prohibition of alcohol in the first half of the twentieth century. Far more certain and widespread, though, is the negative connotation of the term that is usually used to describe the specific subset of prohibition policies that outlaw any expression: censorship. The costs of censoring any expression are the flip sides of the many benefits that flow from freedom of expression in general. Likewise, the costs of censoring 'pornography' or sexual expression in particular are the flip sides of the many benefits that flow specifically from freedom for this important type of expression.

After defining some key terms, this chapter discusses both the benefits of free expression in general, including sexual expression, and the costs of suppressing any expression. It then focuses on the particular forms of sexual expression that have been targeted by some influential feminists, and addresses the benefits of freedom for such expression, as well as the costs of suppressing it. These feminists have advocated the prohibition of 'degrading' sexual expression, arguing that such a prohibition would advance women's equality and safety. As this chapter explains in detail, though, such prohibition would in fact undermine women's rights, as well as the rights of sexual orientation minorities and human rights in general.

---

1   For their work on the footnotes, editing and proofreading of this piece, Professor Strossen thanks her chief aide, Steven Cunningham (NYLS '99), her assistant, Danica Rue (NYLS '09), and her research assistant, Jackie Ferrari (NYLS '08).

Definitions of 'pornography' and related key terms

Before discussing the great individual and societal costs of censoring pornography, I must make a few explanatory comments about the meaning of that key term, along with a few other, closely related, terms. I will focus on the US legal system and culture, although the issues I address are of universal concern.

Pornography and obscenity

Pornography is not a legal term of art; it is not the label for any category of expression that is deemed to be unprotected under the free speech guarantee in the First Amendment to the United States Constitution. In contrast, as discussed below, 'child pornography' is a specific legal term, designating a category of sexual expression that the US Supreme Court has held to be beyond constitutional protection.

In everyday parlance, the term 'pornography' has a stigmatising connotation, typically designating whatever sexual expression the person using it dislikes. For example, when the press, politicians and public initially became aware of the Internet, concern abounded about the alleged evils of 'cyberporn', which immediately became the target of many censorial measures. Likewise, certain feminists who have advocated censoring sexual expression that they consider 'degrading' to women have demonised such expressions with the term 'pornography', whereas they approvingly refer to other sexually explicit expression as 'erotica'.

In contrast with these negative connotations of the word 'pornography' in current usage, its dictionary definition according to *Webster's International Dictionary* (1986: 239) is 'sexually explicit expression that is designed to be sexually arousing or exciting'. Even the USA, with its sexually prudish cultural traditions, has never sought to outlaw all pornography, in that literal dictionary sense. To the contrary, the US Supreme Court has stressed that most sexual expression is constitutionally protected free speech. As the Court declared when it first addressed this topic in 1957, 'sex, a great and mysterious motive force in human life, has indisputably been a subject of absorbing interest to mankind through the ages; it is one of the vital problems of human interest and public concern.'[2]

Nonetheless, in the next breath, the Court concluded that a subcategory of sexual expression, which it labelled 'obscenity', is not entitled to constitutional protection because of its feared harmful impact. Specifically, the Court has held that obscene expression may be suppressed because it might lead to antisocial attitudes on the part of the individual viewer, and it may lower the 'moral tone' of the community in which it is viewed, although the Court has acknowledged that these feared harms have not been established through actual evidence.[3] The Court has crafted a three-part definition for illegal obscenity: the material must appeal to the 'prurient' interest in sex, and it must be 'patently offensive', according to 'contemporary community standards'; in addition, the material must lack 'serious' value, according to prevailing national standards.[4]

Child pornography

The Supreme Court has upheld government power to outlaw 'child pornography', sexually explicit expression that is produced by using actual minors, because minors are presumed not sufficiently mature to make truly voluntary, informed decisions about participating in such productions. In short, child pornography is outlawed because of the harm it causes to unconsenting, immature performers, resulting from the production process.[5] In sharp contrast, obscenity is outlawed because of a completely distinguishable harm it allegedly causes: harm to the minds of consenting, mature viewers, resulting from the viewing

---

2   Roth v. United States, 354 US 476, 487 (1957).
3   Paris Adult Theatre I v. Slaton, 413 US 49, 60 (1973).
4   Miller v. California, 413 US 15, 24 (1973).
5   Ashcroft v. Free Speech Coalition, 535 US 234 (2002).

process. In short, laws that criminalise child pornography are examples of child labour laws, which are designed to protect children from exploitation, rather than examples of censorship laws, which are designed to protect adults from expression.

Concept of 'pornography' that degrades women, advocated by some feminists

Starting in the late 1970s, some influential feminists have advocated prohibiting an allegedly different category of sexual expression, as distinct from the traditionally prohibited category of 'obscenity', with its concern for upholding the community's traditional moral values. Instead, they target sexual expression that, in their view, 'degrades' women, thus fostering discrimination or violence against women. A model law incorporating this proposed new prohibition was drafted in 1983 by writer Andrea Dworkin and law professor Catharine MacKinnon. The MacDworkinite model law labels the newly targeted sexual expression as 'pornography', and defines it as 'the sexually explicit subordination of women through pictures and/or words' (MacKinnon, 1985). All US courts that have considered this proposed definition of prohibited sexual expression, including the Supreme Court, have held that it violates the free speech guarantee in the US Constitution.[6] In contrast, in 1992 Canada's Supreme Court incorporated this definition into Canadian obscenity law, holding that it is consistent with Canadian constitutional norms.[7]

I said above that the MacDworkinite concept of illegal pornography prohibits 'an *allegedly* different category of sexual expression', in contrast with the category that is deemed 'obscene', because both concepts are inescapably vague. Both turn on subjective value judgements, with the result that both endanger most, if not all, sexual expression.

---

6   American Booksellers Association v. Hudnut, 598 F. Supp. 1316 (D. Ind. 1984), aff'd., 771 F. 2d 323 (7th Cir. 1985), *aff'd. mem.*, 475 US 1001 (1986).

7   [1992]1 S.C.R. 452 (Can.).

There are 'special costs' of prohibiting sexual expression

Prohibiting expression entails the same general costs as those resulting from all prohibition policies. In particular, any prohibition policy that outlaws voluntary, consensual conduct by mentally competent, mature individuals – whether it be consuming a certain chemical substance or consuming certain words or images – imposes similar basic costs on individuals and society. Any such prohibition policy deprives individuals of freedom of choice, and it also diverts society's limited resources away from conduct that harms third parties.

In contrast with other prohibition policies, censorship exacts an especially great toll on individual freedom of choice, since self-identity is tied especially closely to ideas and expression. For that reason, national constitutions and international human rights instruments explicitly protect choices about what expression to convey, and what expression to receive, whereas they protect other personal choices, such as those involving sexual conduct among consenting adults or the ingestion of chemical substances, only implicitly or not at all.

Definitions are going to suffer from inevitable vagueness

Even beyond the special tolls upon individuals and society resulting from prohibition of expression, there are still further tolls resulting from prohibition of sexual expression in particular. That is because any such prohibition is inherently difficult to formulate, or to enforce, with any clarity or predictability.

As explained above, even advocates of prohibiting some sexual expression recognise that most such expression should be protected under constitutional free speech guarantees. Consequently, the censorship advocates must articulate criteria for distinguishing the category of sexual expression that should assertedly be unprotected. Whether the unprotected category of sexual expression is claimed to be 'patently offensive' to prevailing community morals, as under the traditional obscenity concept, or whether the unprotected category is claimed to be 'degrading' to women, as under the MacDworkinite feminist approach, the same definitional and enforcement problems arise.

Intractable definitional problems are inherent in any effort to single out for prohibition any category of sexual expression based on its alleged harm to the minds of its viewers, in contrast with some more concrete, ascertainable harm. In effect, this kind of prohibition creates a 'thought crime', criminalising the viewing of certain words or images because they will allegedly give rise to 'immoral' or 'degrading' thoughts. Such thought crimes are inherently inconsistent with individual freedom, as eloquently explained in John Stuart Mill's classic essay, *On Liberty*: 'Over himself, over his own body and mind, the individual is sovereign.' Therefore, 'the only purpose for which government may rightfully exercise ... power ... over any individual is to prevent harm to others. His own good, either physical or moral, is not a sufficient warrant' (Mill, 1859: 7). Even beyond the unwarranted invasions of individual freedom – with no countervailing societal gain – arising from thought crimes in general, the particular thought crimes of 'obscenity' or MacDworkinite 'pornography' create further problems in light of their value-laden definitions, which necessarily centre on the irreducibly subjective concepts of 'immorality' or 'degradation', respectively.

In contrast, when expression is prohibited because of some tangible harm to some third party, it is easily and clearly defined in terms of that specific harm. For example, pornography produced by using children, whose immaturity makes them incapable of voluntarily consenting to such productions, harms the children's bodies and minds. Accordingly, illegal child pornography, which is unprotected by the First Amendment, is defined strictly in terms of that harm, as sexually explicit productions made with minors. The US Supreme Court struck down Congress's 1996 effort to expand the definition of illegal child pornography to include material that appears to depict minors, but does not actually do so, precisely because the expanded definition encompassed material that does not cause the specific harm that justifies outlawing depictions of actual children.[8] To cite another example, defamatory expression is outlawed because of, and hence defined in terms of, its adverse impact on its subject's reputation.

Since the sexual realm is uniquely personal, choices about sexual expression are likewise. As the Supreme Court observed, 'One man's vulgarity is another man's lyric.'[9] In the context of the feminist debate about pornography, this famous epigram could be paraphrased as: 'One woman's degrading scene is another woman's liberating scene.'

Given the inevitable subjectivity in determining which sexual words or images should be banned, it has proved impossible both to formulate clear definitions of the targeted expression and to enforce any such definition in an even-handed and predictable manner. The US Supreme Court's experience concerning obscenity is illustrative. The Justices have wrestled with various definitions, but have been unable to craft one that does not turn on subjective value judgements. This insoluble problem is highlighted by former Justice Potter Stewart's well-known statement in a 1964 obscenity case: 'I shall not today attempt further to define [obscenity] ...; and perhaps I could never succeed in intelligibly doing so. But I know it when I see it.'[10]

Along with Justice Stewart, none of us could intelligibly articulate a neutral standard for judging sexual expression in general, but all of us can recognise particular works that we ourselves find less appealing, and more offensive, to our own personal tastes and sensibilities. Each of us, though, including each prosecutor, each judge and each juror, sees a different 'it'. In reality, then, any definition of prohibited sexual expression functions as a subjective Rorschach test for law enforcement officials, rather than as an objective legal standard for protecting sexual expression against unwarranted prosecutions or convictions.

In addition to being unable to provide a coherent definition of the sexual expression that is subject to prohibition, the Supreme Court has

---

8   Free Speech Coalition, 535 US 234.
9   Cohen v. California, 403 US 15, 25 (1971).
10 Jacobellis v. Ohio, 378 US 492, 498 (1985).

also been unable to explain why particular sexual expression satisfies that definition, or does not. In many obscenity cases, the Justices simply have issued conclusory rulings, noting only that they either 'affirmed' or 'reversed' lower court decisions as to whether a particular expression satisfied the Court's definition of proscribable obscenity; the Justices were apparently unable to concur on any opinions explaining the rationales for their conclusions.[11]

In sum, the Court has failed to provide any meaningful guidance to law enforcement authorities, or to would-be distributors of sexual expression, as to which expression is constitutionally protected and which is subject to criminal prosecution. It is therefore impossible to predict what expression will be targeted for prosecution and conviction, and which convictions will be sustained by appellate judges. For this reason, many Supreme Court Justices, other judges and other constitutional law experts have concluded that laws prohibiting obscenity or other sexual expression are unconstitutional on the ground that their 'undue vagueness' denies 'due process of law'. Since the laws do not, and cannot, give fair notice of precisely what expression they prohibit, they deprive individuals who are prosecuted or convicted under them of liberty and/or property without 'due process'.[12]

Prohibition is likely to lead to arbitrary, discriminatory enforcement and chilling expression

As with any unduly vague law, laws prohibiting any category of sexual expression necessarily delegate enormous discretion to the enforcing authorities to decide which expression to single out for prosecution or conviction. This largely unfettered discretion imposes significant special costs, even beyond those resulting from other (non-vague) laws prohibiting expression.

---

11 See, for example, Redrup v. New York, 386 US 767 (1967).
12 See, for example, Pope v. Illinois , 481 US 497, 507 (1987) (Brennan, J. dissenting); ibid., 504–5 (Scalia, J. concurring).

First, in selecting which sexual expression to target, out of the whole universe that could plausibly be deemed contrary to either moral values or sexual politics, the enforcing authorities will act arbitrarily at best, discriminatorily at worst. The targets will necessarily reflect the individual tastes and values of those who are empowered to make the decisions about prosecution and conviction; all such officials will, along with Justice Stewart, 'know it when [they] see it'. From the perspective of anyone else, who necessarily has different individual tastes and values, the targets will appear to have been chosen randomly or arbitrarily. This problem is well illustrated by two prosecutions in Broward County, Florida, in 1990, against the very same song, 'As Nasty As They Wanna Be', by the rap group 2 Live Crew. Purporting to apply the very same 'community standards', since both prosecutions occurred in the same jurisdiction, the decision-maker in one case (a judge) decided that the song was obscene and convicted, but the decision-maker in the other case (a jury) decided that the song was not obscene and acquitted (Rimer, 1990).

Even worse than the arbitrary enforcement of laws censoring sexual expression is their discriminatory enforcement, singling out expression that conveys ideas that are disfavoured by those who wield political power, or which are conveyed by or addressed to members of groups that lack political power. As explained below, laws aimed at sexual expression have disproportionately suppressed speech by political dissidents, as well as speech associated with racial, gender and sexual orientation minority groups.

Yet another special cost that flows from the unavoidably subjective criteria for prohibiting sexual expression is their chilling effect. It is impossible to predict which sexual expression will be the subject of an enforcement action under any such criteria, including those laid out in the Supreme Court's obscenity rulings, and those laid out in the MacDworkinite model law. A plain reading of these nebulous 'standards', as well as their actual enforcement history, underscores that they could plausibly be applied to most, if not all, sexual expression, including expression that is widely viewed as having serious artistic or other merit (Strossen, 2000: 63). Consequently, authors, artists, bookshop owners and others who produce or distribute material with any sexual content are driven to engage in self-censorship, to avoid the enormous tangible and intangible costs of defending against accusations of distributing sexual expression that is demonised as illegal 'obscenity' or 'pornography'. For this reason, prohibition laws deprive the public of not only the vast amount of sexual material that is actually subject to enforcement actions, but also the immeasurably vaster amount that is never produced owing to the reasonable fear that it could be subject to such actions.

There are benefits of free speech and costs of suppression of expression in general

As former US Supreme Court Justice Louis Brandeis declared in a famous free speech opinion, the framers of the US Constitution 'valued liberty both as an end and as a means'.[13] Freedom of expression is intrinsically important to all individuals, allowing them to express their own ideas and emotions, and to seek out expression from others consistent with, and formative of, their own identities and values. Freedom of expression is also important instrumentally, promoting both personal relationships and broader concerns of our social and political communities. It facilitates the exchange of ideas and information, which is especially important in democratic and capitalist societies, as a precondition for informed public policymaking and the free economic marketplace. This instrumental function is well captured by the 'marketplace of ideas' metaphor.[14]

Associated with these basic benefits of free expression are a number of correlative benefits, summarised below.

---

13 Whitney v. California, 274 US 357, 375 (1927) (Brandeis, J. concurring).
14 See, for example, Abrams v. United States, 250 US 616, 630 (1919) (Holmes, J. dissenting).

- Freedom of expression affords an outlet for ideas or emotions that might be expressed in antisocial, violent, illegal conduct if expression were stifled.
- Freedom of expression fosters a community with an attitude of tolerance towards diverse and unpopular ideas, speakers and groups. When people are routinely exposed to dissident and provocative views, and permitted to express their own views, no matter how unpopular with their peers, they become at least more tolerant, and perhaps even accepting, of 'difference'. Such increased tolerance could well reduce not only suspicious or hostile attitudes but also discrimination or violence towards those perceived as 'other' (Chemerinsky, 2006).
- Freedom of expression has always been especially important for members of various minority causes and groups, in order for them to develop their own sense of identity and solidarity, and also to organise and advocate for their rights.

Because censorship targets expression on the rationale that it fosters harmful conduct, it diverts societal resources from other, more constructive, measures that would directly address the actual harmful conduct. Censorship is a 'feel-good' purported 'solution' for the designated problems, which allows politicians to claim unjustified credit for 'doing something', but the symbolic action of censorship is ineffective at best, counterproductive at worst. For example, anti-porn feminists blame certain sexual expression for promoting discrimination and violence against women. Any such 'book-blaming' strategy, however, displaces responsibility from the men who actually engage in discriminatory or violent conduct against women. Moreover, it diverts societal resources from policies that prevent and punish such conduct (Strossen, 2000).

The benefits of freedom and costs of suppression of sexual expression in particular

Since sexuality is a uniquely important element of everyone's individual sense of self, and everyone's sense of connection to other individuals and groups, sexual expression is likewise uniquely important. It enables us to explore, develop and communicate about our sexual self-identities, and to make the inherently important, life-altering choices we all face in the realm of sexuality, including choices relating to sexual orientation, sexual partners and intimacies, sexual health and prevention of sexually transmitted infections, contraception, abortion and pregnancy.

Freedom of sexual expression has always been especially important for members of sexual orientation minorities and for women. For lesbian, gay, bisexual and transgendered ('LGBT') individuals, and those who are questioning their sexual orientation, it is critically important to have access to information about sexuality, as well as the opportunity to communicate freely with other LGBT individuals. For women, information about sexual and reproductive health and options has been essential not only for their individual and family lives, but also for facilitating their equal opportunities in the public sphere. In reaffirming women's reproductive rights under the US Constitution, the US Supreme Court has stressed the vital interconnection between women's freedom in the sexual sphere and their equality in the economic and political arenas.[15]

I will now summarise some of the other major benefits that flow from freedom of sexual expression:

- Given the rampant spread of HIV and other sexually transmitted infections, including among minors, freedom of sexual expression promotes health, and may well even be life-saving.
- Freedom of sexual expression is essential for reducing unintended pregnancies; in the USA, a full one half of all pregnancies are unintended (Sonfield, 2003).

---

15   Planned Parenthood v. Casey, 510 US 1309, 1313 (1994).

- Many key public policy and political debates centre around sexual issues, including abortion, AIDS and other sexually transmitted infections, censorship of the Internet and other media, contraception, gender discrimination, LGBT rights, rape and sexual assault, and sexual harassment. Some advocates of prohibiting sexual expression assert that such censorship is consistent with the free speech guarantee in the US Constitution because that guarantee extends only, or principally, to expression about public policy issues. Even assuming (only for the sake of argument) that any such qualification could fairly be read into the unqualified language of the Constitution's free speech clause, it still would not justify suppressing sexual expression, in light of the integral role that sexual issues and expression play in the public policy arena. As the famous feminist slogan recognises, 'The sexual is political'.
- Many new media have been developed specifically to facilitate people's abiding fascination with sex and sexual expression. Pornographic words and images have been widely credited with helping to make the VCR and computers household appliances. As *New York Times* columnist John Tierney noted in an article aptly entitled 'Porn, the low-slung engine of progress': 'sometimes the erotic has been a force driving technological innovation; virtually always, from Stone Age sculpture to computer bulletin boards, it has been one of the first uses for a new medium' (Tierney, 1994).
- Sexual expression has been credited with stimulating the development of artistic styles and movements in various media, including film (Linker, 1996).
- Sexual expression is closely interconnected with scientific research in many vital areas, including those that are directly related to sexual and reproductive health, and those that are indirectly connected, ranging from population planning to stem cell research.
- The legal fictions that are invented in an attempt to justify singling out certain sexual expression for suppression can be extended to other expression too, thus creating at least a risk of even wider

suppression. A good example of this cost of sexual censorship is the 'secondary effects' doctrine that the US Supreme Court has cited, in a few controversial decisions, as purportedly justifying strict zoning laws that expressly single out bookstores, cinemas and other 'adult' businesses on the basis of the sexually explicit content of the expressive materials they sell or display.[16]

If the Court acknowledged that these laws regulate the targeted expression on the basis of its sexual content, then it would likewise have to acknowledge that such laws are presumptively unconstitutional as violating the 'bedrock' free speech requirement that government may never suppress speech because its content is disfavoured by officials or the majority of the community.[17] To circumvent this cardinal free speech principle, the Court has said that the laws were not in fact targeting the expression's content, but rather its alleged 'secondary effects', such as increasing crime or decreasing property values in the surrounding vicinity. This legal fiction has been seized upon by government officials who seek to justify laws that prohibit or restrict other kinds of expression, including classic political protest.[18] As a number of dissenting Justices have noted, the Court would likely do less damage to free expression on balance if it candidly created special, discriminatory rules for regulating sexual expression, rather than purporting to formulate content-neutral rationales that also endanger non-sexual expression.[19] Of course, the optimal approach would be to enforce the content-neutral First Amendment mandate that 'no law' may 'abridg[e] the freedom of speech', regardless of the subject matter of such speech, sexual or otherwise.

---

16 See, for example, City of Renton v. Playtime Theaters, Inc., 475 US 41 (1986).
17 See, for example, Texas v. Johnson, 491 US 397 (1989).
18 See, for example, Boos v. Barry, 485 US 312, 320–21 (1988).
19 See idem. at 334–5 (Brennan, J. concurring in part and concurring in the judgement).

The costs of suppressing the sexual expression targeted by MacDworkinite feminists

As explained above, the feminists who have advocated prohibition of 'degrading' sexual expression argue that such a prohibition would advance women's equality and safety. Accordingly, it is important to note the special costs of this particular type of sexual censorship, specifically in terms of women's equality and safety, as well as the closely interrelated concerns of reproductive freedom and the rights of LGBT individuals.

Censoring sexual expression undermines women's rights

I will list the most important specific reasons why suppressing what the MacDworkinites stigmatise as 'pornography' actually undermines the critically important goals of reducing discrimination and violence against women. I will then elaborate briefly on some of these reasons.

- Censoring pornography would suppress many works that are especially valuable to women and feminists (Strossen, 2000: 199–215).
- Any pornography censorship scheme would be enforced in a way that discriminates against the least popular, least powerful groups in our society, including feminists and lesbians (ibid.: 217–46).
- It would perpetuate demeaning stereotypes about women, including the claim that sex is bad for us (ibid.: 107–18).
- It would perpetuate the disempowering notion that women are essentially victims (ibid.: 48, 114–18, 274–5).
- It would divert resources from constructive approaches to countering discrimination and violence against women (ibid.: 266–79).
- It would harm women who voluntarily work in the sex industry (ibid.: 179–86).
- It would harm women's efforts to develop their own sexuality (ibid.: 161–78).

- It would strengthen the power of political and religious advocates of authoritarian policies, whose patriarchal agendas would curtail women's rights (ibid.: 12–13, 82, 90–91).
- Finally, by undermining free speech, censorship would deprive feminists of a powerful tool for advancing women's equality (ibid.: 30–32, 224–9).

Just as free speech has always been the strongest weapon for advancing equal rights causes, censorship has always been the strongest weapon for thwarting them. Ironically, the explanation for this pattern lies in the very analysis of those feminists who want to curb 'degrading pornography'. They contend that women are relatively disempowered and marginalised. Precisely for this reason, it makes no sense to hand the power structure yet another tool that it can use to further suppress them. Consistent with the analysis of the pro-censorship feminists themselves, the government will inevitably wield this tool, along with others, to the particular disadvantage of already disempowered groups (Dworkin, 1985). This conclusion is consistently confirmed by the enforcement record of censorship measures. The pattern of disempowered groups being disproportionately targeted extends even to censorship laws that are allegedly designed for their benefit. Accordingly, in the one country that has enforced the MacDworkin concept of illegal 'pornography', Canada, the major censorship targets have been feminist bookshops and LGBT bookshops.

Laws permitting the suppression of sexual expression have regularly been used to suppress information essential for women's rights, including reproductive freedom. In the United States, anti-obscenity laws have consistently been used to suppress information about contraception and abortion. The first federal anti-obscenity statute in the USA, the 1873 'Comstock Law', was repeatedly used to prosecute pioneering feminists and birth control advocates early in the twentieth century (Blanchard, 1992: 748). Its targets included Margaret Sanger, the founder of Planned Parenthood (ibid.: 766–7).

Sanger also had the dubious distinction of being one of the first victims of a new form of censorship that was applied to the then-new medium of films. The Supreme Court had ruled in 1915 that movies were not protected 'speech' under the First Amendment.[20] One of the first films banned under that decision was *Birth Control*, a 1917 picture produced by and featuring Margaret Sanger.[21] Until the second half of the twentieth century, film censors in the USA continued to ban films concerning not only birth control, but also other sexually oriented subjects of particular interest to women, including pregnancy, abortion, non-marital children, prostitution and divorce (Karst, 1990: 129).

The most recent laws targeting sexual expression in a new medium, those that have regulated cyberspace starting in the mid-1990s, again reflect the consistent historical pattern: that such laws, no matter how well intended, have a disproportionate adverse impact on women's rights, as well as reproductive freedom and rights of sexual orientation minorities. In the American Civil Liberties Union's many lawsuits that have successfully challenged cyber-censorship laws as violating constitutional free speech rights, the courts have concurred that prime targets of all these laws include expression concerning women's sexual and reproductive health and options, as well as expression concerning LGBT sexuality.[22]

For instance, one of the ACLU's clients in the groundbreaking 1997 case of *Reno* v. *ACLU*,[23] the Supreme Court's first ruling concerning freedom of cyberspeech, was Planned Parenthood Federation of America. During the ACLU's first decade of existence, one of our clients was Planned Parenthood's Founding Mother, Margaret Sanger. As I noted above, she was repeatedly harassed under the Victorian-era

---

20   Mutual Film Corp. v. Indus. Comm'n of Ohio, 236 US 230, 244 (1915), *overruled by* Joseph Burstyn, Inc. v. Wilson, 343 US 495 (1952).

21   Message Photo-Play Co. v. Bell, 166 NYS 338 (1917).

22   See, for example, ACLU v. Reno, 217 F.3d 162, 171 (3rd Cir. 2000); ACLU v. Reno, 31 F.Supp. 473, 491 (E.D.Pa. 1999); Reno v. ACLU, 521 US 844, 871 (1997); ACLU v. Reno, 828 F.Supp. 824, 870–872 (E.D.Pa. 1996).

23   See, for example, Reno v. ACLU, 521 US 844 (1997).

Comstock Law, the first national anti-obscenity law, which criminalised the information she conveyed about women's reproductive health and options. Sadly, more than three-quarters of a century later, the ACLU had to defend the organisation that Sanger founded against the Internet era's first national cyber-censorship law, which criminalised the very same information. Likewise, just as Sanger herself was censored when she conveyed birth control information via the then-new medium of film, the organisation that she founded is now facing censorship when it conveys the same information via the now-new medium of the Internet.

In the one country that has adopted a feminist-style anti-pornography law, we can observe the familiar pattern for all measures targeting sexual expression, harming the very people and causes it was supposed to help. In 1992, in *Butler* v. *The Queen*,[24] the Canadian Supreme Court incorporated the MacDworkinite concept into Canada's obscenity law, holding that such law would henceforth bar sexual materials that are 'degrading' or 'dehumanising' to women. The primary victims of Canada's brave new censorship regime have been the writings and bookshops of women, feminists, lesbians and gay men (Feminist Bookstore News, 1993).

The *Butler* ruling had been spearheaded by the Women's Legal Education and Action Fund (LEAF), a Canadian anti-pornography organisation that MacKinnon co-founded. Even LEAF, however, was soon forced to repudiate its purported victory in this case. In 1993 LEAF leaders and anti-censorship activists in Canada issued a joint news release that condemned Canadian officials' enforcement of *Butler* 'to harass and intimidate lesbians and gays', as well as 'bookstores, artists, AIDS organizations, sex trade workers, and safe sex educators' (LEAF, 1993).

Within the first two and a half years after the *Butler* decision, approximately two-thirds of all Canadian feminist bookshops had materials confiscated or detained by Canadian customs officials on the ground that these materials were 'degrading' or 'dehumanising'. Ironically, some of

---

24   1 SCR 452 (1992) (Can.).

that feminist material has been suppressed on the ground that it is allegedly degrading and harmful not to women, but rather to men (Feminist Bookstore News, 1993). In the ultimate irony, two of the earliest books to be seized under *Butler* at the US–Canada border had been written by Andrea Dworkin herself (Barton, 1993; Nerenberg, 1993)! According to Canadian customs officials, these feminist anti-pornography tracts illegally 'eroticized pain and bondage' (Scott, 1993).

Censoring sexual expression undermines rights of sexual orientation minorities

As former Stanford Law School dean Kathleen Sullivan has written, 'In a world where sodomy may still be made a crime, gay pornography is the *samizdat* of the oppressed' (Sullivan, 1992). In light of the long-standing and ongoing legal and societal discrimination faced by lesbians and gay men, materials depicting and exploring their sexuality are especially important, serving to educate and liberate. Yet precisely because of LGBT individuals' second-class legal status, expression about them is especially vulnerable to censorship. That conclusion is borne out by the experience under recently enacted cyber-censorship laws, as noted above, and also under MacDworkin-style laws, despite their allegedly egalitarian rationale.

The MacDworkin model law permits the suppression of any sexually oriented expression, regardless of the genders or the sexual orientations of the individuals depicted (Strossen, 2000: 106). This law's intended antipathy towards gay sexual expression was underscored by a leading gay activist, John Preston (1993), drawing on his experience in working with Andrea Dworkin at a centre for LGBT individuals: 'Dworkin used to run a lesbian discussion group in the center. One of her favourite antics ... was to deface any ... material that promoted male homosexuality ... I've come to understand that it's the expression of any male sexuality that she feels fuels the oppression of women in our society. That makes gay men not allies, but a big part of the problem.'

Further demonstrating her equal-opportunity condemnation of all sexual expression, Dworkin has also denounced lesbian pornography as 'an expression of self-hatred' (Brest and Vandenberg, 1987). These censorial views have been echoed by other anti-pornography feminists (Strossen, 2000: 169).

Even more significant than the pornophobic feminists' non-discriminatory denunciations of homosexual and heterosexual sexual expression is the fact that any censorship measure would be enforced by government officials and legal systems that reflect society's pervasive homophobia and heterosexism. Thus, it is not surprising that, in the real world, under the first feminist anti-pornography scheme to go into operation, in Canada, lesbian and gay erotica has borne the brunt of the censorship. As one LEAF lawyer observed, too many Canadian judges and other officials who enforce *Butler* believe that all homoerotic expression is 'degrading' (Busby, n.d.: 17).

Canada's LGBT bookshops have been so persistently harassed that, according to Bruce Walsh of the Canadian anti-censorship coalition Censorstop, 'every gay bookstore in this country has attempted to sell their bookstores, but nobody wants to buy them' (Reddin, 1993).

One of Canada's LGBT bookshops, Little Sisters Bookstore in Vancouver, brought a lawsuit against the government (Wente, 2000), arguing that its enforcement of *Butler* violated not only freedom of speech, but also equality rights, under Canada's Charter of Rights and Freedoms (Makin and Alphonso, 2000). Even LEAF, *Butler*'s prime proponents, filed a brief in this case, acknowledging that *Butler* was, after all, not good for (at least) those women and feminists who happen to be lesbian (Makin, 2002). In the Little Sisters case, the Canadian Supreme Court unanimously recognised that Canadian officials were systematically harassing Little Sisters and other LGBT bookshops under the *Butler* ruling, but the majority nonetheless refused to alter that ruling.[25]

In addition to the direct government censorship of LGBT expression

---

25   Little Sisters Book and Art Emporium v. Canada (Minister of Justice), [2000] CarswellBC 2442, [2000] SCC 69, [2000] 83 BCLR (3d) 1.

under *Butler*, the decision has also incited massive self-censorship. In an effort to forestall costly customs seizures, police raids and court battles, bookshop owners avoid ordering periodicals whose previous issues have been confiscated. As a result, the lesbian erotic magazines *Bad Attitude* and *On Our Backs* have effectively been banned in Canada, according to Janine Fuller, manager of Little Sisters. Likewise, to avoid incurring harassment by Canadian customs officials, Oxford University Press refused to distribute in Canada philosopher Richard Mohr's book *Gay Ideas: Outing and Other Controversies* (Human Rights Watch Free Expression Project, 1994).

Censoring sexual expression undermines human rights more broadly

As I have explained above, no matter what category of sexual expression is targeted for censorship, its inevitably vague contours will endanger all sexually oriented words and images. Moreover, any suppression of sexual expression will inevitably endanger free speech more generally, as well as other human rights. One reason, which I have already noted, is that laws prohibiting sexual speech have always targeted views that challenge the prevailing orthodoxy and powers not only in terms of sexual mores, but also on other political, religious, cultural or social issues. Sexually explicit speech has been banned by the most repressive regimes, including communism in the former Soviet Union, Eastern bloc countries and China; apartheid in South Africa; and fascist or clerical dictatorships in Chile, Iran and Iraq. Conversely, recent studies of Russia have correlated improvements in human rights, including women's rights, with the rise of free sexual expression.

In places where real pornography, i.e. sexually explicit expression, is conspicuously absent, political dissent is labelled as such. The communist government of the former Soviet Union suppressed political dissidents under obscenity laws. In 1987, when the Chinese communist government dramatically increased its censorship of books and magazines with Western political and literary messages, it condemned them as 'obscene', 'pornographic' and 'bawdy'. The white supremacist South African government banned black writing as 'pornographically immoral'. In Nazi Germany and the former Soviet Union, Jewish writings were reviled as 'pornographic', as were, respectively, any works that criticised the Nazi or Communist Party (Dershowitz, 1986: 36). Even in societies that generally respect human rights, including free speech, the terms 'obscenity' and 'pornography' tend to be used as epithets to stigmatise expression that is politically or socially unpopular. Obscenity laws have often been enforced against individuals who have expressed disfavoured ideas about political or religious subjects. One of the earliest British obscenity prosecutions, in the eighteenth century, was brought by the Tory government to imprison its leading Whig opponent, John Wilkes. In early American history, anti-obscenity laws were directed at speech that was offensive to the prevailing religious orthodoxy.

The pattern holds today. Obscenity laws in the USA have regularly been used to suppress expression of those who are relatively unpopular or disempowered, because of their ideas or their membership in particular societal groups. Recent major US obscenity prosecutions have attacked the rap music of young African-American men, and homoerotic works by gay and lesbian artists. Likewise, the National Endowment for the Arts has been attacked for its funding of art exploring feminist or homoerotic themes (Strossen, 2000: 56–7). UCLA law professor Kenneth Karst (1990: 103–4) provides intriguing insights into the link between sexual freedom, including free sexual expression, and freedom from discrimination:

> The suppression of Unreason is rooted in the same fears that produce group subordination: men's fear of the feminine, whites' fear of blackness, heterosexuals' anxiety about sexual orientation. Historically, all these fears have been closely connected with the fear of sexuality. It is no accident that the 1960s, a period of sexual 'revolution', also saw the acceleration of three movements that sought major re-definitions of America's social boundaries: the civil

rights movement, the gay liberation movement, and the women's movement.

For the reasons Professor Karst articulates, free sexual expression is integrally interconnected with equality, hardly at odds with it, as argued by the pro-censorship feminists. Indeed, free sexual expression is an essential aspect of all human freedom, as eloquently explained by Dr Gary Mongiovi (1991), who teaches at St John's University in New York:

> Sexual expression is perhaps the most fundamental manifestation of human individuality. Erotic material is subversive in the sense that it celebrates, and appeals to, the most uniquely personal aspects of an individual's emotional life. Thus, to allow freedom of expression and freedom of thought in this realm is to ... promote diversity and nonconformist behavior in general ... It is no coincidence that one of the first consequences of democratization and political liberalization in the former Soviet Union, Eastern Europe and China was a small explosion of erotic publications ... Suppression of pornography is not just a free-speech issue: Attempts to stifle sexual expression are part of a larger agenda directed at the suppression of human freedom and individuality more generally.

References

Barton, P. (1993), 'How Otto Jelinek guards our morals', *Toronto Star*, 29 May, p. H3.

Blanchard, M. (1992), 'The American urge to censor: freedom of expression versus the desire to sanitize society, from Anthony Comstock to 2 Live Crew', *William and Mary Law Review*, 33: 741–8.

Brest, P. and A. Vandenberg (1987), 'Essay: politics, feminism, and the constitution: the anti-pornography movement in Minneapolis', *Stanford Law Review*, 39: 607–41.

Busby, K (n.d.), *LEAF and Pornography: Litigating on Equality and Sexual Representations* (unpublished).

Chemerinsky, E. (2006), *Constitutional Law: Principles and Policies*, Aspen Law & Politics, sec. 11.1.2.

Dershowitz, A. (1986), 'What is porn?', *ABA Law Journal*, 36, 1 November.

Dworkin, A. (1985), 'Against the male flood: censorship, pornography, and equality', *Harvard Women's Law Journal*, 1: 20–21.

Feminist Bookstore News (1993), 'Canada customs hits feminist stores and others', *Feminist Bookstore News*, March/April.

Human Rights Watch Free Expression Project (1994), 'A ruling inspired by US anti-pornography activists is used to restrict lesbian and gay publications in Canada', February, pp. 8–9.

Karst, K. (1990), 'Boundaries and reasons: freedom of expression and the subordination of groups', *University of Illinois Law Review*, 95: 103–4 and 129.

LEAF (Women's Legal Education and Action Fund) (1993), 'Historic gathering condemns targeting of lesbian and gay materials and sex trade workers', LEAF News Release, Toronto, Canada: LEAF.

Linker, K. (1996), 'Film, feminism, psychoanalysis, and the problem of vision', in K. Brougher (ed.), *Art and Film since 1945: Hall of Mirrors*, Los Angeles, CA: Museum of Contemporary Art.

MacKinnon, C. (1985), 'Pornography, civil rights, and speech', *Harvard Civil Rights-Civil Liberties Law Review*, 20(1): 1–2, 22–60.

Makin, K. (2002), 'Judging the Charter: part 2; this case ... is out of control', *Globe and Mail*, Toronto, Canada, 8 April.

Makin, K. and C. Alphonso (2000), 'Gay book-sellers win Supreme Court case; Customs agents blasted for harassment', *Globe and Mail*, Toronto, Canada, 16 December, p. A1.

Mill, J. S. (1859), *On Liberty*, Serendipity, *www.billstclair.com/Serendipity/on_lib.html*, accessed 5 September 2006.

Mongiovi, G. (1991), 'Letters to the Editor', *Civil Liberties*, Spring/Summer, p. 2.

Nerenberg, A. (1993), 'Fear not, brave Canadian, Customs stands guard for thee', *Gazette*, Montreal, Canada, 22 January, p. 2.

Preston, J. (1993), 'Whose free speech?', *Boston Phoenix*, 8 October.

Reddin, B. (1993), 'O for Christ's sake Canada', *PDXS*, Portland, OR, 30 August–12 September, p. 3.

Rimer, S. (1990), 'Rap band members found not guilty in obscenity trial', *New York Times*, 21 October, p. 1.

Scott, S. (1993), 'Porn police: who decides what to ban at the border?', *Gazette*, Montreal, Canada, 14 April, pp. A1, A15.

Sonfield, A. (2003), 'Preventing unintended pregnancy in the US', www.guttmacher.org/pubs/ib2004n03.html.

Strossen, N. (2000), *Defending Pornography*, 2nd edn, New York: New York University Press.

Sullivan, K. (1992), 'Book review', *New Republic*, 28 September, pp. 35–40.

Tierney, J. (1994), 'Porn: the low-slung engine of progress', *New York Times*, 9 January.

Tribe, L. (2003), *American Constitutional Law*, 3rd edn, New York: Foundation Press, sections 12–16.

Webster's International Dictionary (1986), Springfield, MA: Merriam-Webster Inc.

Wente, M. (2000), 'Counterpoint: bad porn, good porn, Little Sisters', *Globe and Mail*, Toronto, Canada, 16 March.

8 MEDICAL DRUGS AND DEVICES
Alexander Tabarrok

Introduction

Most governments ban all new medical drugs and devices. The ban is lifted only when a government agency grants its approval. Getting government approval is time-consuming and expensive. In the USA, for example, it takes more than ten years and costs more than $800 million to bring a new drug to market (DiMasi et al. 2003).[1] Lengthier and more extensive testing of new drugs has benefits and costs. More testing increases the safety and effectiveness of those drugs that reach the market, but more testing means fewer new drugs since many drugs become uneconomic to produce as costs increase. More testing also delays the use of beneficial drugs, drugs that could have reduced mortality and morbidity had they been available earlier. In short, regulation may deter and delay medical progress. We survey the research that compares the benefits and costs of drug regulation.

For two reasons our focus will be on evaluating the US Food and Drug Administration (FDA). First, although the principles are similar everywhere, more research has been done on the FDA than its counterpart in other countries. Second, the US pharmaceutical market is the largest and most profitable in the world. If US regulations increase the cost of drug research and development, fewer new drugs will be produced not just in the USA but in the world. There are lessons to be drawn from the

---

1   Even without FDA regulations, drug firms would spend substantial sums to research and develop new drugs, so not all of the time or cost of bringing a drug to market is directly attributable to the FDA. FDA requirements, however, do impose substantial costs; see Adams and Branter (2004) for some estimates.

European system of drug regulation, however, and we will make reference to these further below.

We examine four sources of evidence: 1) studies that estimate the effect on new drug introductions of regulatory cost increases; 2) comparisons of safety and patient welfare in Europe and the USA during the 1970s and 1980s when the USA lagged behind Europe in the speed of new drug introductions; 3) comparisons of safety and patient welfare following the speed-up of approval times owing to the Prescription Drug User Fee Act; and 4) examinations of off-label prescribing.[2] The last area is of special interest because off-label prescribing gives us a window on a world with much less regulation. Overall, the evidence suggests that FDA prohibitions have reduced patient welfare.

FDA regulations and new drug introductions

Sam Peltzman (1973) wrote the first serious cost–benefit study of the FDA. He focused his attention on the 1962 Kefauver-Harris Amendments to the Food, Drug, and Cosmetics Act of 1938, which significantly enhanced FDA powers. The amendments added a proof-of-efficacy requirement to the existing proof-of-safety requirement, removed time constraints on the FDA disposition of New Drug Applications (NDAs), and gave the FDA extensive powers over the clinical testing procedures drug companies must use to support their applications. Using data from 1948 to 1962, Peltzman created a statistical model to predict the yearly number of new drug introductions. During 1948–62, the model tracks the actual number of new drug introductions quite well, as indicated by Figure 8.

Because Peltzman's model tracks the pre-1962 drug market well we have some confidence that, *if all else had remained equal*, the model would also roughly track the post-1962 drug market. Peltzman's model, in other words, estimates the number of new drugs that would have been

---

2   We draw extensively from Klein and Tabarrok (2002).

Figure 8   **Drug loss due to 1962 increase in FDA powers**
New NCEs

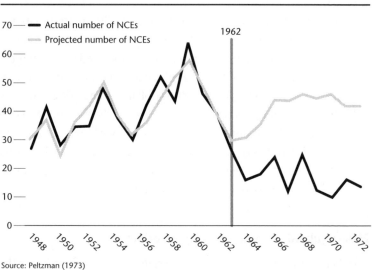

Source: Peltzman (1973)

produced if the FDA's powers had not been increased in 1962. Thus, by comparing the model results with the *actual* number of new drugs, we can draw an estimate of the effect of the 1962 amendments. The model predicts a probable post-1962 average of 41 new chemical entities (NCEs, or new drugs) approved per year. The actual number of new drugs per year in this period was sixteen.

The average number of new drugs introduced pre-1962 (40) was also much larger than the post-1962 average (16). Thus, whether one compares pre- and post-1962 averages or compares the results from a forecast with the actual results, the conclusions are the same: the 1962 Amendments caused a significant drop in the introduction of new drugs. Using data of longer span, Wiggins (1981) also found that increased FDA regulations raised costs and reduced the number of new drugs. Even if FDA regulations have not improved safety, they might be redeemed if they reduced the proportion of inefficacious drugs on the market. Using a variety of tests, however, Peltzman (1973) found little evidence to suggest a decline in the proportion of inefficacious drugs reaching the market since 1962. Thus, he concluded, '[the] penalties imposed by the marketplace on sellers of ineffective drugs prior to 1962 seem to have been enough of a deterrent to have left little room for improvement by a regulatory agency' (ibid.: 1086). Similarly, in their survey of the literature, Grabowski and Vernon (1983) concluded, 'In sum, the hypothesis that the observed decline in new product introductions has largely been concentrated in marginal or ineffective drugs is not generally supported by empirical analyses' (p. 34).

Comparison with other countries

Time to approval has historically been years shorter in Europe than in the USA. The difference between the time of a drug's availability in Europe and that in the USA has come to be called the *drug lag* (Grabowski, 1980; Kaitin et al., 1989; Wardell, 1973, 1978a, 1978b; Wardell and Lasagna, 1975). In recent years, however, the FDA has improved and perhaps Europe has slowed so the drug lag has been eliminated (Healy and Kaitin, 1999). We discuss some reasons for the FDA's improvement below. What is significant for our purposes is that from approximately 1970 to 1993 the FDA clearly lagged significantly behind its counterparts in the United Kingdom, France, Spain and Germany (Kaitin and Brown, 1995). This fact gives us a basis for comparison: during the period of consistent drug lag, did the delay correspond to greater safety? Put another way: did speedier drug approval in Europe lead to a scourge of unsafe drugs in Europe?

It is impossible to know all of a drug's side effects before it reaches the market.[3] Thus, as a matter of probability, drug lag will sometimes

---

3   Suppose that a drug has a serious side effect in 1 out of every 1,000 patients. Even in a large and expensive clinical trial of 4,000 patients the chances of spotting this problem are slight – especially if the condition being treated is also life-threatening. Yet a serious side effect in 1 out of every 1,000 patients is troubling in a patient population that may

result in improved safety, thalidomide being the classic example. But does drug lag improve safety overall? If the US system resulted in appreciably safer drugs, we would expect to see far fewer post-market safety withdrawals in the United States than in other countries. Bakke et al. (1995) compared safety withdrawals in the USA with those in Great Britain and Spain, each of which approved more drugs than the USA during the same time period. Yet approximately 3 per cent of all drug approvals were withdrawn for safety reasons in the USA, approximately 3 per cent in Spain, and approximately 4 per cent in Great Britain. There is no evidence that the US drug lag brought greater safety. Wardell and Lasagna (1975) concluded their comparison of drug approvals in the USA and Great Britain by noting: 'In view of the clear benefits demonstrable from some of the drugs introduced into Britain, it appears that the United States has lost more than it has gained from adopting a more conservative approach' (p. 105). Although the FDA no longer lags behind Europe, it is drug delay which kills, not drug delay relative to Europe. What the drug delay issue suggests is that at or near current levels of testing the marginal benefit of testing is low.

Mutual recognition as reform

The European system of drug approval has benefited from a combination of harmonisation of standards and decentralisation of standard testers. Under the 'mutual recognition procedure' (formally established in January 1995 via an amendment to 75/319/EEC but having evolved over many years) a firm that has a drug approved in one member state can apply to have that approval recognised by two or more other member states (Abraham and Lewis, 2000). The member states have 90

---

number in the millions. The mathematics, combined with the costs of clinical trials, guarantee that patients will also always be experimental subjects. Post-market surveillance can speed discovery of post-market problems and should be a key feature of any drug safety system. The USA has a particularly weak post-market surveillance system.

days to challenge a request for recognition but recognition is expected in principle. A challenged request does not automatically result in a rejection. Instead a challenged request is sent for arbitration before the EU's Committee for Proprietary Medicinal Products (CPMP).

A firm may submit a drug application to any of the member states, thereby bypassing states with slow approval procedures.[4] Member states can charge fees for evaluating pharmaceuticals and so have an incentive to encourage customers by offering efficient review procedures. All member states, however, must evaluate pharmaceuticals according to harmonised standards set centrally.

The mutual recognition procedure speeds approval and avoids needless duplication of resources. Klein and Tabarrok (2002) suggest that the USA should recognise European drug approvals. If a product is approved in the EU why should it not be available in the USA within, say, 90 days? German and Italian patients and doctors do not refuse drugs that have not been approved in the United States – evidently they do not hold the FDA in great esteem. Why should US patients not have the same access to drugs as Europeans? Japan, Canada, Australia and other countries with advanced medical review systems could also benefit from a mutual recognition procedure.

The EU procedure of competing drug evaluators also raises the possibility of non-state evaluators of new drug applications. Miller (2000), for example, argues that the FDA should become 'primarily a *certifier of certifiers*, rather than a *certifier of products*' (p. 106). Opening up drug evaluation to the private market could potentially increase efficiency and speed approval time with no loss in safety, just as competition has worked in the EU system.

Critics fear a 'race to the bottom', but private quality certification has a long and successful history in the market for electrical and other devices (Campbell, 2000). Underwriters Laboratories Inc. (UL), for

---

4   A firm may also submit directly to the CPMP, the centralised procedure. Biotechnology products must use the centralised procedure. See Abraham and Lewis (2000) for more on European regulatory procedure.

example, is a private, not-for-profit, product-safety testing and certification organisation with customers throughout the world. The UL mark certifies that the product has passed the UL Standard. Applying for a UL mark is voluntary but many governments and retailers require that products be certified by a Nationally Recognised Testing Laboratory (NRTL), of which UL is one example. The US Occupational Safety and Health Organisation (OSHA) acts as a certifier for NRTLs, just the role that Miller (2000) suggests for the FDA. (In fact, the FDA does have a small third-party review programme for low-risk medical devices.) A race to the bottom would destroy UL's reputation for probity, the source of its revenues, and would result in decertification by OSHA.

The Prescription Drug User Fee Act

Pre-1992 figures indicated that on average it took the FDA two and a half years to review an NDA and sometimes up to eight years. Often, the cause of delay was not the difficulty of the application but simple backlog. Despite the inefficiency of spending millions to research new drugs only to have applications sit unexamined for months or even years, Congress was unwilling to increase FDA appropriations. Thus was born the Prescription Drug User Fee Act (PDUFA) of 1992. PDUFA offered firms a deal – if you pay a submission fee, in essence an earmarked tax, the FDA will promise to use the fees to hire more drug evaluators to speed review times.

PDUFA has been a big success – the FDA's budget is significantly larger because of PDUFA fees but firms are better off because speedier approval times more than justify the fee. Olson (2004) estimates that PDUFA reduced approval times by 34 per cent. Berndt et al. (2005) find large increases in consumer and producer welfare under PDUFA and no statistically significant difference between safety withdrawals pre- and post-PDUFA.

Off-label prescribing

When the FDA evaluates the safety and efficacy of a drug, the evaluation is made with respect to a specified use of the drug. Once a drug has been approved for some use, however, doctors may legally prescribe the drug for other uses. Approved uses are known as *on-label* uses, and other uses are considered *off-label* uses. Amoxicillin, for example, has an on-label use for treating respiratory tract infections and an off-label use for treating stomach ulcers.

For the on-label treatment of respiratory tract infections, amoxicillin has been tested and passed muster in all three phases of the IND clinical study; phase I trials for basic safety and phase II and phase III trials for efficacy. For the treatment of stomach ulcers, however, amoxicillin has not gone through FDA-mandated phase II and phase III trials and thus is not FDA approved for this use. Indeed, amoxicillin will probably never go through FDA efficacy trials for the treatment of stomach ulcers because the basic formulation is no longer under patent. Yet any textbook or medical guide discussing stomach ulcers will mention amoxicillin as a potential treatment, and a doctor who did not consider prescribing amoxicillin or other antibiotics for the treatment of stomach ulcers would today be considered highly negligent. Off-label uses are in effect regulated according to the FDA's pre-1962 rules (which required only safety, not efficacy), whereas on-label uses are regulated according to the post-1962 rules.

FDA defenders suggest that an unregulated market for drugs would be a medical disaster. Do patients and doctors shrink in fear from uses not certified by the FDA? Not at all. Most hospital patients are given drugs that are not FDA approved for prescribed use. In a large number of fields, a majority of patients are prescribed at least one drug off-label. Off-label prescriptions are especially common for AIDS, cancer and paediatric patients, but are also common throughout medicine. Doctors learn of off-label uses from extensive medical research, testing, peer-reviewed publications, newsletters, lecture presentations, conferences, advertising, Internet sources and trusted colleagues. Scientists and doctors, working through professional associations and organisations, make official determinations of 'best practice' and certify off-label uses in standard reference compendia such as the *US Pharmacopoeia Drug Indications, The American Hospital Formulary Service Drug Information* and pharmacopoeia developed in-house by large health maintenance organisations. Doctors use this information to try to make the best decisions for their patients. Medical decisions are most often made in uncertainty and partial ignorance, so there is rarely a single best decision, and different doctors and different patients choose different treatments. New information constantly flows into this system as outcomes accumulate, epidemiological studies reveal new correlations, scientists propose theoretical explanations, researchers design and embark on new clinical studies, scientific institutions arrive at new judgements, and pharmaceutical companies create new drugs. As this medical knowledge grows and develops, information flows in a decentralised fashion, and doctors adjust their decisions accordingly.

The difference between the on-label and off-label markets is not that the off-label market is 'unregulated' but that it is unregulated by the FDA, a centralised and coercive authority. In approving or rejecting a new drug, the FDA makes a decision everyone must obey. Heterogeneity among patients in both preferences and circumstances is great. A drug that can save the life of A may be dangerous to B even if A and B have the same disease. An athlete and a college professor with the same disease may choose different courses of treatment. The FDA's 'one size fits all' policy is not appropriate for every patient.

The off-label market is regulated by thousands of doctors and patients acting in a decentralised manner. Compared with the FDA, this market adjusts quickly to new information, shows less sign of biased incentives, and allows a more precise adjusting of treatment decisions to preferences and the particular conditions of time and place (Tabarrok, 2000). The off-label market operates with much less government intervention than the on-label market and provides a good idea of the benefits to be had from reducing FDA control over approval decisions.

By their actions and words, doctors tell us that they believe in off-label prescribing (ibid.; Klein and Tabarrok, 2008). Why do doctors prescribe drugs off-label? For one thing, as mentioned above, physicians have many sources of information about drugs other than the FDA, such as the peer-reviewed scientific literature or information from other countries. This medical knowledge can advance faster than the FDA is able to approve or test drugs. Also, standard therapies sometimes fail and patients are heterogeneous. *Notice that each of these reasons is also a reason to allow physicians to prescribe new drugs that are not yet FDA approved.*

Indeed, because drugs prescribed off-label have not been through FDA-prescribed efficacy trials there is a logical inconsistency in allowing off-label prescribing and requiring proof of efficacy for the drug's initial use (Tabarrok, 2000; Klein and Tabarrok, 2008). Logical consistency would require us *either* 1) to oppose off-label prescribing and favour initial proof of efficacy, *or* 2) to favour off-label prescribing and oppose initial proof of efficacy. Experience recommends the second option.

The *Consumer Reports* model

A wide variety of evidence indicates that patient welfare would be improved with less drug regulation. On this basis and out of a deep respect for patient autonomy, Higgs (1994) suggests that the FDA and other drug agencies should be eliminated. Elimination is unlikely and may be undesirable but there are many opportunities for reform that stop short of elimination. Mutual recognition and competitive drug evaluators have already been mentioned. Off-label prescribing suggests moving back to a safety-only testing system. More generally, drug agencies should shift from drug paternalism to patient consumerism.

The FDA currently works on a paternalistic model: one choice to rule them all. But another approach, what I call the *Consumer Reports* model, would meet the needs of diverse healthcare consumers much better. *Consumer Reports*, a magazine run by a non-profit foundation, doesn't try to replace consumer choice. Instead, by carefully evaluating and testing new products and providing this information to readers, *Consumer Reports* helps consumers to make better choices. Similarly, a less paternalistic FDA would provide more information to patients and doctors, but it would also leave more choices in their hands because only patients and their doctors have the particular knowledge that allows each patient to be treated as an individual.

A consumer-oriented FDA does not mean an end to the agency. On the contrary, an FDA reorganised on the *Consumer Reports* model would produce and disseminate more information to patients and doctors, it would be more independent of the industry, and it would be more willing to counter puffed-up pharmaceutical industry advertising.

A consumer-oriented FDA, for example, could help consumers decide which drug is best for them by testing products in head-to-head comparisons. Imagine how much less useful *Consumer Reports* would be if it issued only 'acceptable' or 'not-acceptable' recommendations – but this is precisely the focus of the FDA.

Consumer Reports also conducts its own testing (or contracts that testing out to independent labs) while the FDA relies on the pharmaceutical manufacturers to test their own products – an inherent conflict of interest. We have already noted that given Congress's unwillingness to fund the FDA, PDUFA is an excellent law that cuts delay in the approval of new drugs. But one doesn't have to be a conspiracy theorist to be concerned when industry pays the salaries of its regulators. A consumer-oriented FDA would lose the power to ban products before sale but it would be funded independently of pharmaceutical manufacturers and it could thus better advise consumers and physicians.

Conclusion

Banning new medical drugs and devices until expensive and time-consuming tests have been conducted according to the dictates of a centralised agency has resulted in drug lag and drug loss. Overall, drug regulation has reduced patient choice and welfare. Rather than paternalism and banning, patient welfare would be better served by drug agencies built on a *Consumer Reports* model of independent testing, information collection and dissemination of information and advice.

References

Abraham, J. and G. Lewis (2000), *Regulating Medicines in Europe*, New York: Routledge.

Adams, C. and V. V. Brantner (2004), 'Estimating the costs of new drug development: is it really $802m?', Working paper, http://papers. ssrn.com/s013/papers.cfm?abstract_id=640563.

Bakke, O. M., M. Manocchia, F. de Abajom, K. Kaitin and L. Lasagna (1995), 'Drug safety discontinuations in the United Kingdom, the United States, and Spain from 1974 through 1993: a regulatory perspective', *Clinical Pharmacology and Therapeutics*, 58(1): 108–17.

Berndt, E. R., A. H. B. Gottschalk, T. Philipson and M. W. Strobeck (2005), 'Assessing the impacts of the Prescription Drug User Fee Acts (PDUFA) on the FDA approval process', *Forum for Health Economics & Policy*, Forum: Frontiers in Health Policy Research, 8(2), *www.bepress.com/fhep/8/2*.

Campbell, N. (2000), 'Exploring free market certification of medical devices', in R. D. Feldman (ed.), *American Health Care: Government, Market Processes and the Public Interest*, New Brunswick, NJ: Transaction Publishers and the Independent Institute.

DiMasi, J. A., R. W. Hansen and H. G. Grabowski (2003), 'The price of innovation: new estimates of drug development costs', *Journal of Health Economics*, 22(2): 151–85.

Grabowski, H. G. (1980), 'Regulation and the international diffusion of pharmaceuticals', in R. B. Helms (ed.), *The International Supply of Medicines*, Washington, DC: American Enterprise Institute for Public Policy Research.

Grabowski, H. G. and J. M. Vernon (1983), *The Regulation of Pharmaceuticals: Balancing the Benefits and Risks*, Washington, DC: American Enterprise Institute for Public Policy Research.

Healy, E. and K. Kaitin (1999), 'The European Agency for the Evaluation of Medicinal Product's centralised procedure for product approval: current status', *Drug Information Journal*, 33: 969–78.

Higgs, R. (1994), 'Banning a risky product cannot improve any consumer's welfare (properly understood), with applications to FDA testing requirements', *Review of Austrian Economics*, 7(2): 3–20.

Kaitin, K. I., and J. Brown (1995), 'A drug lag update', *Drug Information Journal*, 29: 361–73.

Kaitin, K. I., N. Mattison, F. K. Northington and L. Lasagna (1989), 'The drug lag: an update of new drug introductions in the US and UK, 1977 through 1987', *Clinical Pharmacology and Therapeutics*, 4: 121–38.

Klein, D. B and A. Tabarrok (2002), 'Is the FDA safe and effective?', Oakland, CA: Independent Institute, www.FDAReview.org.

Klein, D. B and A. Tabarrok (2008), 'Do off-label drug practices argue against FDA efficacy requirements? Testing an argument by structured conversations with experts', *American Journal of Economics and Sociology*, forthcoming.

Miller, H. (2000), *To America's Health: A Proposal to Reform the Food and Drug Administration*, Stanford, CA: Hoover Institution Press.

Olson, M. K. (2004), 'Perspective: explaining reductions in FDA drug review times: PDUFA matters', *Health Affairs*, Web exclusive, 30 January, http://content.healthaffairs.org/cgi/content/abstract/hlthaff.w4.s1v1.

Peltzman, S. (1973), 'An evaluation of consumer protection legislation: the 1962 Drug Amendments', *Journal of Political Economy*, 81(5): 1049–91. Reprinted in G. J. Stigler (ed.) (1988), *Chicago Studies in Political Economy*, Chicago, IL: University of Chicago Press.

Tabarrok, A. (2000), 'Assessing the FDA via the anomaly of off-label drug prescribing', *Independent Review*, 5(1): 25–53.

Wardell, W. M. (1973), 'Introduction of new therapeutic drugs in the United States and Great Britain: an international comparison', *Clinical Pharmacology and Therapeutics*, 14(5): 773–90.

Wardell, W. M. (1978a), 'A close inspection of the "calm look"', *Journal of the American Medical Association*, 239(19): 2004–11.

Wardell, W. M. (1978b), 'The drug lag revisited: comparisons by therapeutic area of patterns of drugs marketed in the US and Great Britain from 1972 through 1976', *Clinical Pharmacology and Therapeutics*, 24: 499–524.

Wardell, W. M. and L. Lasagna (1975), *Regulation and Drug Development*, Washington, DC: American Enterprise Institute for Public Policy Research.

Wiggins, S. N. (1981), 'Product quality regulation and new drug introductions: some new evidence from the 1970s', *Review of Economics and Statistics*, 63: 615–19.

9 PROSTITUTION[1]

John Meadowcroft

Introduction

Prostitution is the provision of sexual services for payment.[2] Although prostitution has not existed in every known human society, it is a practice that has existed for millennia in every continent of the world and within many different cultures, hence its popular soubriquet as 'the world's oldest profession'. Prostitutes and their clients may be male or female, although most popular and scholarly attention has focused on the employment of female prostitutes by male clients. This is perhaps not surprising given that female-for-male prostitution constitutes the majority of commercial sexual relationships, but significant male homosexual prostitution also exists, as well as some male-for-female and lesbian prostitution (Diana, 1985; Perkins and Bennett, 1985; Ringdal, 2004). Hence, as Ericsson (1980: 349) has commented, 'rather than constituting a dichotomy between the sexes, prostitution has the characteristic that a considerable portion of the prostitutes are men, and a small minority of the customers are women'. Despite its prevalence, prostitution is illegal in large parts of the world, and where it is nominally legal many of the activities necessary for prostitution to take place are illegal.

---

1   I would like to thank Adrian Blau and an anonymous referee for their comments on an earlier version of this chapter. The usual caveat applies.

2   Definitional difficulties may arise, however, because such an arrangement may exist within some marriages and other relationships that involve 'the purchase of intimacy' (Edlund and Korn, 2002; Zelizer, 2005). Edlund and Korn (2002) have attempted to overcome this problem by defining prostitution as the purchase of sex that is non-reproductive from the purchaser's point of view. This definition does not completely resolve the difficulties, but it is probably as close to a workable definition of prostitution as is possible.

This chapter will argue that the prohibition of prostitution and other attempts by governments to curtail the market for sexual services infringe the basic rights of citizens and constitute bad public policy. First, such interventions infringe the basic rights of individuals to freely engage in sexual relations with partners of their choice; it is morally wrong for the state to seek to prevent adult women and men freely choosing their sexual partners. Second, they impose costs on prostitutes, their clients and society as a whole that are not justified by the benefits derived.

After this introduction, this chapter will set out the different prostitution markets that have developed in contemporary societies and the three standard legal regimes that govern prostitution. It will then present the principal arguments that are advanced for prohibiting prostitution, all of which are variants of the 'harm principle', and show why these arguments should be rejected. An optimal legal regime that should govern prostitution will then be proposed.

Prostitution: markets and legal regimes

To judge whether or not prostitution should be prohibited it is first necessary to understand what prostitution involves and the different prostitution markets that exist in most developed countries.

Prostitution is a huge global industry. Figures for its size must be estimates, but Moffatt's (2005: 193) conservative estimate puts global income from prostitution at US$20 billion annually. In the UK context, a 2003 study by Glasgow City Council estimated that over £6 million is spent annually in the city on female-for-male prostitution.[3]

Prostitution markets

Prostitution describes a wide range of activities that take place in a number

---

3   BBC News website, 'Men spend £6.6m on sex in Glasgow', http://news.bbc.co.uk/1/hi/ scotland/glasgow_and_west/5007898.stm.

of different contexts. As Diana (1985: 3) has written: 'The stratification of prostitution and its organization are quite varied and more complex than usually imagined. Categories also overlap on one basis or another.' Nevertheless, three basic prostitution markets can be identified.[4]

Street prostitution is the most visible form of prostitution, where prostitutes openly solicit for clients in public streets and often provide services in public places. Almost all major North American and European cities have a 'red light district' where street prostitution takes place. Although this is often away from residential areas, prostitution may constitute a public nuisance where transactions take place openly in the street, people with no involvement in prostitution may be subject to solicitation and there is likely to be increased crime (or fear of crime) caused by a transient population involved in clandestine activity. In street prostitution, prostitutes (and their clients) are vulnerable to robbery and other forms of violent attack. Indeed, the murder rate for active female street prostitutes in the USA has been calculated at 459 per 100,000, meaning that street prostitutes are eighteen times more likely to be murdered than other women of similar age and race (Potterat et al., 2004). Third parties may be involved in street prostitution, usually by providing some form of protection to the prostitute. The horror stories presented by opponents of prostitution almost always concern street prostitutes, many of whom are extremely vulnerable and damaged people; in the developed world the great majority of street prostitutes are probably hard drugs users who do little more than earn money to maintain their drug supply. While street prostitution is the most visible form of prostitution, it represents a small proportion of the entire prostitution market; it has been estimated that street prostitutes constitute only 20 per cent of female prostitutes and 5 per cent of male prostitutes, proportions that may have further declined as the advent of the Internet and cheap mobile phones have facilitated the growth of other prostitution markets (Cameron et al., 1999).

4   In the USA, a fourth prostitution market exists centred on the provision of sexual services at truck stops (see, for example, Diana, 1985).

The second market for prostitution is the brothel, or as they are sometimes euphemistically known, 'saunas' or 'massage parlours'. Here, a number of prostitutes work in premises specifically used for this purpose, often on a shift or rota system. The brothel will usually employ a receptionist, or 'maid'. Larger brothels may employ security guards and/or CCTV. Many brothels in developed countries now advertise on the Internet, listing details of services provided and fees charged. Brothels do not create a public nuisance in the same way as street prostitution, although those living close to a well-used brothel may experience some disturbance. In many developed countries, notably Australia, Germany, Holland and the state of Nevada in the USA, brothels are legal and government regulated to ensure condom use and tax compliance (Diana, 1985; Fleiss and Labi, 2003; Perkins and Bennett, 1985; Ringdal, 2004).

The third prostitution market is for escort or 'call girl' services. Escorts are independent prostitutes who meet clients in their own homes or in the client's home or hotel room, though many escorts outsource client screening and introduction to an escort agency. The public nuisance caused by escort services is minimal; a person's neighbour, friend or even partner may work as an escort without their knowledge. In many developed countries the market for escorts (and to a lesser extent brothel prostitutes) has become highly developed, as indicated by the websites created by clients to facilitate the sharing of information about and the 'rating' of different escorts and agencies (Diana, 1985; Fleiss and Labi, 2003; Perkins and Bennett, 1985; Ringdal, 2004).[5]

Moffatt and Peters (2004) have shown that UK-based female prostitutes working in brothels and as escorts typically earn three times the wages of manual workers and twice the wages of non-manual workers. They calculated the average annual income of an inner London brothel

---

5   Escort review websites have become an important source of information about prostitution in the UK, informing a number of academic papers, such as Moffatt and Peters (2004).

worker or escort to be more than £50,000 per annum,[6] an income often received tax free and without the requirement of formal qualifications or work experience usually necessary to earn such a salary.

Legal regimes governing prostitution

Prostitution tends to be governed by one of three legal regimes. First, where prostitution and all concomitant activities are legal, including 'pimping' – the management of prostitutes by a third party. This is the current legal status of prostitution in a number of countries, including Austria, Singapore and Switzerland.

The second and most common regime, which is found in Australia, Germany, Holland, Hungary, the UK and the state of Nevada in the USA, permits prostitution and most of the acts that facilitate it, but some (though not always all) third-party actions are illegal. Such a regime is intended to minimise the prevalence of prostitution and protect prostitutes from exploitation by predatory 'pimps' or 'madams'.

In the third regime prostitution is illegal, as are all acts connected with prostitution. This is the legal position throughout the Islamic and Arab world and also in Sweden. In some countries, such as Iran and Somalia, prostitution is punishable by death. The legal regime introduced to Sweden in 1999 by the Act Prohibiting the Sale of Sexual Services is particularly noteworthy, as it criminalises the purchase of the services of a prostitute, so that it is clients, rather than prostitutes, who are criminalised.

Even where prostitution is nominally legal, there can be a number of legal barriers to it becoming an occupation like any other. Most notably, in many countries, including the UK, it is illegal for prostitutes to employ third parties to provide security and other services. There also remains

---

6   A comparable figure (after adjusting for inflation) of an annual income of $30,000–$100,000 for New York escorts has been cited by Satz (1995). Escorts working for the former 'Hollywood Madam' Heidi Fleiss were said to be paid four- and five-figure sums per night for the provision of sexual services to her exclusive clientele (Fleiss, 2002).

a powerful body of opinion that engages in political lobbying for the prohibition of prostitution. Following the successful campaign to outlaw prostitution in Sweden, a similar campaign is ongoing in Norway, and in September 2007 it was reported that UK government ministers were considering bringing forward similar proposals.[7] This chapter will now consider the principal arguments advanced for the prohibition of prostitution.

The prohibition of prostitution: for and against

The principal arguments advanced for the prohibition of prostitution are all variants of the 'harm principle'. As set out in the Introduction to this collection, the harm principle, most famously articulated by John Stuart Mill (1859 [1985]), states that legal restrictions on individual liberty can be justified only to prevent harm to others. This principle is an important basis of criminal law in all civilised societies (although it may take its authority from different sources) and debate on the appropriate scope of the law often involves judging whether or not an act harms other people (Feinberg, 1984). Hence, advocates of the prohibition of prostitution have sought to demonstrate that it causes harm.

Two principal variants of this argument can be identified. First, that prostitution harms the prostitute, usually because it is believed to necessarily involve the exploitation of women who work as prostitutes. Second, it is argued that the existence of prostitution constitutes a harm to society or imposes externalities on others not directly engaged in it.

Harm to the prostitute

Probably the most enduring argument against prostitution is that prostitution is necessarily harmful to those who sell sexual services. At the heart of this argument is the view that no one would freely choose to

---

7   'Men who buy sex could face prosecution', *Guardian*, 10 September 2007, p. 1.

be a prostitute and that therefore prostitution must necessarily involve exploitation, coercion or at the very least result from desperation. This argument is most frequently applied to female prostitutes, who are claimed to be disempowered and marginalised in what are said to be contemporary patriarchal societies.

The view that female prostitution must involve the exploitation of women is central to the arguments of feminists who oppose prostitution. Female prostitutes are considered to be women who have been denied the choice of alternative occupations, principally as a result of poverty: 'Prostitution is a choice based on a lack of survival options ... What do women need in order to escape prostitution? They need a living wage. Specifically their list of needs includes housing, job training and medical care including substance abuse treatment' (Farley, 2005: 2; see also Pateman, 1988: ch. 7).

Such depictions of prostitution are applied not only to street prostitutes, or to women who have been trafficked into prostitution, but are said to apply to all women who work as prostitutes: 'the distinctions other people make between whether the event took place in the Plaza Hotel or somewhere more inelegant are not the distinctions that matter ... The circumstances don't mitigate or modify what prostitution is' (Dworkin, 1997: 140–41).

This perception that prostitution is inherently exploitative of women is often explicitly informed by Marxist views of the exploitation alleged to be inherent within all capitalist societies; the prostitution of women is a more raw form of the exploitation deemed to be endemic within capitalism. Hence, according to Rowbotham (1972: 65): 'Just as the prostitute gives the substitute of love for money, so the worker hands over his work and his life for a daily wage.'

According to Pateman (1988: ch. 7) prostitution is a product of 'patriarchal capitalism', but there is also said to be a qualitative difference between the exploitation of women in prostitution and the exploitation of the male workforce within capitalism; whereas men simply sell their labour to their employer, the integral relationship between body and self means that when a woman enters into prostitution 'she is thus selling *herself* in a very real sense' (ibid.: 207).

Hence, it is claimed that the physically invasive nature of prostitution means it is not a 'dirty job' like many other 'dirty jobs', or just one example of capitalist exploitation among many: 'sweatshops are vicious but they don't involve invasion of all your body's orifices on a daily basis for years into the future' (Farley, 2005: 4). The key feature of prostitution, then, is said to be that it infringes women's right of self-ownership of their own bodies. On this basis, prostitution is said to constitute a harm.

This view that prostitution necessarily involves the exploitation of women so that all female prostitutes are victims of harm has been hugely influential in shaping public perceptions of prostitution and in informing public policy. This can be seen in the Swedish prohibition legislation of 1999, which regards 'prostitution ... as an aspect of male violence against women and children', so that it is 'officially acknowledged as a form of exploitation of women and children' (Ministry of Industry, Employment and Communications, 2004: 1).

Empirical evidence, however, does not support the claim advanced by opponents of prostitution that sex work is undertaken only by women (and men) who have no alternative as a result of either desperation or coercion. A number of empirical studies have shown that prostitutes are drawn from across the socio-economic spectrum. Studies of female escorts, for example, have found a number to be university graduates earning relatively large sums of money relatively quickly while searching for other jobs. These are women who do have alternative employment opportunities and have not entered into prostitution as the only alternative to destitution (Diana, 1985; Perkins and Bennett, 1985; Satz, 1995). Indeed, one of the most comprehensive studies of prostitution in the USA found that a third of female prostitutes came from high-income backgrounds (Diana, 1985: 45).

Also, *contra* to the claim of feminists who oppose prostitution that prostitutes are so disempowered and lacking in choice that they must submit to any act that a client demands (for example: Dworkin, 1997: 140; Farley, 2005: 3), empirical evidence shows that prostitutes often engage in protracted negotiations with clients as to what they will or will not do and the fee to be paid for specific services (Diana, 1985; Pheterson, 1996). Hence, as Pheterson (1996: 39) describes, 'In practice, the sexual activity, like the fee, is open to negotiation. The whore makes an offer or the customer makes a request; she is the one who must agree to the final terms.' Indeed, the high incomes earned by many sex workers constitute further evidence that they are not powerless, as substantial bargaining power must be necessary to negotiate such lucrative pay rates.

Prostitution, then, is one of many activities that people are willing to undertake when the benefits accrued exceed the costs incurred. In any society where people are not sustained by manna from heaven but must work for their subsistence, people must inevitably undertake activity that involves personal costs – assuming that they prefer leisure to work. There are, as Wertheimer (1992: 215) has described, 'negative *elements* in virtually all employment contracts, indeed, in virtually all uncontroversially beneficial transactions', but, 'We do not say that a worker is harmed by employment ... We assume that the benefits that the worker receives from employment are greater than the costs.'

Hence, to show that an individual has been compelled by their economic circumstances to carry out actions that they would otherwise not undertake, or which involve personal costs, does not demonstrate that that person has been exploited or coerced, or is acting out of desperation. Rather, it shows that other more desirable alternatives required the cooperation of others, for example people willing to work to provide their subsistence while they enjoy leisure, and that such cooperation has been legitimately denied. As Ericsson (1980: 346) has pointed out, 'to say that hustling very clearly has economic causes ... is entirely acceptable, so long as we are also prepared to say the same about "lawyerism"'. If prostitutes enter prostitution for economic reasons, that simply makes prostitution an occupation like any other, whether the law, medicine or window cleaning.

Moreover, if individual women and men have a right to choose their sexual partners, then that must include choosing to engage in sex in return for money if they so wish. Hence, Farley's (2005: 1) statement that 'women have a right NOT to be prostitutes' must logically also imply that women (and men) *have a right to be prostitutes*. If this is not the case then it must follow that an external authority has the power to determine who women (and men) may have sex with, a position that seems incompatible with any notion of self-ownership, personal freedom or empowerment.

The idea that women cannot choose to engage in commercial sexual relationships whereas men can make such choices without being exploited or coerced would seem to suggest that women are incapable of participating in the sexual realm without protection by government. For women to be more than second-class citizens surely means accepting that they can choose to use their bodies as they see fit, even if that means engaging in prostitution.

Indeed, Pheterson (1996: 37–8) has argued that the automatic attribution of victim status to women who are prostitutes is a product of 'traditional female socialization [that] discourages women from talking about sex, from asking for money in any situation' and hence is part of the 'normative imposition of female sexual and financial dependency'. For Pheterson, it will only be when women are deemed capable of choosing to engage in prostitution on the same basis as men that they will have achieved genuine liberation and sex equality. Accordingly, it is not prostitution which perpetuates the subordination of women, but the belief that women cannot freely choose to sell sexual services and therefore that female prostitutes are necessarily victims.

Harm to society

The second category of harm frequently attributed to prostitution involves harm to people who have no direct involvement in the sex industry. At the most basic level, prostitution is said to impose externalities on the wider society by contributing to the spread of sexually transmitted diseases, causing a public nuisance, being linked with drug abuse and other forms of criminality, and undermining stable relationships and thereby contributing to the break-up of marriages and families.

A pragmatic approach to prostitution that seeks to minimise such harms alleged to be caused by prostitution has characterised public policy in many developed countries, although the reduction of the occurrence of prostitution to as close to zero as possible is generally the long-term goal of policy.

Many of the harms attributed to prostitution, however, must also apply to a wide range of sexual activities, including adulterous affairs and one-night stands (Fabre, 2006: 163). Hence, to argue that prostitution should be outlawed on such a basis should logically imply that other non-commercial sexual relationships that may also contribute to the spread of diseases and the dissolution of marriages should also be prohibited. Such a suggestion is not particularly far fetched, of course, given that this is exactly the approach taken in a number of strict Islamic countries, such as Iran and Saudi Arabia, where adultery (like prostitution) is a serious crime. If it is to be argued that prostitution should be prohibited on such grounds, then it also has to be shown why adulterous affairs or more general promiscuity should not be similarly outlawed.

Many of the harms cited above are a direct result of the legal status of prostitution and can be ameliorated if it and the activities necessary for it to take place are situated firmly within the law. The fact that prostitution exists in a legal grey area in most countries leads those who engage in it to operate in a similarly hazy world, where at worst prostitution may be controlled by organised criminal enterprises. This links prostitution with other criminal activities, such as drug dealing, and exposes prostitutes and their clients to the attentions of criminals. The criminalisation of the provision of third-party services to prostitutes also makes it more difficult for sex workers to employ security measures without recourse to criminal enterprises.

It is because prostitution is either illegal or exists in a legal grey area in so many countries that the trafficking of women for prostitution can take place, although the extent of such criminality has almost certainly been exaggerated by the opponents of prostitution for political reasons (Weitzer, 2007a, 2007b). Moreover, it is only work that takes place in the black economy which is prone to such criminality; legal, regulated sectors of the economy do not encounter similar problems of trafficking and person abuse. The way forward here can be illustrated by the example of Australia's largest brothel, Daily Planet, which floated on the stock market in May 2003; such a company is no more likely to be involved in people trafficking and forced labour than Tesco or Wal-Mart. Putting the sex industry on a similar footing to other sectors of the economy is the only way to end this category of harm associated with prostitution.

It should be added that there is little evidence that prohibition decreases the incidence of prostitution. Rather, evidence suggests that prostitution is highly impervious to measures that increase its pecuniary and non-pecuniary costs. Evidence from Europe and North America suggests that the legal status of prostitution in a particular country or US state has little bearing on the number of prostitutes relative to the whole population. Rather, population density appears to be the key determinant of the prevalence of prostitution, probably because social controls (notably social stigma) may be greater in sparsely populated rural areas and a critical mass of clients is required to make prostitution viable, which is more likely to be found in an urban setting (MacCoun and Reuter, 2001; Moffatt, 2005).

A more fundamental argument that prostitution constitutes a harm to society rests on the belief that prostitution is immoral or intrinsically wrong. It is argued that even if prostitution is undertaken in such a way that it does not cause any public nuisance, and even if those who engage in prostitution do so willingly, the very existence of prostitution is nevertheless corrosive of society's moral fabric and therefore it should be outlawed. This view that the requirements of societal morality (whatever that might mean and however it might be determined) trump the rights of individuals to engage in voluntarily acts underpins religious condemnations of prostitution (and a host of other activities deemed similarly immoral) and some of the critiques of prostitution articulated by feminists.

According to feminist opponents of prostitution, it is one of a number of social institutions that perpetuate the general perception that women are inferior to men, and that their principal value lies in their ability to provide sexual satisfaction to men. According to Satz (1995: 64): 'Commercialized sex ... [sustains] a social world in which women form a subordinated group. Prostitution is wrong insofar as the sale of women's sexual labor reinforces broad patterns of sex discrimination ... contemporary prostitution contributes to, and also instantiates, the perception of women as socially inferior to men.'

Similarly, Pateman (1988: 199) has argued that prostitution is part of a sex industry that 'continually reminds men – and women – that men exercise the law of male sex-right, that they have patriarchal right of access to women's bodies'.

Hence, prostitution is said to constitute a harm, not just to those women who engage in prostitution, but also to women without direct experience of prostitution who must live in a society in which male and female attitudes are in some way conditioned by the existence of prostitution. In this sense, it is argued that all women have practical experience of prostitution, as they inhabit a world that is structured by prostitution and other patriarchal institutions.

It has to be questioned, however, whether prostitution reinforces the power that men supposedly hold over women, or whether it does quite the reverse. It would seem that, *contra* to Pateman's claim, men who are required to pay for sex have *less* of a 'right of access to women's bodies' than those who have sex for free.

Moreover, the assertion that women form a single class or group with a single shared experience is not grounded in empirical evidence. In reality, each individual is shaped by their own subjective, personal experiences and values. Such experiences and values will of course be socially and culturally situated, but they will not be identical to those of all other people who share the same sex, age, race or economic position.

If all women do share one common experience, however, it is not clear why that experience should be the experience of women who work as prostitutes, rather than, say, women who are successful lawyers, senior politicians or university professors.

Furthermore, if all women's experience is shaped by the fact that some women are prostitutes, then the same must logically apply to men. Given that some women and some men are prostitutes, the experience of women and men must be identical in this respect, and therefore prostitution ceases to be particularly oppressive of women.

The public and the private

In the context of the harm principle, Mill's (1859 [1985]) principal intention was to delineate the appropriate spheres of private and public morality. That is, to set out what were private matters of individual concern and what were public matters of government concern. Without such a distinction the potential scope of government interference in people's lives is limitless. For Mill, it was only those actions that directly impacted on others which fell within the realm of public morality and were therefore an appropriate target for legislation; those actions that did not directly impact on others fell within the realm of private morality and were therefore a matter of individual conscience.

While some feminists have argued that 'the personal is political', in fact personal matters must be a matter for each individual, so that 'the personal is personal' (McElroy, 1995: 125). Hence, as McElroy (ibid.: 125–6) has written, the sex lives of consenting adult men and women are a personal matter outside of the political, or public, realm: 'There is a political door that closes to separate and protect individuals from society. People call this protection by different names: the Bill of Rights, self-ownership, individual rights, or natural law. In the shadow of this protection, individual women make decisions about matters that concern them and them alone. For example, they decide about sex.'

The harm principle, then, is not intended to open up the possibility of seemingly limitless government intervention by enabling people to claim that they have been harmed by acts undertaken by other consenting adults in private. Rather, the harm principle is intended to close down and limit the grounds on which government can intervene by delineating the separate public and private spheres of human action. However one might draw such a boundary, the sex lives of consenting adults must belong in the private sphere.

An optimal legal regime

A quarter of a century ago, Ericsson (1980: 336) noted that all discussion of prostitution began from the starting point that prostitution was undesirable. Though there are now some exceptions within the academic literature, such an approach continues to dominate policy discussions of prostitution to this day. For example, a 2004 UK government consultation paper on prostitution began with the words: 'Prostitution can have devastating consequences for the individuals involved and for the wider community' (Home Office, 2004: 5). Of course, the same could be said of driving, but no government consultation paper on road transport would begin with a similar statement. But people continue to drive because they judge that the benefits derived exceed the costs incurred, and likewise prostitution continues because prostitutes and their clients also judge that the benefits outweigh the costs. The most appropriate starting point for devising an optimal legal regime for prostitution is to recognise the benefits that people derive from it.

For sex workers, prostitution provides a way of earning a relatively high income with relatively short, flexible working hours and without the requirement of formal qualifications. While it is not an occupation that everyone would contemplate, there is evidence that some people do find it a rewarding form of work that enables them to provide what they consider to be an important service to others (Diana, 1985: ch. 2; Fleiss, 2002; Perkins and Bennett, 1985: ch. 11).

For clients, prostitution provides an opportunity to enter into sexual and intimate relationships outside the standard realm of dating and commitment. There are a wide variety of reasons why people may wish to do this. Perhaps the most common reason is to achieve sexual satisfaction that is not otherwise possible, perhaps because long-term partners are unable or unwilling to provide it or because there is no long-term partner. Some clients may be disabled, or be too unattractive to find a sexual partner outside of the commercial realm. Others may use prostitutes because they may wish to have sex with a partner more attractive than they otherwise would be able to obtain. Some clients may wish to engage in sex with a wide variety of partners, or simply without the ties of a committed relationship. Prostitution also enables people to explore their sexuality and different sexual practices outside the context of a committed relationship; it is one way in which people are able to engage in 'experiments in living'. There is also evidence that many clients of escorts desire emotional as well as physical intimacy – indeed, demands made by clients in this regard may be a significant psychological burden placed upon prostitutes (Lever and Dolnick, 2000; Monto, 2000; Perkins and Bennett, 1985).

As Perkins and Bennett (1985: 222) have written on the basis of their international empirical study of sex work, prostitution should be understood as a social service that enables people to work through a variety of needs and desires:

> We see [prostitution] as a social service providing a sexual outlet
> for the possibility of sexual fulfilment that may help to prevent
> the traumatisation of many men, and in some cases psychological
> disturbance. Even those who find it regrettable, or less than perfect,
> might come to see it as one of the helping professions, a service like
> medicine, social work or the law which helps people cope with their
> problems.

Hence, a more accurate opening statement of a consultation paper on the subject would be: prostitution can generate positive benefits for the individuals involved and for the wider community.

An optimal legal regime for prostitution must legalise prostitution and all the activities that facilitate it, including the actions of third parties who manage sex workers or provide services to them for financial gain. Such a legal framework will ensure that prostitutes may employ agencies to screen clients or work together in brothels that employ appropriate security and provide other services, such as healthcare. The complete legalisation of prostitution would bring the industry within the tax system and facilitate the detection of criminal behaviour.

Where there is criminal exploitation of people who do not enter prostitution through choice, such crimes can and should be dealt with via existing legislation dealing with kidnapping, sexual offences and employment practices. Moving prostitution from the black and grey economies into the white economy would greatly facilitate this.

Externalities, or public nuisance, principally associated with street prostitution would also be addressed within this legal framework; even where prostitution itself is legal, most street prostitution will remain outside existing laws and regulations governing street trading and tax compliance. As such, under an optimal legal regime it will be possible for the police and other agencies to intervene to curb street prostitution where appropriate, though on the basis of street trading without relevant licences and tax evasion rather than specific prostitution offences.

Conclusion

The prohibition of prostitution is an example of bad public policy founded upon a series of fallacious arguments that have gained wide currency, in part because relatively few people are willing to challenge them in public. This chapter has shown that prostitution is a mutually advantageous exchange voluntarily entered into by adult women and men. Many of the harms associated with prostitution are in fact the result of its quasi-legal or illegal status in many countries. Prostitution should fall within the private sphere of personal morality rather than the public sphere of government legislation; it is morally wrong for government to dictate the sex lives of consenting adults.

References

Cameron, S., A. Collins and N. Thew (1999), 'Prostitution services: an exploratory analysis', *Applied Economics*, 31: 1523–9.

Diana, L. (1985), *The Prostitute and Her Clients*, Springfield, IL: Charles C. Thomas.

Dworkin, A. (1997) *Life and Death: Unapologetic writings on the continuing war against women*, New York: Free Press.

Edlund, L. and E. Korn (2002), 'A theory of prostitution', *Journal of Political Economy*, 110(11): 181–214.

Ericsson, L. O. (1980), 'Charges against prostitution: an attempt at a philosophical assessment', *Ethics*, 90: 335–66.

Fabre, C. (2006), *Whose Body Is It Anyway?*, Oxford: Oxford University Press.

Farley, M. (2005), *Unequal*, San Francisco, CA: Prostitution Research and Education Center.

Feinberg, J. (1984), *Harm to Others: The Moral Limits of the Criminal Law*, vol. 1, New York: Oxford University Press.

Fleiss, H. (2002), *Pandering*, Los Angeles, CA: 1 Hour Entertainment.

Fleiss, H. and N. Labi (2003), 'In defense of prostitution', *Legal Affairs*, September/October.

Home Office (2004), *Paying the Price: A consultation paper on prostitution*, London: TSO.

Lever, J. and D. Dolnick (2000), 'Clients and call girls: seeking sex and intimacy', in R. Weitzer (ed.), *Sex for Sale: Prostitution, Pornography and the Sex Industry*, London: Routledge.

MacCoun, R. J. and P. Reuter (2001), *Drug War Heresies: Learning from Other Vices, Times and Places*, Cambridge: Cambridge University Press.

McElroy, W. (1995), *XXX: A Women's Right to Pornography*, New York: St Martin's Press.

Mill, J. S. (1859 [1985]), *On Liberty*, London: Penguin Classics.

Ministry of Industry, Employment and Communications (2004), *Prostitution and Trafficking in Women*, Stockholm: Ministry of Industry, Employment and Communications.

Moffatt, G. (2005), 'The economics of prostitution', in S. W. Bowmaker (ed.), *Economics Uncut*, Cheltenham: Edward Elgar.

Moffatt, G. and S. A. Peters (2004), 'Pricing personal services: an empirical study of earnings in the UK prostitution industry', *Scottish Journal of Political Economy*, 51(5): 675–90.

Monto, M. A. (2000), 'Why men seek out prostitutes', in R. Weitzer (ed.), *Sex for Sale: Prostitution, Pornography and the Sex Industry*, London: Routledge.

Pateman, C. (1988), *The Sexual Contract*, Cambridge: Polity.

Perkins, R. and G. Bennett (1985), *Being a Prostitute: Prostitute Women and Prostitute Men*, London: Allen and Unwin.

Pheterson, G. (1996), *The Prostitution Prism*, Amsterdam: Amsterdam University Press.

Potterat, J., D. Brewer, S. Muth, R. Rothenburg, D. Woodhouse, J. Muth, H. Stites and S. Brody (2004), 'Mortality in a long-term open cohort of prostitute women', *American Journal of Epidemiology*, 159(8): 778–85.

Ringdal, N. (2004), *Love for Sale: A Global History of Prostitution*, trans. R. Daly, London: Atlantic Books.

Rowbotham, S. (1972), *Women, Resistance and Revolution*, London: Penguin.

Satz, D. (1995), 'Markets in women's sexual labor', *Ethics*, 106(1): 63–85.

Weitzer, R. (2007a), 'The facts about the slave trade', *Foreign Affairs*, 86(3): 164–5.

Weitzer, R. (2007b), 'The social construction of sex trafficking: ideology and institutionalization of a moral crusade', *Politics and Society*, 35(3): 447–75.

Wertheimer, A. (1992), 'Two questions about surrogacy and exploitation', *Philosophy and Public Affairs*, 21(3): 211–39.

Zelizer, V. A. (2005), *The Purchase of Intimacy*, Princeton, NJ: Princeton University Press.

10 GAMBLING
Robert Simmons

Introduction

This chapter examines the attempts by various local and national governments to restrict the supply of gambling to potential consumers. I explore general reasons for restrictions and offer a critique of available evidence on adverse side effects. Particular case studies are examined to show how combinations of producer interests and effective political lobbying restrict the expansion of gambling opportunities in ways that reduce potential consumer welfare. Among the cases considered are the recent United Kingdom Gambling Act 2005, which restricts the development of large casinos, and attempts to restrict or ban betting via the Internet in the USA.

The UK's gambling sector generated £660 million in revenues in 2005, according to *Screen Digest International*, and is forecast to grow to £1.6 billion in 2010 (Barton and Smith, 2006). Growth forecasts are also strong for the USA, Asia and Australia. Forecasts of strong growth of gambling activity are based on increased disposable income, especially among young adults, and a demand for more variety of leisure pursuits. On the supply side, the growth of the Internet has led to an increase in the number of suppliers offering gambling products online with easy access for consumers. Interactive gambling via mobile phones also offers substantial opportunities for betting. The gambling sector is therefore characterised by rising consumer demand and rapidly changing technology, both of which represent challenges for governments and industry regulators.

Prohibition of gambling varies considerably by country. In the USA, seven states do not have lotteries (including, ironically, the 'home' of American gambling, Nevada). Casinos (excluding those on Indian reservations) are present in just eleven states (Kearney, 2005). Sports betting is legal only in Nevada, New Jersey and Oregon. As we shall see, the USA is at the time of writing about to pass a bill to prohibit Internet gambling. In contrast, the UK has a proliferation of betting opportunities through licensed off-course bookmakers, amusement arcades and Internet providers. It is the casino sector which has been relatively restricted in the UK, and recent policy discussion has focused on the possibility of casino liberalisation and expansion.

Why restrict gambling? A public choice perspective

Sauer (2001) offers a general public choice model of gambling restrictions. This takes as a starting point that governments do not impose restrictions on a whim but are responsive to lobbying by interest groups. Sauer posits two groups in society. Group G is pro-gambling and its welfare falls as restrictions are imposed that lower the level of gambling. This group is prepared to spend money on political action to reduce gambling restrictions. Although Sauer does not state this explicitly, this group is likely to come from within the gambling industry. In opposition to the pro-gambling group, there is an anti-gambling group A, which is prepared to devote resources to restrict gambling. This group may be a coalition of churches and morally outraged people who dislike gambling. A key feature of group A's welfare is that it rises as restrictions on gambling are increased. In blunt terms, the anti-gambling group gains satisfaction from imposing its preferences on others.

Sauer's public choice model is a neat device for theorising about gambling restrictions where there is a powerful anti-gambling lobby (as evidenced by the aggressive stance taken by church groups in the USA). But the model is less applicable where gambling is already entrenched and where a variety of gambling opportunities are already in place, as in the UK and Australia. In these jurisdictions the market structure of gambling needs explicit attention as monopolistic producers erect entry barriers against new competitors. Producer interests within the gambling sector mean that companies offering one type of gambling product (e.g. amusement arcades in Britain) will fear competition from another type of gambling product (e.g. casino gaming) which can be viewed as a potential substitute for consumers. Then the incumbent operators will have a motive to erect entry barriers against the new competition. This will then induce lobbying efforts to dissuade legislators from removing restrictions currently placed on the rival sector.

Pathological and problem gambling

A pathological gambler is one who gambles 'because of a compulsion ... [for these people] gambling is a source of neither fun nor wealth' (Quinn, 2001). A pathological gambler is, then, one who is physiologically and psychologically addicted in a similar way to hard drug users; gambling is a habit that must be fed. A 'problem gambler', rather loosely defined, is someone who is at risk of becoming addicted to gambling.

Earl Grinols is an American economist who has spoken strongly against the expansion of gambling in the USA. He argues that 30 to 50 per cent of gambling revenues in the USA derive from problem and pathological gamblers (Grinols, 2004). In a sequence of papers of which Grinols and Mustard (2001) is a clear example, Grinols argues that pathological and problem gambling contributes substantially to crime, bankruptcy, suicide, illness of various forms (stress related, cardiovascular, anxiety, depression and various cognitive disorders) and family costs (divorce, separation, child abuse, child neglect and domestic violence). Treatment of such problems imposes costs on society (policing, healthcare, counselling services, etc.). According to Grinols, pathological gamblers are more likely than non-gamblers to have been bankrupt and to have been arrested. Such people, it is alleged, are likely to turn to crime to finance their gambling habit.

There are two problems with the somewhat emotive picture of pathological gambling portrayed by Grinols and other anti-gambling writers. First, the nature of the *social* cost of pathological gambling is actually rather blurred. For example, some (such as Walker and Barnett, 2000) would suggest that 'family costs' are internalised within households and do not fall on society. Yet many, if not most, citizens would welcome stronger action by the authorities to intervene to protect women against domestic violence, and this would then be considered as a social cost in the broader sense of men doing harm to their partners.

The difficulty with assessment of pathological gambling is that the externalities are less visible and harder to identify, in terms of resource costs, then externalities from smoking or alcoholism, for example. A further problem is that vices tend to be complementary: Forrest and Gulley (2005) find from UK Family Expenditure Survey data that players involved with six types of gambling tend also to smoke and drink. By extension, one would not be surprised to find that pathological gamblers also smoke and drink heavily. Isolating the social cost of gambling from these other vices is then necessary for an informed discussion of social costs.

Much discussion of gambling addiction implies that the addict is seen as a victim who is not exercising rational choice. This lack of rationality can then be invoked to justify prohibition of addictive goods and services, including gambling. But it is worth noting an alternative view of *rational* addiction proposed by Becker and Murphy (1988). They argue that consumption of addictive goods is both rational and planned for, with a degree of foresight. Moreover, people become addicted not only to alcohol, narcotics and gambling but also to more general activities including work, eating, listening to music and attending sports events. In this alternative perspective, gambling addiction is a by-product of forward-looking rational choice.

Notwithstanding arguments over 'rational addiction', it is now a matter of convention that every jurisdiction contemplating liberalisation of its gambling laws gives serious consideration to the question of the consequences for the level of pathological gambling. Potential harm to others from compulsive gambling is accepted as a social cost that should be reduced to some extent. Indeed, the UK casino industry has agreed to support substantial extra research funding into problem gambling as an explicit component of gambling reforms. But measurement of the incidence of pathological gambling and its social costs is extremely difficult and several attempts at quantification are biased or just back-of-envelope calculations based on arbitrary assumptions (see Walker, 2006, for examples of both arbitrary and biased studies). As such, these estimates are capable of manipulation by skilled lobbyists and by newspapers hunting for sensationalist stories, outcomes that arguably impeded objective assessments on the path to the UK's recent attempt at gambling reform, as we shall see below (Collins, 2006). It is highly doubtful that reducing the social costs of pathological gambling *to zero* is a socially optimal solution to the problems raised by legalised gambling. The level of pathological gambling that would be socially acceptable, given rising consumer demand for gambling, is still unclear in all jurisdictions.

As an example of a possible framework for regulation of gambling explicitly designed to mitigate the incidence of pathological gambling, consider Quinn (2001). Quinn is an experienced counsellor of pathological gamblers in the USA. He offers twenty proposals specifically geared towards limiting the adverse effects of pathological gambling in US casinos. These are, in summary:

- High distances of casinos from population centres.
- Restriction of admission to adults.
- Restrictions on opening hours.
- Reduction of artificial stimulation (bright lights, noise) from gaming machines.
- Ban on alcohol and tobacco in the gambling area.
- Ban on sitting in the gambling area.
- Ease of egress from machines and gambling tables.
- Slower speed of machines.

- Equal payout rates for all machines.
- Make complementary inducements illegal.
- Limited advertising with strong ethical controls.
- Information on payouts and odds of winning to be made available.
- Casinos to recognise and identify pathological gamblers.
- Casinos to keep away from treatment of pathological gambling.
- But casinos to share knowedge of problem gamblers' habits with clinical specialists.
- Gambling to be paid for by cash only, not credit.
- Casinos *not* to offer complementary activities to gambling.
- Casinos *not* to be business partners with any part of government, local or national.

Taken together, these restrictions look excessive. Consumers would be denied choice and the entertainment value of the gambling experience, 'fun', would be reduced. Implementation of these restrictions would raise costs and reduce profits for operators. Since both consumers and producers would see their welfare lowered, these reforms would lead to a Pareto-inferior outcome.

The anti-gambling lobby tends to view problem gamblers as a misled, ill-informed group who need to be saved from the harm they may inflict on themselves and their families. This begs the question of the rationality of gambling behaviour. Here, economists do not have a uniform answer. Broadly, the prominent economic theories of gambling behaviour include:

- Expected utility theory, which specifies a weighted average utility across several outcomes; in its plainest form this theory has difficulty in rationalising the coexistence of gambling and insurance choices. The standard response following Friedman and Savage (1948) is to invoke a utility function that exhibits risk-averse behaviour (purchase of insurance) and risk-loving behaviour (gambling) at different levels of wealth. This response has been much criticised and is argued by some economists to be inconsistent with experimental evidence.

- Prospect theory, following Kahneman and Tversky (1979), which states that people weight the probability of loss differently to the probability of winning. In this 'nearly rational' theory, individuals are risk-loving over potential losses and risk-averse over potential gains. People also put greater weight on losses than on gains. These different probabilities are exhibited in a 'probability weighting function'. In this function, people subjectively distort the probabilities of events so the probability weighting function has an inverted S-shape. This means that small probabilities are exaggerated while large probabilities are understated (Cain et al., 2008). The theory is mathematically complex but several economists maintain its usefulness in explaining why people bet at long odds in lotteries and horse races. In prospect theory, individuals find it difficult to distinguish between different long-odds probabilities. For example, two bets on winning a lottery jackpot prize of 14 million to one and 10 million to one would be observationally equivalent to the bettor yet would show up as substantial differences in a probability weighting function. Cain et al. (ibid.) offer an extension of the Kahneman-Tversky theory in which individuals are less averse to losses over small-stake gambles than large ones. They also posit that probability distortions are smaller for gains than for losses. With these extensions Cain et al. show that prospect theory can explain gambling on favoured outcomes and the favourite-long-shot bias (where favourites are under-bet relative to outsiders) in horse racing.

Empirical evidence suggests that gamblers make rational decisions, given that they have made the seemingly irrational decision to gamble in the first place. Both Forrest et al. (2000) and Guryan and Kearney (2005) find that lottery players, in the UK and USA respectively, do respond to changes in lottery takeout rates largely as economic theory predicts. Forrest et al. (forthcoming) find evidence of substitution away from bookmaker betting towards lottery play when the lottery takeout rate falls ('effective price' is less) in a rollover draw that gives better value to the player. In contrast to this view of gambler rationality, Guryan and Kearney (2005) find that lottery players mistakenly bought tickets from stores that advertised sales of winning tickets, a variant on the gambler's fallacy.

Out of the evidence on gambler rationality, perhaps the best consensus is that the betting market contains a mix of bettors with different attitudes to risk, different gambling preferences and different levels of interest and expertise in betting outcomes. 'Professional' gamblers coexist with amateurs who enjoy gambling as just 'fun' and who see gambling as a consumption activity rather than an investment (Forrest et al., 2002). Economic evidence does point against the notion that *all* gamblers are misguided, vulnerable people who are seduced into an activity that they subsequently lose control over.

Gambling and crime

An association of legitimate gambling with crime cannot be denied and is a serious concern, especially when organised crime is involved. The fear of organised crime partly explains the strong resistance to gambling deregulation in the USA. But establishing a causal empirical relationship between new forms of gambling and crime is difficult. Also, some of the measures of the social costs of crime attributed to gambling are based on questionable assumptions (Walker, 2006).

A recent study by Grinols and Mustard (2006) on the impact of US casino openings on crime has appeared in a prestigious academic journal and so deserves close attention. Grinols and Mustard argue that crime increased in US counties that had casino openings, compared with those that did not, over the period 1977 to 1996. Moreover, crime was not just redistributed across neighbourhoods; apparently casinos 'created' crime. Converting the estimated impacts of new casinos on crime into social cost figures gives the authors' headline figure of $75 per adult per year, and this represents 'between 8 and 30' per cent of the social costs of crime, depending on category of crime.

Crime can be raised by casino openings through externalities such as prostitution and extortion, greater pay-offs to criminals with more opportunities for crime, and crime committed by pathological gamblers who need to finance their gambling habit. Crime reduction could occur as earnings in the locality increase and economic development lowers local unemployment rates. Casinos create labour market opportunities for low-skilled workers, and some of these might be on the margin of a choice between criminal and legitimate economic activities.

The basic model of crime used by Grinols and Mustard has per capita local crime rates determined by a set of control variables and a variable indicating the presence of a casino. This model of crime is estimated for a range of property and violent crime categories. There are a number of methodological weaknesses in Grinols and Mustard's approach, outlined as follows. First, the population at risk from casino-related crime is the local population plus visitors. As Walker (2006) points out, after a casino opens the numerator in the authors' crime definition increases (owing to the extra visitors) while the denominator is constant by construction. So crime rates will be overstated purely by measurement error. Second, the presence of other attractions is posited to be constant over time, yet other consumer facilities will most likely have been developed over the twenty-year sample period. These would include shopping malls, cinemas and sports stadia, all of which attract both visitors and crime. The investigator needs to isolate the impacts of casinos from the effects of these other developments on crime. Third, if the presence of other attractions is plausibly taken to be positively corre-lated with crime, then the estimated impact of casino presence on crime is overstated. Fourth, the authors lack data on police resources at county level, but extra policing would deter crime to some extent, according to the economic model. Fifth, the authors have just one estimation method, which specifies separate intercepts for each county so as to incorporate unknown factors into the set of constant terms. But for dynamic panel data of this kind the authors need to address issues of non-stationarity of the data, possible break-points in crime rates, endogeneity of the lagged values of the dependent variable and serial correlation of the error term. A full treatment would entail comparison of several estimation methods, and a single method cannot be relied upon.

Hence, there are a number of reasons for questioning the validity of a casino–crime relationship in the Grinols–Mustard study. But the study can be used as a basis for further empirical refinement using better data on visitors, alternative indoor leisure attractions to casinos, and police resources. As it stands, clear evidence of a strong causal link between casinos and crime has yet to be established.

The UK gambling reforms: road to nowhere?

In 2005, six years after an official *Gambling Review Report* was launched and four years after this report was published (Department for Culture, Media and Sport, 2001), the UK government finally implemented its long-awaited Gambling Act. This replaced the Gaming Act of 1968, generally regarded as out of date and irrelevant to a society in which technological change and consumer tastes in the gambling sector have changed radically. The UK government's road to reform passed through several official documents. Although the legislation covered many aspects of gambling, the reforms that attracted the most publicity related to casinos, where high-price machine gaming would ostensibly be liberalised (Collins, 2006).

The Gambling Review Report (Budd Report) (2001)

Chaired by a prominent economist, Alan Budd, with free market proclivities, this substantial report proposed, *inter alia*, the introduction of casino slot machines with unlimited prizes. Gaming machines would, however, be limited to a maximum of eight machines per table. Once 80 tables had been reached, there would be no maximum number of machines. The *Gambling Review Report* did not set limits on the number of casinos, and market forces were implicitly taken to determine the number of these, subject to suitable licensing criteria, including lack of access by children, adequate infrastructure and avoidance of public nuisance.

A Safe Bet for Success (2002)

This official response to the Budd Report accepted the notion of very high slot machine jackpots but left open the criteria for limits on the numbers of machines. Otherwise, reforms proposed in the *Gambling Review Report*, such as abolition of the 24-hour waiting period for casino membership and new, more open methods of licensing casinos, were accepted. As suggested by Budd, a new Gambling Commission would regulate (but not license) gambling activity in the UK, although lotteries were excluded from consideration. Licensing would be undertaken by local authorities.

Draft Gambling Bill (2003)

Again, most of the proposals in *A Safe Bet for Success* appeared in a draft Bill which then went to a joint House of Commons and House of Lords committee for scrutiny. One change was a limitation on the ratio of machines to tables of three to one, down from eight to one recommended by Budd. The draft Bill now specified, contrary to Budd, the size of small casinos to be determined by floor space devoted to table games (5,000 to 10,000 square feet) whereas Budd defined a small casino as one with fewer than 80 tables.

At this stage the only mention of 'resort casinos' or 'mega-casinos' modelled along the lines of Las Vegas casino hotels was in a Government Position Paper of August 2003. This concept was absent from the draft Bill. The category of 'resort casino' made its official appearance in the next stage of the legislative process.

Scrutiny Committee Report (2004)

This proposed a three-tier structure for casinos: small, large and resort casino. Small casinos would have a maximum three-to-one ratio of machines to tables. Large casinos would have a higher (unspecified) ratio. Resort casinos would have a still higher machine : tables ratio with a maximum number of machines to be set at 1,250.

Consultation period (2005)

With a general election imminent in 2005, the UK government did not want to appear controversial in pushing legislation through quickly, so a consultation period was allowed. In this period, an anti-gambling lobby developed momentum, and this led to large-scale changes in the eventual legislation. The ingredients of a backlash against liberalisation of Britain's gambling laws relating to casinos were:

- Consultancy reports such as NERA (2003), which highlighted the risks of pathological and problem gambling from a more liberal casino regime.
- Protectionist interests including amusement arcade operators (BACTA), bookmakers and bingo operators, all of which faced new threats to revenues from a larger and stronger casino sector.
- An aggressive media campaign promulgated by scare stories of gambling addiction in various newspapers, especially the *Daily Mail* (one of the few occasions when this conservative organ would find itself in agreement with the socialist *Guardian*).
- Opportunistic opposition by Conservative and Liberal Democrat politicians desperate to score political points off an incumbent government with a large majority (Collins, 2006).

In contrast to the US experience of gambling deregulation, and Sauer's public choice model described above, British church groups were rather less powerful and influential in their opposition to casino liberalisation, although religious interests did make known their views against reform.[1]

Whereas the opponents of reform had a simple agenda – to block and dilute reforms – those sympathetic to new legislation had no common voice. Potential investors in new large casinos included several prominent Las Vegas leisure groups such as MGM Grand and Harrah's, and these were seriously contemplating large-scale investment in partnership with local authorities and existing leisure interests, such as Glasgow Rangers, Sheffield United and Manchester City football clubs, each located in areas with above-average social and economic deprivation indicators. Collins (2006) counts 27 such areas which expressed serious interest in hosting large casinos, largely to reap the benefits from economic regeneration of inner-city areas.

Gambling Act (2005)

The coalition of anti-gambling groups was largely successful in that only one 'resort casino' was permitted (as an 'experiment') in the final legislation. In the discussion stage, eight 'regional' casinos had been mooted with a 1,250-machines limit and unlimited payouts. So this was reduced to just one. The anti-gambling lobby scored a further victory, however, when in July 2007 incoming prime minister Gordon Brown refused to give support for a licence to be granted to Manchester for the single (monopoly) large-scale casino permitted under the Gambling Act. Instead, the prime minister promised a report on the 'social effects' of gambling by September 2007. This report was expected to emphasise the alleged growth in the incidence of problem gambling from 0.6 to 0.8 per cent of the adult population in 1999 to 2.0 per cent, according to leaked newspaper reports based upon unpublished research by the National Centre for Social Research carried out by academics at the University of Birmingham on behalf of the Gambling Commission.

---

1   This means that the term 'unholy' used by Peter Collins (2006) to describe the coalition of interests of groups opposed to UK casino reform needs to be modified.

Even without Prime Minister Brown's U-turn, the Gambling Act did not address the potential for 'integrated casino complexes' which would combine a casino with other leisure activities (theatres, restaurants, hotels, golf courses and theme parks) along the lines of Las Vegas hotels. Opportunities could have been taken to develop complementary leisure facilities, which could make strong inroads into urban renewal in decaying and run-down resorts and communities such as Blackpool (Collins, 2006). Moreover, integrated leisure complexes with wider holiday appeal might reduce at least some of the risks associated with criminality which some researchers have been concerned about (Grinols and Mustard, 2006).

Eadington (2005) suggests that casino liberalisation and deregulation have proceeded too slowly in Europe compared with Asia, where resort casinos have been developed. He makes the interesting observation that some eastern European countries such as Latvia and Lithuania will be less shy of making progress towards opening up growth of casinos. When this happens, the potential for imitation and 'domino effects' should not be understated as tourists opt for these countries for a wider choice of entertainment and leisure opportunities. Then, resistance to change in western Europe will be likely to break down as competition in the casino-based leisure market increases. Much the same occurred in the USA as residents of states without gambling facilities drove across state boundaries to riverboat casinos, leading to new casino openings in their own states.

The growth of sports betting

Back in the 1950s and 1960s sports betting was limited to horse race betting (with off-course betting in licensed bookmakers made legal in 1960) and the football pools game. Now, in the UK, gamblers can bet on a variety of sports by telephone, by mobile phone and on the Internet, as well as in betting shops. They can also bet on game outcomes other than match or tournament results. Index (or 'spread') betting, where gamblers can buy or sell positions on events, rather like stocks and shares, has become popular.

As with most new forms of gambling, the growth of events-based sports betting is due to greater disposable incomes, especially for highly educated, professional young people, and a demand for variety. The football pools game, where bettors predict the identity of eight drawn fixtures from a set of Saturday football matches, still exists but predominantly draws an older clientele. With a very high takeout, greater than the 50 per cent of the National Lottery main draw, the pools game represents poor value compared with fixed-odds bets on football results. Revenues to pools companies have declined, especially since 1994, when the National Lottery began to offer effective competition in the long-odds/large-prize/low-skill gambling market (Forrest, 1999).

The portfolio of sports betting opportunities now caters for a range of risk preferences. For example, bettors with high income levels who prefer a high-risk/high-return betting option will try their luck on the index betting market. Those who prefer a less risky gamble with shorter odds will place their bets on fixed-odds match results. The rapid growth of sports (especially football) betting in the UK has taken place in a liberal environment where entry has been largely tolerated, with some notable exceptions. The British bookmaking sector remains concentrated, with William Hill, Ladbroke and Coral as the dominant three, but a strong independent sector flourishes as a competitive fringe.

In contrast, sports betting in mainland Europe tends to be the preserve of monopoly betting firms such as France's Pari-Mutuel-Urbain (PMU), owned by the racing industry and sanctioned by government. France has the largest horse racing sector, by turnover, outside the UK, with 255 racecourses. PMU's betting is characterised by high volume and high takeout of around 30 per cent compared with around 20 per cent in the more competitive UK off-course betting sector. But winnings as a proportion of stakes have risen to 72 per cent in 2004, caused mainly by competition from Internet betting.

In Spain and Germany, there is growing pressure to deregulate the sports betting markets and open up competition. In Germany this pressure is being applied through the courts, and there is always the threat of anti-trust pressure at European Union level. The standard economist's prediction from deregulation, if it does occur in Spain and Germany, is greater choice and lower takeout rates for the consumer.

Among the growth of betting services over the last decade one particularly interesting phenomenon is the emergence of 'betting exchanges', which enable gamblers to place a bet for or against a particular outcome. This outcome could be virtually anything. These exchanges help match those who wish to place a bet with those who would like to accept this bet. The betting exchange simply takes a commission from the winner of the bet.

A key feature of betting exchanges is their ability to provide betting services without bricks and mortar. They do not need to set up shops as they are able to match bettors on either side of the market. The players who accept bets are acting like bookmakers, and anecdotal evidence suggests that many of these are professionals. With no capital investment, little overheads and no need for a bookmaker's licence, barriers to entry into the bookmaker betting market are substantially eroded. Lower transactions costs arise for the bettor, and the bookmaker betting market becomes contestable.

The company Betfair, based in the UK, was the first mover in the betting exchange market. Bookmakers derive their profit from the overround (sum of odds-based probabilities of outcomes minus one), which, as noted above, can be as high as 20 per cent in some British horse races. In contrast, since Betfair takes its commission from the winner of any betting transaction, it has no overround and the profit margins are therefore smaller than for bookmakers. Betfair therefore offers a lower takeout rate and a better-value bet for the gambler. Smith et al. (2006) offer evidence from matched data on UK horse racing from betting exchanges. They find that transactions costs, and profit margins, were indeed lower for betting exchanges than for traditional bookmakers. Smith et al. go on to show that these reduced transactions costs allowed betting exchanges to improve information flows to consumers. One measurable outcome in the horse race betting sector was a closer correspondence of objective probabilities of horse race outcomes to probabilities derived from betting odds from betting exchanges as opposed to traditional bookmakers; betting exchanges exhibited greater market efficiency. In particular, the 'favourite–long-shot' bias typically observed in horse race betting markets, where favourites offer a better-value wager than outsiders, was generally absent for bets placed with betting exchanges. The favourable consequences of increased competition offered by betting exchanges were, according to Smith et al., increased productive and allocative efficiency.

Despite the increase in price competition, Betfair has just 2–3 per cent of the bookmaker betting market, by turnover, in the UK. Although the established British bookmakers have not succeeded in sustaining effective entry barriers against betting exchanges, their market dominance has not been substantially eroded.

In contrast, the state-owned Australian totaliser board has successfully resisted expansion of Betfair into the Australian betting market. To date, only the smallest state of Tasmania has licensed Betfair's operations and other states are unlikely to follow suit. Competition therefore remains restricted in the Australian betting market.

The growth of gambling on the Internet

Much of the strong growth in gambling activity worldwide has been through Internet gambling sites. Christiansen Capital Advisers (2005) estimated the volume of global Internet gambling to be $3.1 billion in 2001 and $12.0 billion in 2005, with a prediction of $24.5 billion for 2010 (see Figure 9). Around 40–60 per cent of these values are attributable to bets originating from the USA. The dominant categories of Internet betting are, first, casino-style games and, second, sports betting.

Figure 9   **Estimated and predicted global Internet gambling revenues**
Revenue, $bn

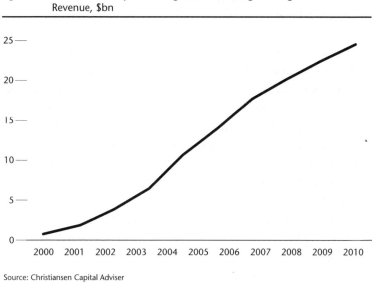

Source: Christiansen Capital Adviser

Prohibition in the USA

In the USA the 1961 Wire Act made it illegal for organisations to accept bets on sporting events or contests made by telephone or wire transfer across state boundaries. The applicability of this Act to Internet betting has remained in doubt, and to resolve this ambiguity two Republican congressmen moved the 2006 Unlawful Internet Gambling Enforcement Act, which was signed into law by President Bush in October, having successfully passed through Congress and Senate. The main features of the Act are to:

- Extend the definition of betting in the Wire Act to cover wagering on sporting events, lotteries and games of chance.
- Prohibit gambling businesses from accepting non-cash payments (credit card and electronic transfers).

- Permit enforcement agencies to remove or disable Internet betting sites that break the new law.[2]

The rationales offered for this legislation by Congressman Good-latte were that Internet gambling damaged gamblers and their families, 'drained' dollars from the USA and was a vehicle for money laundering. The 'harm to gamblers' argument suggests that problem gambling is exacerbated by the Internet medium. There is some evidence from analysis of questionnaires completed by hospital patients by Ladd and Petry (2002) that people who used the Internet as the medium for their gambling had characteristics of gambling addiction. But their sample of patients from Connecticut was only 389 in total and only 31 of these reported that they were involved in Internet wagering. This is much too small a sample on which to base inferences about problem gambling being exacerbated by availability of Internet gaming.

The 'drained dollars' argument looks like protectionism. When US prohibition of Internet gaming was first proposed, the governments of Antigua and Costa Rica objected that the US proposals ran counter to World Trade Organization (WTO) agreements on access to US markets for Third World service providers.[3]

Subsequently, the WTO ruled that the US ban on Internet gambling unfairly targeted offshore casinos, specifically those in Antigua and Costa Rica. Interestingly, the WTO qualified this verdict by stating that the USA could continue its restrictions against online betting provided that these were similarly applied to remote US interstate betting on horse races. This parity of treatment has not materialised, making the application of US Internet restrictions appear discriminatory in practice.[4]

---

2   In July 2006, the English CEO of BetonSport PLC, an Internet betting firm based in Antigua and Costa Rica, was arrested on charges relating to violation of the 1961 Wire Act.

3   In 2005, online betting firms based in Antigua employed 3,000 people out of a population of just 68,000.

4   For more details on the WTO ruling, see R. Blakely, 'WTO rules against US web casino crackdown', *The Times*, 30 March 2007; R. Blakely, 'US offshore gambling rules "illegal"', *The Times*, 31 March 2007; and 'WTO rules against US net gambling ban

The complaint about money laundering fails to recognise that this is already practised through conventional media, and it is not clear how or why Internet betting increases the scope for money laundering.

Recently, Nobel Prize-winning economist Gary Becker (2006) entered the debate on the prohibition of Internet gambling. Becker considers the rationalisation of prohibition offered by Congressman Goodlatte to be a smokescreen for a deeper concern: that Internet gambling 'threatens Government revenue and other advantages from taxing and tightly regulating forms of gambling'. Becker argues that gambling is generally less addictive than drinking or smoking and that gambling addicts can find ways to gamble with or without the aid of the Internet medium. He prefers a libertarian approach to Internet gambling involving low tax rates and less regulation so as to generate greater consumer choice and higher consumer surplus.

Licensing and regulation in the UK

In contrast to the USA, other jurisdictions have followed a 'regulate and tax' policy towards Internet betting. From 2007, remote or Internet gaming will be allowed onshore in the United Kingdom, as one of the provisions of the new Gambling Act.[5]

This is part of a deliberate policy to retain existing gambling in the UK and facilitate growth of the sector. Among the appeals to offshore firms of relocation to the UK would be, the government argues, the enhanced reputation that would go with being associated with and supervised by high-quality regulation offered by the new Gambling Commission.

In 2001, the UK government initiated a radical change in taxation policy applied to gambling. Previously, bookmaker betting was subject to a turnover tax. The emergence of Internet betting meant that gamblers

---

– again', Pinsent Mason newsletter *OUTLAW News*, 3 April 2007, www.out-law.com/page-7928.

5   Prior to 2007, UK-registered Internet betting firms had to be run offshore.

had opportunities to bet offshore in locations such as the Channel Islands and Gibraltar. Internet betting firms located offshore could offer lower overrounds as their costs were substantially less than 'bricks and mortar' high-street betting shops. In 1996, turnover tax was 6.75 per cent of turnover, and this represented a further inducement to bet offshore.

The UK Customs and Excise commissioned a study of gambling taxation by three economists based at Nottingham. Their study, summarised in Paton et al. (2002), recommended the abolition of the turnover tax and its replacement by Gross Profits Tax. This policy was introduced by the UK government in October 2001 and was well received by gamblers and bookmakers alike. The new tax also had the benefit, for the UK government, of retaining some (though reduced) tax revenue that would otherwise have been lost as several bookmakers had threatened to move their operations offshore.

Actually, the UK government had negotiated a deal with the leading bookmakers that the tax regime would change. In return, the bookmakers agreed to remain onshore. Specifically, UK Internet betting would remain in or be repatriated to the UK in return for a government commitment to a 15 per cent rate of Gross Profits Tax on betting (Europe Economics, 2005).

Paton et al. (2002) and Vaughan Williams (2006) argue that the new Gross Profits Tax generates a more efficient market outcome than the previous turnover tax. Betting turnover has increased; in the off-course horse race betting sector a declining trend in turnover up to 2001 was reversed. Bookmakers experienced lower profit margins but higher turnover and profits overall (Vaughan Williams, 2006). According to Vaughan Williams, the new tax regime helps the betting sector compete more effectively with overseas competition. This last claim deserves further scrutiny as gambling opportunities now exist in a number of offshore locations with small licence fees, low or even zero rates of gambling tax and low or zero rates of corporate tax. Table 2 below summarises tax regimes in five offshore jurisdictions, each friendly to Internet gambling firms.

Table 2 **Gambling licence fees and taxation in five locations, 2005**

Location	Licence fee £ p.a.	Gambling tax	Corporate tax rate
Alderney	75,000	Zero	Max 20%; zero by 2008
Antigua	26,600 (betting) 39,800 (gaming)	3% of gross handle	Zero
Gibraltar	2,000	1% of turnover/ gaming yield, range £85,000 to £425,000	Zero for exempt status
Isle of Man	100 to 25,000 (betting) 35,000 (gaming)	1.5% or 10% or 15% of gross win depending on origin of bet	Zero
Malta	4,800	0.5% of turnover with maximum £320,000 p.a.	4.17%

Source: Europe Economics (2005)

Since UK firms continue to face 17.5 per cent Value Added Tax and 30 per cent Corporation Tax, the UK tax position looks uncompetitive against the offshore locations listed in Table 2. This raises a question of how sustainable the present 15 per cent Gross Profits Tax would be for UK Internet betting firms. Europe Economics (2005) argues that, since the UK government receives no revenue from offshore Internet gambling, a Gross Profits Tax on Internet betting of 2 per cent is as high a level as can be applied without losing large volumes of gambling business to locations such as Gibraltar and the Channel Islands. The UK government's next concern would be whether the 15 per cent tax rate applied to onshore bookmakers will in turn be sustainable in the face of more intense offshore competition. Thus more intense global competition is likely to generate downward pressure on tax rates, but as Becker (2006) points out, this will deliver benefits to consumers. Generating high tax revenues from gambling is not a good policy objective from an economic welfare perspective.

In summary, the USA's prohibitionist stance will be difficult and costly to monitor and enforce. It will restrict choice and deny opportunities for consumers and business.

Large numbers of gamblers are capable of maximising individual or household satisfaction subject to budget constraints. Policy that restricts access because a small number of gamblers lose control and develop addictive behaviour therefore seems excessively paternalistic. Certainly, policy towards other 'vices' such as alcohol consumption – which delivers rather more obvious externalities in the form of violent, unruly and generally antisocial behaviour – does not usually follow the same prohibitionist stance. Hence, a 'license and regulate' approach, as advocated by Clarke and Dempsey (2001), is more effective than prohibition, less costly in resources and raises consumer surplus.

Conclusion

Rising consumer disposable incomes and increased demand for variety in leisure and entertainment provision have stimulated a large growth in demand for gambling. The growth of Internet betting is widely forecast to be especially strong over the next decade. Yet, as this chapter has shown, jurisdictions continue to restrict or even prohibit the growth of gambling in various ways.

In the USA, restrictions on gambling can be rationalised by Sauer's (2001) public choice model, in which an affluent and vocal anti-gambling lobby has been historically rather successful in limiting the expansion of gambling opportunities. In the UK, regulation of gambling has always been largely pragmatic, and the role of producer interests in sustaining barriers to entry in the face of potential competition goes some way to explaining the British government's cautious approach to deregulation and reform in its latest Gambling Act.

In the various discussions of the pros and cons of the removal of prohibition of, or restrictions on, gambling, two issues appear to have been seriously underplayed. The first is consumer satisfaction. The removal of prohibition or restrictions has the potential to raise consumer surplus, the difference between price paid and willingness to pay. As Kearney (2005) points out, insufficient research has been undertaken on the impact of greater availability of legalised gambling on consumer utility.

The second issue that needs to be addressed by both academics and policymakers is the market structure of the gambling industry. Governments, national or regional, have monopoly power over the issue of licences to operate gambling activities. Such licensing is generally accepted as a means to protect consumers against unscrupulous operators and to protect vulnerable groups such as children. But licensing necessarily creates economic rents and consumer welfare is raised by increased dissipation of rents away from monopolistic producers (whether publicly owned or private). A competitive process is necessary for rent dissipation.

In this chapter I have examined some examples in which rents from licensing of gambling services have not been fully dissipated. In the UK, the potential for liberalisation of casino gaming was not fully explored, owing partly to lobbying pressure exerted by existing interests among operators in amusement arcades, bookmaker betting and bingo (Collins, 2006). Pressure from the UK anti-gambling lobby to restrict casino liberalisation and expansion has focused on the alleged growth in the incidence of problem gambling. But liberalisation and expansion would deliver substantial consumption benefits that should not be ignored. The UK government could provide large sums for expenditure on public education to help offset the adverse effects of problem gambling and aggregate social welfare would still rise. A more balanced view of costs and benefits, with sensible research estimation and calibration, is needed to inform UK government policy.

In Australia, the refusal of state governments to allow Betfair to operate a betting exchange sustains higher takeout rates and margins for state bookmakers. Again, market efficiency and consumer surplus would be greater if betting exchanges were tolerated. In the USA, plans to prohibit Internet betting will raise transactions costs for bettors (who will simply take their business offshore) and reduce consumer surplus. The recently imposed ban on Internet betting also appears to be contrary to the principles of free trade and has already been questioned by the World Trade Organization.

There is a need to disentangle moral and ethical arguments against gambling from the operation of anti-competitive producer interests. The anti-gambling lobbies in both the UK and USA have been effective in using claims and evidence of alleged pathological and problem gambling in their submissions against the liberalisation of gambling. Precisely because such claims are being used by producer interests, and also because there is no effective lobby for consumer interests, it is essential that the evidence produced on the social costs of gambling is subjected to the most careful scrutiny.

The image of gamblers often presented by those who wish to prohibit or restrict gambling is one of foolhardy and ignorant people, incapable of rational action. Such people, it appears, will do harm to themselves and others through pathological addiction. This is misleading in the sense that the majority of gamblers do respond to takeout rates, changes in game design and new gambling products much as economists predict (Forrest et al., 2000; Guryan and Kearney, 2005). The losers from legalised gambling tend be consumers who are misinformed about the characteristics of gambling products (Kearney, 2005). One essential step on the path to gambling reform is to make information on odds, takeout rates and potential losses far more visible and accessible. For example, in the UK television competitions abound in which answering a simple multiple-choice question successfully leads to a large prize (cash, holiday, event tickets, etc.). The odds of winning the prize are not shown but ought to be. Both those for and those against gambling liberalisation can agree on the importance of increasing the level of information about gambling products available to consumers.

References

Barton, E. and M. Smith (2006), *Online gambling: Market forecast and assessment to 2010*, London: Screen Digest International.

Becker, G. (2006), *On Internet gambling, www.becker-posner-blog.com/ archives/2006/08/on_Internet_gam.html*.

Becker, G. and K. Murphy (1988), 'A theory of rational addiction', *Journal of Political Economy*, 96(4): 675–700.

Cain, M., D. Law and D. Peel (2008), 'Bounded cumulative prospect theory: some implications for gambling outcomes', *Applied Economics*, 40, 5–15.

Christiansen Capital Advisers (2005), *Gross Annual Wager Data, www. ccai.com*.

Clarke, R. and G. Dempsey (2001), 'The feasibility of regulating gambling on the Internet', *Managerial and Decision Economics*, 22: 125–32.

Collins, P. (2006) *The UK Gambling Act (2005): Lessons for legislators*, Mimeo, University of Salford, Centre for the Study of Gambling.

Department for Culture, Media and Sport (2001), *Gambling Review Report*, www.Culture.gov.uk/Reference_library/Publications/ archive_2001/gamb_rev_report.htm.

Eadington, W. (2005) 'The future of casinos in Europe', *Society for Study of Gambling Newsletter*, 39.

Europe Economics (2005), *Remote Gambling Taxation: A report for the Remote Gambling Association*, London: Europe Economics.

Forrest, D. (1999) 'The past and future of the British football pools', *Journal of Gambling Studies*, 15: 161–72.

Forrest, D. and O. D. Gulley (2005), *Characteristics of Lotto players and Correlations with Spending on other 'Vices'*, Mimeo, University of Salford, Centre for the Study of Gambling.

Forrest, D., O. D. Gulley and R. Simmons (2000), 'Testing for rationality in the UK National Lottery', *Applied Economics*, 32: 315–26.

Forrest, D., O. D. Gulley and R. Simmons (forthcoming), 'The relationship between betting and lottery play', *Economic Enquiry*.

Forrest, D., R. Simmons and N. Chesters (2002), 'Buying a dream: alternative models of demand for lotto', *Economic Inquiry*, 40: 485–96.

Friedman, M. and L. Savage (1948), 'The utility analysis of choices involving risk', *Journal of Political Economy*, 56: 279–304.

Grinols, E. (2004), *Gambling in America: Costs and Benefits*, New York: Cambridge University Press.

Grinols, E. and D. Mustard (2001), 'Business profitability vs. social profitability: evaluating the social contribution of industries with externalities and the case of the casino industry', *Managerial and Decision Economics*, 22: 143–62.

Grinols, E. and D. Mustard (2006), 'Casinos, crime and community costs', *Review of Economics and Statistics*, 88: 28–45.

Guryan, J. and M. S. Kearney (2005), 'Lucky stores, gambling and addiction: empirical evidence from State Lottery sales', Cambridge, MA.: National Bureau of Economic Research Working Paper no. 11287.

Kahneman, D. and A. Tversky (1979), 'Prospect theory: an analysis of decision under risk', *Econometrica*, 2: 263–91.

Kearney, M. S. (2005), 'The economic winners and losers from legalized gambling', *National Tax Journal*, 58: 281–302.

Ladd, G. and N. Petry (2002), 'Disordered gambling among university-based medical and dental patients: a focus on Internet gambling', *Psychology of Addictive Behaviors*, 16: 76–9.

NERA (National Economic Research Associates) (2003), *Gambling Liberalisation and Problem Gambling*, London: NERA.

Paton, D., D. Siegel and L. Vaughan Williams (2002), 'A policy response to the e-commerce revolution: the case of betting taxation in the UK', *Economic Journal*, 57: 247–63.

Quinn, F. (2001), 'First do no harm: what could be done by casinos to limit pathological gambling', *Managerial and Decision Economics*, 22: 133–42.

Sauer, R. (2001), 'The political economy of gambling regulation', *Managerial and Decision Economics*, 22: 1–15.

Smith, M., D. Paton and L. Vaughan Williams (2006), 'Market efficiency in person-to-person betting', *Economica*, 73(292): 673–89.

Vaughan Williams, L. (2006), 'Betting tax policy in the UK: some history, some theory and some evidence', Mimeo, Nottingham Trent University Betting Research Unit.

Walker, D. (2006), 'Quantification of the social costs and benefits of gambling', Paper presented at 5th Annual Alberta Conference on Gambling Research.

Walker, D. and A. Barnett (2000), 'The social costs of gambling: an economic perspective', *Journal of Gambling Studies*, 15: 213–21.

11 HUMAN BODY PARTS FOR TRANSPLANTATION

Mark J. Cherry

Regulatory failures

... some observers have suggested that organ donation rates might be increased through incentives – either financial incentives such as paying for funeral costs or non-financial incentives such as preferential access to donated organs. The report recommends against offering such incentives at this time for a variety of reasons. Financial incentives might disproportionately affect the poor or other marginalized groups, and might also cause a drop in donations for altruistic reasons if people see donated organs as goods with a certain market value. And non-financial incentives, such as reciprocity agreements, might disadvantage those who are less informed about organ donation and therefore increase existing social inequality. (Institute of Medicine, 2006a: 2; see also 2006b)

Whereas the members of the United States Institute of Medicine committee on increasing rates of organ donation were aware that current altruism-based policies of organ procurement are not adequate to meet medical demand, they were unwilling to recommend in favour of market-based solutions. While the Institute of Medicine committee encouraged increased use of non-heart-beating donors,[1] their

---

1   Heart-beating donation may occur either in the case of a living donation – such as living kidney donation – or in the case of deceased donation – such as a brain-dead donor, whose heart is kept beating through the use of medical technology. When non-heart-beating donation occurs in controlled circumstances, it is only after determination of death by cessation of cardiopulmonary function for an appropriately specified period of time. The Institute of Medicine committee recommended cessation for at least five minutes as documented by electrocardiographic and arterial pressure monitoring (2006b: 134). In uncontrolled circumstances, a patient who has died, typically outside of the hospital, may be assessed for possible organ donation. One of the challenges for non-

recommendations primarily focused on increasing social solidarity and community-directed altruism:

> Instead, the goal should be to move toward a society where people see organ donation as a social responsibility. In such a society, donating organs would be accepted as a normal part of dying, and in cases where a person died without recording a specific choice about donating his or her organs, the surviving family members would be comfortable giving permission. (Institute of Medicine 2006a: 2; also 2006b)

As a simple extension of current US policy, it is likely that such a recommendation will lead only to an increasing gap between patients in need of transplants and the number of available organs. In the USA alone, more than seven thousand people die every year while waiting for an organ transplant (UNOS, 2006). According to the UK National Health Service, more than four hundred patients in the UK died in 2005 while waiting for transplant. Many others endure pain and distress, at times even in hospitals on life support, while queuing for available organs. In 2005, in the USA, only approximately 28,000 of the more than 96,000 patients waiting for solid organ transplants (kidney, liver, heart, lung, pancreas, intestine) received them – a tragedy by any standard. Regarding kidney transplantation alone, it is predicted that by 2010 there will be some 650,000 patients in the USA who will require dialysis or transplantation, with approximately 100,000 waiting for a transplant (Xue et al., 2001; Hippen, 2005). While demand for transplantable organs has risen, the national growth rate of organ donation has been relatively stagnant since 1997.[2] Living donation has exceeded

heart-beating donation is tissue damage due to lack of oxygen.

2 The situation is often even more challenging in other countries. In Australia, for example, donor rates fell 7 per cent in 2005, as compared with 2004 (Australian Nursing Federation, 2006). In Romania, the number of donations has fallen to remarkably low levels: 'Irinel Popescu, a specialist in liver transplants, says donor numbers have been steadily falling. "There were 21 organ donors in 2001, 13 in 2002, eight in 2003, and this year we're heading for another negative record: there have been only three in the first 6 months"' (Ionescu, 2004: 491). Despite the severe lack of donated organs, selling one's own organs, such as a redundant kidney, or the organs of a deceased family member, is illegal in Romania.

cadaveric donation nearly every year since 2000, with living unrelated donation accounting for some 29 per cent of all living donation in the USA.

As illustrated by the Institute of Medicine committee's summary conclusions, a core policy challenge is that within bioethics and medical jurisprudence the proposition that the market encourages scientific excellence and virtue in medical research and practice is usually met with considerable scepticism. Market systems are decried as advantaging the wealthier and healthier members of society. Market-based research and practice, it is typically claimed, substitutes profit-seeking behaviour for truth-seeking behaviour, and thus fails to protect the most fundamental interests of persons and public health. The literature does not usually regard the market as leading to the appropriate use of resources, the protection of human subjects, or the development of high-quality and innovative medical products and services. To put the matter starkly, profiting from the provision of healthcare services (such as transplantation) or the sale of scarce medical resources (such as human organs) is viewed as morally suspect. An additional and often hidden presupposition – frequently assumed rather than argued – is that justice requires state action to mitigate the influence of social contingencies and natural fortune. As a result, calls for significant, wide-ranging and extensive governmental regulation – including continued prohibition of the selling of human organs for transplantation – are ubiquitous. Public policy in the USA and in most of the world currently forbids outright any market-based solution to the scarcity of organs for transplantation (see Cherry, 2005a: Appendix).

In order to assess market-based policy realistically one must also consider the background risks involved in a medical enterprise bereft of the healthcare incentives of the commercial sector. The adequate framing of future public policy requires critical assessment of which strategies for procurement and allocation would most improve access to human organs, thereby saving lives, reducing human suffering and advancing healthcare outcomes, as well as increasing the efficient and effective use of scarce resources, while at the same time avoiding significant moral harms, such as the exploitation of persons. As I will argue, each of these challenges would be best met by openly crafting a market for the procurement and allocation of transplantable human organs.

Improving access to transplantation

Commercial markets in human organs are typically denounced as inappropriately commodifying the human body. As a recent editorial in *The Lancet* asserted without argument:

> Ethical arguments have been made for and against the practice, with the pro side generally contending that legitimizing a market for organs would increase their availability. But human livers and kidneys are not commodities, and hospitals are not just another convenient locale for money to change hands. Trade in human organs is immoral and ought to be outlawed around the world. (Lancet, 2006: 1118)

The author of the editorial conveniently leaves unstated the fact that surgeons, nurses, hospital administrators and staff charge significant amounts of money for access to their goods and services – that is, *a great deal of money changes hands in hospitals.*

Selling human organs for profit is held to be necessarily degrading, as well as incompatible with basic human values, such as social justice and individual liberty, and important social goals, including equality and a spirit of altruism. The human body, it is urged, ought not be treated as mere property. The market is viewed as corrosive of the 'gift-of-life' sentiments, social beneficence and community solidarity which, it is claimed, ought to characterise organ procurement. Altruistic donation is perceived as an expression of important human values, social solidarity and community commitments. As illustrated, though, a market is perceived as commodifying human organs as products for sale and trade, thereby undermining the essential gift-exchange dimensions of organ donation that purportedly bind the community together. Human organs are characterised as medical resources to be used to support public interests and social goods.

To emphasise, it is not just that organs are to be gifts, donated in the spirit of altruism and social solidarity; organs are to be nationalised as a public resource. Human organs are to be understood as a scarce public resource and allocated on the basis of acceptable medical criteria and appropriate social goals, rather than private gain. The core challenge is, therefore, permissibly to enhance access to transplantable organs, while also improving healthcare outcomes relative to the current system of altruistic donation.

The usual circumstance of transplant patients without a private donor is an evermore significant wait time. Given increased demand for human organs, and a concurrently increased queuing time, median waiting times for patients with less common blood types and highly sensitised recipients have not been accurately calculated since 1998, because less than 50 per cent of these patients have received a transplant since listing (Xue et al., 2001; Hippen, 2005). As queuing time for transplantable organs has increased, so too have direct and indirect health risks. Patients with end-stage renal failure not due to diabetes have a mortality rate of approximately 60 per cent at five years while waiting for organs; mortality rates are worse for patients whose renal failure is due to diabetes. Yet, in the Netherlands, for example, the wait time for deceased-donor kidney transplantation is in the range of four to five years (de Klerk et al., 2005). Even queuing for less than six months has long-term negative health impacts relative to pre-emptive transplantation (Meier-Kriesche and Kaplan, 2002; Abou Ayache et al., 2005). Over time the body becomes more fragile, creating significant risks of poor post-transplant outcomes. As the median wait time increases, it will eventually surpass the lifespan of many patients on dialysis.

Public policy that expands the number of living donors would multiply the availability of transplantable organs, such as kidneys, bone marrow, and liver segments.[3] If such a policy also engaged families to make available organs from recently deceased relatives, this would also increase availability of non-redundant organs, such as hearts from brain-dead and cadaver donors. Expanding the pool of living and non-living donors, including non-heart-beating donors,[4] would then save lives and reduce suffering.

Market-based procurement and distribution of human organs demonstrates significant potential for improving access to transplant-able organs. A policy that embraced financial incentives and other valuable benefits for donors would likely realise a considerable improve-ment in the number and quality of organs. For example, a market would allow families to sell the organs of a deceased loved one, rather than just to donate them. The knowledge that their families would benefit might persuade many more people to become organ donors. Other individuals might be willing to consider a futures contract in which they agree to sell their usable organs upon death to a particular buyer and have the money paid to their descendants. Others might wish to sell a redundant internal

---

3   In Iran living unrelated kidney donation is compensated and governmentally regulated. It has effectively eliminated the renal transplant waiting list (see Ghods and Nasrollah-zadeh, 2005; Bagheri, 2005; Ghods, 2004). There is some indication of negative vendor psychosocial outcomes that should be addressed as the programme goes forward (Zar-gooshi, 2001). Such negative outcomes must be addressed regarding living organ donors as well. In India some of the data suggest that while selling kidneys increases the number of organs available for transplant, the compensation is insufficient adequately to help those who sell a kidney (Goyal et al., 2002). The India data, though, are ambiguous partly because the market is illegal and unregulated, leaving vendors without adequate recourse for fraud or ill treatment. It may be that the reported negative implications, such as con-tinuing vendor impoverishment and lack of adequate follow-up, would be straightfor-wardly solvable by legalising the market, tracking results and correcting for unwanted outcomes, for example by increasing payments to organ vendors.

4   In the USA more than 22,000 individuals who would likely be suitable non-heart-beating donors die each year of cardiac arrest outside of hospitals (Institute of Medicine, 2006b). Whereas this group represents a largely untapped source of organs, it would still be insuf-ficient to meet demand (Brook et al., 2003). Transplant centres have also begun using more organs from 'marginal donors'; that is, 'donors that would not have been consid-ered suitable for donation previously' (Humar, 2004: S410). The positive is that more or-gans are available for transplant; the negative is that often such transplants yield inferior results, such as greater complications.

organ, such as a kidney, while still living. Some might find this a valuable way of obtaining resources to improve their life circumstances; indeed, some might view it as heroic – saving the life of another at some risk to themselves. We accept paid rescue workers, who risk their lives to save others, in many areas of life (ski rescue teams, firefighters, and so forth). To be sure, intentionally obstructing a life-saving rescue attempt is typically judged as morally blameworthy, and frequently as legally culpable. Why not in organ transplantation?

Barter markets would open up related possibilities, such as organ trading, in which the families of those in need of transplant trade with each other for the necessary healthy organs – for example, a slice of healthy liver might be exchanged for a healthy kidney, or perhaps paired donor kidney exchanges (Delmonico et al., 2004). At Johns Hopkins University Hospital, in July 2003, surgeons performed a 'triple swap' kidney transplant operation in which three patients, who were not tissue compatible with their own willing donors, exchanged the donor's kidney for a kidney from another of the three donors. Each donor provided a kidney to one of the three transplant patients. In a British case, a father who was not a sufficiently good tissue match to donate to his son offered one of his kidneys to the British cadaveric donor pool in exchange for placing his son on the national cadaveric waiting list for a kidney. He offered a cost-neutral option for a trade in kind (Sells, 1997).

Other market-based incentives include organ entitlements, or higher priority on the waiting list for those families whose members donated organs, the payment of funeral expenses, or various tax credits. Here, one might consider allowing donors, or their families, to take tax deductions for the fair market value of the organs, or perhaps utilise a system of tax credits against income or inheritance taxes owed for the organ's value. These two examples would be governmentally managed systems for the purchase of organs. Both policies would ensure that donors were compensated for the market value of their body parts, while actively encouraging an increase in available organs, without raising direct healthcare costs. Moreover, each case is little different to the current system of organ donation, except that donors or their families receive financial or other valuable compensation.

Churches and other charitable organisations could play a significant role in such a market-based system. One might envision individuals donating rights in organs directly to local churches, which would guarantee high-quality healthcare for surgery and minimise other risks associated with donation. The organs could then be sold to the wealthy to raise funds to purchase healthcare, food and medicine, or be made available to the impecunious. Such organisations could raise money to provide organs to those who could not otherwise purchase them, or could act as organ brokers for the poor to advantage those poor themselves. One might also imagine particular religious groups or corporations supporting organ drives, modelled after the drives to increase the blood supply. The market creates social and political space to explore additional opportunities and incentives for organ procurement without thereby forbidding other types of incentives and opportunities.

Some have raised concerns that permitting organ sales will curtail altruistic donation or intimidate charitably inclined donors. One might argue that the existence of financial incentives for organ procurement undermines the freedom to donate one's organs. If an organ market is created, while only some will exercise the liberty to sell, the freedom of all to donate will thereby be limited. The Institute of Medicine committee on organ donation, for example, concluded that permitting commercial sales would 'crowd-out' altruistic donation:

> The committee examined financial incentives within the gift model of donation to determine if they would provide additional increases in the rates of organ donation. Hard data on the impact of incentives are lacking, and it may be difficult to obtain reliable data to address these issues. A pilot study of financial incentives for organ donation may set in motion a societal process that is difficult to reverse even after the pilot study itself is abandoned. For example, if people begin to view their organs as valuable commodities that should be purchased, then altruistic donation may be difficult to reinvigorate. (Institute of Medicine, 2006a: 13)

Importantly, this criticism can be turned on its head. Prohibition of an organ market precludes the freedom of all to sell their organs. Given that with a general prohibition on organ vending only some will exercise the freedom to donate, the freedom of all to sell, if they so will, is limited. Lloyd Cohen, for example, has reportedly removed himself from the general donor pool, and has encouraged others to do likewise, as a protest against the laws prohibiting compensation for organ donation (Cohen, 2005: 32). Prohibition of the sale of human organs necessarily 'crowds-out' all commercial-based incentives for increasing access to transplantation.

Even within a market system, private individuals could still donate organs out of charity to family members or to others in need. Presuming that the willingness to donate body parts is motivated by actual, rather than coerced, altruism, those who are willing to donate should still be willing to donate regardless of the existence of a market. For-profit markets in food and medicine exist side by side with food banks, charity hospitals and other not-for-profit programmes. Moreover, most organ donations from living persons are to family members or close friends. The motivations underlying such donations are likely to maintain the same force regardless of the existence of a market: love, beneficence, loyalty, gratitude, guilt or avoidance of the shame of failing to donate. For these donors, their willingness to donate stems from their relationship with the particular patient. Such donations are unlikely to change either in general character (i.e. from donation to sale) or in relative number (i.e. become other than driven by the need of a particular friend or relative).

Indeed, a requirement that organ donation be altruistically motivated, if taken seriously, would likely rule out many donations. Persons who stand to be financially supported by a person needing an organ might have motivations other than 'charity' for donating an organ to a relative. Families sometimes donate out of a self-interested desire to see their loved one continue on in another person or to feel that something good has come from their loved one's death (Siminoff and Chillag, 1999:

40). How pure must one's intentions be for organ transfer to be classified as altruistic?

Market incentives encourage people to raise resources to further personal as well as social interests and goals. With the creation of a market, organ procurement need not be artificially limited to acts of altruism. Incentives would likely lead to an increase in the number of living persons willing to sell internal redundant organs to recipients who are neither family members nor close friends. Incentives would also increase the willingness of families to have the organs of their loved ones harvested upon death. Such public policy would thereby incur significant health benefits for all those in need of a transfer.

Justice, fairness and exploitation

An additional challenge is that access to organ transplantation is seen as raising numerous issues of social justice, such as exploitation and fair access to scarce healthcare resources. Here market-based policy is perceived as raising particularly weighty concerns; for example, that cash payments will attract primarily poor and low-income segments of the population, who will disproportionately bear the healthcare complications of being vendors; that it would coerce poor people into selling their organs, something that in better circumstances they would not consider.

But why would the market necessarily be exploitative? People would be free to negotiate a bargain in which both parties would expect to benefit: on the one side, a life is saved; on the other, a family is provided with significant resources to improve their lives. Perhaps the lure of financial gain would motivate a decision that the vendor would have rejected if he had thought carefully about its full effects on his life. The existence of such miscalculation, though, is an empirical question. If the typical organ vendor agrees to sell because he believes that the expected value of so doing is positive, and the resulting value is positive, then there is no miscalculation and no exploitation on such grounds. The possibility of such miscalculation exists with every commercial transaction; yet, provided that they are approached honestly, commercial transactions are generally speaking neither coercive nor exploitative. Even if the individual is so interested in money that it would, given his values, be irrational to decline the offer, the choice is still plausibly understood as free insofar as he affirms the outcome. Consider the impoverished economics student, who does not wish to become greatly in debt to pay for graduate school. If a rich patient offered this student $2 million to sell a kidney, one might imagine the student thinking: 'Wow! I could never rationally refuse such a wonderful offer of two million dollars, and I would never want to turn it down in any case. I'm very glad that it was made.'

The fear that unscrupulous entrepreneurs would coerce people to part with organs for less than the market price is likely also misplaced. Unlike illicit trading on a black market, a legally regulated market should not suffer from such behaviour. One option would be to set minimum legal prices for organs as a matter of public policy to ensure that sellers are properly compensated. Countries would have to decide how best to regulate the national and international organ trade, but this should be a reasonable extension of current donation practices (Friedman and Friedman, 2006: 962). In Iran, for example, foreigners are not permitted renal transplantation from compensated Iranian living unrelated donors (Ghods and Nasrollahzadeh, 2005; Ghods, 2004).

Moreover, in legitimate markets kindness and personal recognition of the other are often crucial for business, allowing partners to build up trust. Customer satisfaction and professionalism lead to long-term profits. Successful organ procurement and transplantation require the skilled services of many professionals. Even though donor and recipient may meet only once in an organ market, reputations are built on relationships with and among surgeons, hospitals, transplant teams and others who perform specialised services. Hospitals, as providers of highly qualified surgical teams, a suitably sterile environment and medical follow-up, have significant professional incentives to encourage virtuous tendencies in the market. Surgeons would be unlikely to put their reputations at risk by dealing with black-market traders or con-artists. Given a good reputation, others will be much more likely to utilise their services in the future. Professional virtue and medical skill can, therefore, be seen as a profit-maximising strategy.

Perhaps the market is exploitative because people have a moral obligation to provide assistance, a duty to help others in need. If such a duty exists, then demanding compensation to fulfil one's duty may be coercive. It is unclear, however, that even if the existence of such a duty could be demonstrated it would sustain the case against organ sales. Patients dying of organ failure would not usually be described as having special moral obligations to provide potential organ donors with financial income. Indeed, it may be that it is patients with end-stage organ failure who are being exploited. Contrary to the often cited concern that a commercial organ market would exploit the poor, it may be that by offering to sell organs the poor would be exploiting the illness, suffering and fear of death of the rich for personal gain. Yet, in the absence of prior agreements or special moral obligations, it is unclear why those with healthy organs have a moral obligation to donate. Persons have a monopoly over the use of their own bodies and its parts. Intervening in the commerce of transplantable organs brings about exploitation by forcibly preventing others from paying the owner of the organs as much as they are worth to the owner. In short, adequately to assess claims of exploitation, and to establish policy to prevent such exploitation, one must also enquire as to who is in greater need, and thus under more threat of exploitation: the poor who need financial resources, or the patients who are dying of organ failure.

Here, critics of organ vending often claim that only the rich would be able to afford organs, and that the poor would have to suffer in extra-long queues for state-funded transplants. But this consequence is unlikely for several reasons. Since the market would increase the number of organs, making transplantation more readily available, it would reduce queuing time. Consider, for example, two alternative procurement and allocation policies. Under policy A, 100 per cent of the patients spend an average of 24 months queuing for a suitable organ, with a 5 per cent mortality among patients awaiting transplantation. Under policy B, 50 per cent of the patients spend an average of two months queuing, with less than 1 per cent mortality while awaiting transplantation. The circumstance of the remaining 50 per cent of the patients is exactly the same as with policy A. Of the two policies, B may be worse with regard to equality, if judged solely in terms of queuing time and probability of dying while queuing. B is, however, significantly better with regard to healthcare outcomes: waiting time is much less for half of the patients, reducing morbidity and mortality costs. Moreover, with market-based procurement more organs would likely be available, reducing queuing time for the entire waiting list.

Meeting the medical needs of patients who are waiting for transplants is very costly. By reducing waiting times, the market would also save financial resources, which may be particularly important for stretching the budgets of public programmes that address the healthcare needs of the poor. In the USA the Medicare cost of dialysis and transplantation in 2002 was $17 billion; this is expected to increase to approximately $28 billion in 2010. While these individuals represent only 0.5 per cent of Medicare patients, they accounted for approximately 5 per cent of the entire Medicare budget in 2002 (Xue et al., 2001; Hippen, 2005).

Even if the purchased organs predominantly benefited only certain segments of the patient population, such activity would reduce the number of patients on the general waiting lists, thus reducing waiting time for others. Early transplant removes individuals from the queue, shortening the waiting list, reducing suffering, saving lives and money. Still, many decry the practice as immoral 'queue jumping'. Consider similar objections to directed donation:

> Directed donation means a donor family can designate where their loved one's organs can go and to whom they may go. It was created so that if someone became an organ donor and they had a friend or

family member awaiting a transplant, they could help that person. However, this loophole in the donation regulations now means that those with the right social and financial considerations can solicit donations ... This loophole needs to be closed. (Palmeri, 2005: 701–2)

Importantly, however, such 'directed donations' often bring organs into the transplant pool that would otherwise not have been available. Soliciting donors – however much UNOS may oppose it (UNOS News Bureau, 2004) – typically increases access to transplantation (see also MatchingDonors.com).

Perhaps a market in organs for transplantation is exploitative because it commodifies that which should not be commodified – for many, such a practice exemplifies improper commodification. Commodities are marked by 1) objectification (i.e. 'ascription of status as a thing in the Kantian sense of something that is manipulable at the will of persons'); 2) fungibility (i.e. as 'fully interchangeable with no effect on value to the holder'); 3) commensurability (i.e. that 'values of things can be arrayed as a function of one continuous variable'); and 4) money equivalence (i.e. 'the continuous variable in terms of which things are ranked is dollar value') (Radin, 1996: 118). The central question, though, is whether organ markets would likely fare better or worse regarding commodification than other strategies of procurement and allocation.

The challenge for opponents of the market is that organs are in fact manipulable and interchangeable with others of the same kind. This is the very reason why transplantation is medically viable. Whereas one may raise the concern that the market will fail appropriately to weigh and compare economic versus non-economic values, non-market-based strategies for procurement and allocation face similar difficulties. All objectify human organs, treating them as exchangeable objects.

Perhaps organ sales involve an exchange of incommensurable values. Incommensurability represents a concern that the values at stake cannot be relevantly summed and compared. By itself, though, incommensurability does not require that the goods exchanged be precisely commensurable, but rather that the parties transact voluntarily, that deception or other forms of coercion are not employed, and that each is satisfied with the value to be received. This means that what is received in return is worth as least as much to the party as that which was given. As others have noted, one can buy or sell 'priceless' Monet paintings without claiming that the aesthetic or historic value of the artwork is commensurate with the money that is paid (Wertheimer, 1992: 218). Perhaps there is a kind of exploitation, as Elizabeth Anderson suggests, 'when one party to a transaction is oriented toward the exchange of "gift values", while the other party operates in accordance with the norms of the market exchange of commodities. Gift values, which include love, gratitude, and appreciation of others, cannot be bought or obtained through piecemeal calculations of individual advantage' (1990: 89). This account oversimplifies, however: at times one party to a transaction may deliberately sell goods for less than the market value as a subtle gift. This suggests that gift values can in various ways be brought into the market. Moreover, the challenge is relevant if and only if such a dichotomy of intentions exists. Persons who negotiate regarding the fair market value of human organs will not likely experience such conceptual dissonance.

An additional concern is that once there is a market in human organs, all organs will have a price, and those who do not sell their organs will become hoarders of something that is useful to other people and which is financially valuable. Such considerations hold equally against systems of donation. As organ donation became perceived as the standard of care, organs were recast as mere things. Persons who do not donate their organs, or their loved one's organs, at death are seen as immorally withholding life-sustaining medical resources. It is this reconceptualisation of persons as sources of scarce medical resources which in large measure has driven the proposals for 'required request' laws, as well as the state-based coercive 'presumed consent', 'expected donation' or 'routine salvage' systems of organ procurement. Among the proposals to improve access to organs through altruism is 'Living Anonymous Kidney Donation', which would entail the solicitation of living volunteers from the general population to undergo kidney removal surgery and post-operative care without personal connection to the recipient, public recognition of their sacrifice or any sort of compensation (Neyhart, 2004). Indeed, the stated goal of the Institute of Medicine committee, quoted at the very beginning of this chapter, is to re-educate society to appreciate organ donation as a 'social responsibility'; i.e. as a moral duty. Concern to avoid recasting persons as collections of spare parts or as hoarders of a scarce resource is not a challenge particular to the market, and thus is not a legitimate objection to the market; this moral concern must be addressed under any system of organ procurement and allocation.

Moreover, donors, surgeons and recipients alike objectify organs and treat them as fungible. That is, all systems of organ procurement and allocation treat organs as commodities, even donation. On each ground, one has specified a market in human organs, albeit a heavily regulated market, with carefully stipulated conditions for bearing the costs and benefits of procurement, distribution and transplantation. Thus the argument is not about whether human organs should be commodified, but rather about who should receive the resources and who should bear the costs of appropriation and transfer. Insofar as individuals are prohibited from selling their organs, it is a constrained market where donors are required to part with their property without material compensation, while others (including physicians, hospitals and procurement agencies) benefit financially, and the recipient of the transplant benefits physically. That human organs can be transferred only at a price of zero does not thereby reduce the value of such organs to zero. Rather, it transfers the value of the organ from the donor to other parties.

Perhaps organ selling is degrading to vendors and thereby violates their dignity. This degradation is also objectification – that is, a failure to respect in theory and to make space in practice for the human subject as a person (Radin, 1996: 155). The contention is that it is precisely because of the general significance and intimate connection with persons that organs ought not to be sold. The body is part of the basic dignity of the human person; the body possesses a kind of 'sanctity', or perhaps 'sacredness', in the biological order and, therefore, trade in the body and its parts is morally repugnant and should not be permitted.

Here one must adjudicate among moral intuitions and distinguish between justified and unjustified moral repugnance. For example, many have deep intuitions regarding the moral repugnance of abortion and homosexuality, yet these are practices that society permits. Is such repugnance morally justified? In a Western secular moral culture that frequently affirms the merits of abortion on demand, embryo experimentation and, in growing numbers, physician-assisted suicide, there is an obvious irony in the assumption that rhetorically charged moral terms such as 'sanctity', 'sacredness', 'dignity' or even 'repugnance' should bear any moral weight. In the case of organ sales, one must determine whether generalised feelings of moral repugnance are justified, prior to presupposing that such intuitions ought to carry any weight in meeting the burden of proof to proscribe organ sales.

Finally, it is difficult to count a policy as exploitative if, as in the case of legalising organ sales, it increases the number of options open to individuals. More generally, we do not treat someone merely as a means if he consents to be so treated. The commodification of human organs is not an obvious violation of the Kantian maxim to treat persons as ends in themselves in the absence of additional arguments showing that even consensual selling of organs is morally injurious. To conclude that such circumstances are inherently exploitative, one must hold that there is something intrinsically wrong or debasing in selling one's organs, so that even if one does this freely, one has been brought to do something morally injurious to oneself. Such a conclusion is implausible, however, since the action involved in selling an organ is the same as in donating an organ. The primary difference is that money changes hands. The organ market respects vendors as persons and moral agents. Prohibition demeans the poor and others, who may be interested in vending, by considering them unable to make moral decisions about their own fates.

Markets, medical innovation and scientific excellence

An additional challenge for framing transplantation policy is to encourage both medical innovation and scientific excellence. Here, a root concern is with potential conflicts of interest. In research, conflicts of interest arise when a researcher's judgement regarding a primary interest, such as scientific knowledge, is or may be unduly influenced by a secondary interest, such as financial gain (Medical Research Council, 2003: 208; Thompson, 1993). Physicians who are both researchers and clinicians, for example, have competing commitments. The primary goal of clinicians is generally doing what is best for one's patients within certain side constraints, such as patient consent, institutional policy and resource availability. The primary goal of researchers, on the other hand, is the discovery of answers to research questions. Researchers are constrained in how they may utilise subjects who may or may not benefit from the study design; the objective in a scientific inquiry, however, is to follow a protocol to obtain data, to test a hypothesis and to contribute to the base of scientific knowledge. Other conflicts of interest may emerge when researchers perceive certain conclusions as supporting particular moral judgements, socio-political points of view or career advancement. Here the question for transplantation policy is whether the market fares better or worse on such grounds than the current system of altruistic donation.

The central concern is that the market substitutes profit-seeking behaviour for truth-seeking behaviour. The ubiquitous calls for regulation to correct for so-called 'market failures' risk, however, enacting facile and oversimplified solutions to what is a complex problem. It is important to recognise that many of the forces that potentially distort reported transplantation data are independent of the commercial market. Again, both scientists and bioethicists may bring a particular social, political or moral agenda. For example, researchers may be in favour of unfettered access to abortion or to unrestricted research on human embryonic stem cells, and thus be more likely to work with even poorly designed studies that support such moral claims. Or researchers may be politically predisposed to socialised medicine, including government-controlled organ transplantation, and thus perceive all organ procurement and allocation data through such a prejudicial lens. Political, moral and other epistemic and non-epistemic background commitments often play roles in surreptitious or unconscious distortion of scientific data so as to acquire research funding, advance one's social standing in the scientific community or further particular socio-political goals. It would be short sighted, indeed, to overlook the pervasive and subtly nuanced conflicts that desire for renown, professional advancement and moral world view represent, which may at times take precedence over scientific accuracy or the protection of patients (Cherry, 2006).

Here the market will likely fare somewhat better than government-controlled transplantation in that the market preserves and expands niches by providing incentives for developing high-quality or innovative products and procedures. Newly developing technologies that show promise include transplantation with stem cells, cloning, xenotransplantation and tissue engineering (Cascalho and Platt, 2005). It is in the interest of profit maximisation to produce safer transplantation products and procedures as well as to support better access to transplantation. If one is in the business of selling organs, profits would generally be maximised if one provided high-quality organs with low rates of rejection. Given such circumstances, procuring organs from living persons, which usually produces better medical results, will result in higher profits than from cadaveric organs. Organs removed from living persons are more likely to be of significant use to recipients. They have greater vitality and can be screened in advance for defects, diseases or other negative indicators. In contrast, if organs are procured only from the recently deceased, such as accident victims, one loses both vitality and screening opportunities. A central factor jeopardising an organ's viability is the time during which it is without oxygen and other nutrients. Damage due to inadequate oxygen, or ischaemia, begins immediately once the heart stops pumping. As the Institute of Medicine report on organ procurement from non-heart-beating donors points out, such organs have higher discard rates, which leads to increased transplant costs and means that fewer organs are available (Institute of Medicine, 1997). Transplant survival data, though increasingly competitive, are not quite as good as from heart-beating donors (Weber et al., 2002).

Additional challenges include rejection by the recipient and disease transfer. Even a well-preserved organ is more likely to be rejected after transplantation if it does not have the same genetic markers as the recipient. Such failures can be fatal. Moreover, some diseases can be transferred from donor to recipient (for example, HIV). In these areas the open market will have scientific advantages over a system of donation: commercial sale will likely target living donors; provide adequate time to screen for organ viability, disease and potentially deadly immuno-rejections; and have the flexibility to arrange for quick transfer of the organ to avoid significant ischaemia. A central challenge of the black market, for example, is the difficulty of enforcing either appropriate medical standards of practice or quality guarantees for organs. Such challenges can be addressed straightforwardly in an open market.

Conclusion

Innovation, even medical innovation, is frequently driven by the profit motive. The free market offers both the possibility to profit from innovations as well as to raise the capital necessary for experimentation. Moreover, it diffuses political and social authority, freeing innovators to compete with each other as well as to challenge the status quo (Cherry, 2005b). As a result, any adequate assessment of organ transplantation must honestly explore whether market-based policies would more successfully produce high-quality organs and develop innovative transplantation products and techniques, while encouraging virtuous behaviour, than current altruism-based policies. The current regulatory environment increases costs while decreasing organ availability. Its focus on altruism, equality, dignity and fairness leads counterproductively to less efficient organ procurement and allocation, and thereby to greater human suffering and fewer lives saved. Market-based public policy would very likely increase both the quality and the quantity of organs available for transplant, thus leading to direct and indirect health benefits; for example, reduced queuing times and increased transplant viability.

Moreover, as noted, it is important to recognise that factors which lead to conflicts of interest, affecting scientific excellence and medical expertise, are largely independent of the market. Political, moral and other non-epistemic background conditions, such as career development or political goals, often play a significant role in the surreptitious or unconscious distortion of scientific data to maintain research funding and social standing in the scientific community, or to further particular social and political objectives. Finally, the market would provide significant incentives for developing high-quality and innovative transplantation products and services.

In summary, as I have argued elsewhere in more detail (Cherry, 2005a), it is time honestly to consider the hard facts of the public policy challenges: the current altruism-based system of organ transplants is not working adequately, and a market for organ donors and recipients would very likely save lives and considerably reduce suffering. This urgent public health challenge will not be resolved through the rhetoric of altruism, moral repugnancy, exploitation and human dignity. The arguments developed in this chapter leave us with a well-founded basis to criticise current national and international proscription of payments for human organs for transplantation. If this public health crisis is to be adequately addressed and remedied, any future policymaker's assessment must honestly recognise the possibility that the market is the most efficient and effective means of procuring and allocating organs for transplantation.

References

Abou Ayache, R., F. Bridoux, F. Pessione, R. A. Thierry, M. Belmouaz, F. Leroy, E. Desport and M. Bauwens (2005), 'Preemptive renal transplantation in adults', *Transplantation Proceedings*, 37(6): 2817–8.

Anderson, E. (1990), 'Is women's labor a commodity?', *Philosophy and Public Affairs*, 19(1): 71–92.

Australian Nursing Federation (2006), 'Donor rates fall', *Australian Nursing Journal*, 13(9): 8.

Bagheri, A. (2005), 'Organ transplantation laws in Asian countries: a comparative study', *Transplantation Proceedings*, 37(10): 4159–62.

Brook, N. R., J. R. Waller and M. L. Nicholson (2003), 'Nonheart-beating kidney donation: current practice and future developments', *Kidney International*, 63: 1516–29.

Cascalho, M. and J. Platt (2005), 'New technologies for organ replacement and augmentation', *Mayo Clinic Proceedings*, 80(3): 370–78.

Cherry, M. (2005a), *Kidney for Sale by Owner: Human organs, transplantation, and the market*, Washington, DC: Georgetown University Press.

Cherry, M. (2005b), 'The market and medical innovation: human passions and medical advancement', *Journal of Medicine and Philosophy*, 30(6): 555–70.

Cherry, M. (2006), 'Financial conflicts of interest and the human passion to innovate', in A. S. Iltis (ed.), *Research Ethics*, New York: Routledge.

Cohen, L. R. (2005), 'Directions for the disposition of my (and your) vital organs', *Regulation* (Fall), pp. 32–8.

De Klerk, M., K. M. Keizer, F. H. Claas, M. Witvliet, B. Haase-Kromwijk and W. Weimar (2005), 'The Dutch National Living Donor Kidney Exchange Program', *American Journal of Transplantation*, 5(9): 2303–5.

Delmonico, F. L., P. E. Morrissey, G. S. Lipkowitz, J. S. Stoff, J. Himmelfarb, W. Harmon, M. Pavlakis, H. Mah, J. Goguen, R. Luskin, E. Milford, G. Basadonna, M. Chobanian, B. Bouthot, M. Lorber and R. J. Rohrer (2004), 'Donor kidney exchanges', *American Journal of Transplantation*, 4(10): 1553–4.

Friedman, E. A. and A. L. Friedman (2006), 'Payment for donor kidneys: pros and cons', *Kidney International*, 69: 960–62.

Ghods, A. J. (2004), 'Changing ethics in renal transplantation: presentation of Iran model', *Transplantation Proceedings*, 36(1): 11–13.

Ghods, A. J. and D. Nasrollahzadeh (2005), 'Transplant tourism and the Iranian model of renal transplantation program: ethical considerations', *Experimental and Clinical Transplantation*, 3(2): 351–4.

Goyal, M., R. L. Mehta, L. J. Schneiderman and A. R. Sehgal (2002), 'Economic and health consequences of selling a kidney in India', *Journal of the American Medical Association*, 288(13): 1589–93.

Hippen, B. E. (2005), 'In defense of a regulated market in kidneys from living vendors', *Journal of Medicine and Philosophy*, 30(6): 627–42.

Humar, A. (2004), 'Maximizing the donor pool: marginal donors, splits, and living donor liver transplants', *Journal of Gastroenterology and Hepatology*, 19: S410–13.

Institute of Medicine (1997), *Report on Non-heart Beating Organ Transplantation*, R. Herdman, Study Director, and J. Potts, Principal Investigators, Washington, DC: National Academies Press.

Institute of Medicine (2006a), *Organ Donation: Opportunities for action – short report*, Washington, DC: National Academies Press.

Institute of Medicine (2006b), *Organ Donation: Opportunities for action*, Washington, DC: National Academies Press.

Ionescu, C. (2004), 'Organ failure (world report)', *The Lancet*, 364: 491.

Medical Research Council (2003), 'Good research practice', in S. Erickson (ed.), *Manual for Research Ethics Committees*, 6th edn, Cambridge: Cambridge University Press.

Lancet, The (2006), 'Editorial: not for sale at any price', *The Lancet*,
367(9517): 1118.

Meier-Kriesche, H. U. and B. Kaplan (2002), 'Waiting time on
dialysis as the strongest modifiable risk factor for renal transplant
outcomes: a paired donor kidney analysis', *Transplantation*, 74(10):
1377–81.

Neyhart, C. (2004), 'Living anonymous kidney donation: a solution
to the organ donor shortage? Yes, another available resource',
Nephrology Nursing Journal, 31(3): 330–31.

Palmeri, D. (2005), 'Directed donation: what is a transplant center to
do?', *Nephrology Nursing Journal*, 32(6): 701–2.

Radin, M. J. (1996), *Contested Commodities*, Cambridge, MA: Harvard
University Press.

Sells, R. A. (1997), 'Paired-kidney exchange program', *New England
Journal of Medicine*, 337: 1392–3.

Siminoff, L. and K. Chillag (1999), 'The fallacy of the "gift of life"',
Hastings Center Report, 29(6): 34–41.

Thompson, D. F. (1993), 'Understanding financial conflicts of interest',
New England Journal of Medicine, 329(8): 573–6.

UNOS (United Network for Organ Sharing) (2006), *Annual Report of the
US Organ Procurement and Transplantation Network and the Scientific
Registry of Transplant Recipients*, HHS/HRS/OSP/DOT, Rockville,
MD: UNOS, www.optn.org/AR2006/chapter_index.htm.

UNOS News Bureau (2004), 'OPTN/UNOS board opposes solicitation
for deceased organ donation', Press release, www.optn.org/news/
newsdetail.asp?id=374.

Weber, M., D. Dindo, N. Dimartines, P. M. Ambühl and P. A. Clavien
(2002), 'Kidney transplantation from donors without a heartbeat',
New England Journal of Medicine, 347(4): 248–55.

Wertheimer, A. (1992), 'Two questions about surrogacy and
exploitation', *Philosophy and Public Affairs*, 21(3): 211–39.

Xue, J. L., J. Z. Ma, T. A. Louis and A. J. Collins (2001), 'Forecast of the
number of patients with end-stage renal disease in the United States

to the year 2010', *Journal of the American Society for Nephrology*, 12(2): 2753–8.

Zargooshi, J. (2001) 'Quality of life of Iranian kidney "donors"', *Journal of Urology*, 166(5): 1790–99.

12 ALCOHOL
K. Austin Kerr

Introduction

This chapter examines the prohibition of alcoholic beverages in the United States in the early twentieth century. Prohibition arose in the USA principally from two sources, both of which were very much part of the economics of the reform movement. First, Americans from colonial times into the nineteenth century indulged in alcoholic beverages and provided a large market for them. Second, the businesses that supplied the market for alcoholic beverages prospered. Consumption rates were high by modern standards, and seemed to damage the health of the individual drinker, hurt family life and harm the wellbeing of the larger community. These concerns regarding drinking were about the demand for alcoholic beverages. A large number of Americans came to realise that the businesses that supplied alcoholic beverages had an important impact on the consumption of alcoholic beverages. Thus, prohibition was directly economic, with statutes and constitutional amendments proposed and enacted to forbid the manufacture, distribution and sale of alcoholic beverages. Prohibition thus was a set of measures to regulate businesses. To a lesser extent, prohibition was also an effort to regulate personal behaviour.

Background

The production, distribution and sale of alcoholic beverages as commodities of substantial economic importance did not begin until after the expansion of European empires in early modern times. Although alcohol had long been part of people's lives, it was not until the seventeenth century that substantial trading in alcoholic beverages began. The British colonies in North America became an integral part of this trade, and markets, especially for distilled spirits, expanded enormously during the eighteenth century, in the home island, the colonies and elsewhere where British merchants did business (Clark, 1976: 14–18; Courtwright, 2001: 9–30).

During the colonial period, the American distilling industry was an important feature of the British imperial economy, and distilling remained a significant and profitable business after independence. Colonial American entrepreneurs engaged in the rum trade in which they imported molasses from the sugar colonies of the British Caribbean islands and distilled it into liquor, a higher-value commodity. On the fringe of Western development, currency was generally in short supply, and sometimes rum and other spirits served as a medium of exchange. For example, colonial workers constructing public facilities in New York City received rum and other alcoholic beverages as part of their compensation. Also, with the quality of drinking water sometimes questionable, alcoholic beverages were in demand because of the belief that they were more healthful. These beverages included beer and ale brewed in the British tradition. In general, moreover, the propriety of drinking alcoholic beverages was not questioned, and supplying those beverages proved profitable. Although exact statistics are not available, one result was the widespread consumption of alcohol, with rates at least double those of the end of the twentieth century (Rorabaugh, 1979: 225–36).

These conditions changed somewhat after independence from the British Empire. The war for American independence disrupted colonial trade patterns and damaged the rum business. After enactment of the second US constitution in 1789, the federal government installed an improved banking system to facilitate business transactions with currency, as opposed to barter transactions involving high-value commodities such as distilled spirits.

Nevertheless, the old colonial practices persisted, albeit in modified form, with the migration of the American population west of the Appalachian mountains. Rorabaugh (ibid.) has called the first three decades of the nineteenth century in the American west 'the alcoholic republic' because of the large amounts of alcoholic beverages consumed. The American west in this period, like its predecessor colonies on the Atlantic seaboard, was cash poor but agriculturally rich. The lack of efficient and inexpensive means of overland transportation, however, hindered the profitable sale of commodities, especially grain. Farmers and merchants frequently turned to the distillation of maize (called corn in American English), like their colonial forebears, to produce a higher-value product, whiskey, lower in bulk and easier and cheaper to transport.

Drinking and the businesses that supplied whiskey were thus widespread. Modern students of drinking have calculated the annual per capita consumption of ethanol by the drinking-age population. Although precise figures are unavailable for the region as a whole, Clark (1976: 20) estimated the rate in 1810 was about 7 gallons of ethanol. Local reformers reported consumption rates of 10 gallons for Albany, New York, the state capital on the Hudson River, in 1829.

High rates of consumption in both the colonial and early national periods led to public drunkenness that alarmed some public officials. Decrees and statutes began to try to regulate alcohol consumers with fines and jail sentences for drunkenness. And there were early, and futile, efforts to contain trade in alcohol; in 1735 the Governor of Georgia tried to outlaw the importation of 'ardent spirits' into the colony. But drinking was so embedded in Anglo-American culture that juries were typically lenient in reaching judgements, and the law had little impact on consumption. Left alone without government interference, the USA was developing a drunken society.

The emergence of prohibition

The social disorder that alcohol markets and their sating produced led to a widespread reaction by the 1830s. The USA has experienced waves of religious revivals during its history, and the reaction to drunkenness coincided with a lively growth in religious commitments, especially among those persons who followed the Protestant churches associated with the British Reformation. In the emerging religious atmosphere, known as the Second Great Awakening, it was believed that individuals should retain full self-control in order to have a proper relationship with God. In this view, each individual should be free to experience salvation through a direct relationship with God. Those social and economic practices that inhibited or prevented such freedom were anathema. Among the condemned economic practices were the businesses of making, distributing and supplying liquor – lumped together rhetorically as the 'liquor traffic' (in the hierarchy of condemnation, chattel slavery was first, with the liquor traffic typically second). These ideas had become popular by mid-century, especially among Americans of British ancestry. They led to marketing regulations and outright prohibition of the liquor traffic in towns and states across much of the nation.

In addition to the growth of regulatory impulses, there were popular movements to reform the individual drinker through pledges of abstinence or moderation. In 1826, religious and civil leaders in New England formed the American Society for the Promotion of Temperance. The organisation promoted religious revivals combined with the signing of abstinence pledges around the country. By 1834 the society had one million members. Later, in 1840, six drunken men in Baltimore, Maryland, decided on self-reform after one of them attended a temperance meeting. Soon each man agreed to bring a friend to a temperance meeting, where they vowed to live their lives according to the presumed character of George Washington. Out of their enthusiasm the Washington Temperance Society – or Washingtonian Movement – spread to claim 600,000 reformed drunkards as members by 1847. The Washingtonians especially stressed meeting their family obligations by abstaining from drinking. Although it is impossible to measure this precisely, the 'temperance movement' apparently reduced markets for alcoholic beverages considerably.

It was in this context that a movement emerged for outright prohibition of the liquor traffic. In the 1830s and 1840s states and municipalities began enacting legislation to restrict the sale of alcoholic beverages. In 1847 the US Supreme Court ruled that it was constitutional to restrict alcohol sales. Earlier, temperance organisations had begun advocating outright prohibition of the liquor businesses. The eventual leader of the prohibition effort was Neal Dow of Portland, Maine, a seaport and a centre of the rum trade. Dow viewed Portland as especially afflicted with drunkenness and the personal and community miseries associated with alcohol abuse. Active in the temperance movement, Dow asked a barkeeper to refrain from selling liquor to drunks. When the barkeeper refused on the grounds that he enjoyed a business licence to sell liquor to customers, Dow began a crusade to change the law and remove the licence from those doing business as retailers, distributors and manufacturers of alcoholic beverages. In 1851 he succeeded in having the state of Maine pass a prohibition law. Prohibition as an economic policy had begun.

The Maine law established the long-standing goal of the American prohibition movement. The statute banned the manufacture, sale and 'keeping for sale' of intoxicating liquors. It permitted state officials to search and seize illegal beverages and provided jail terms for persons who repeatedly violated prohibition. The law allowed the sale of alcohol for medicinal and industrial purposes, however. It permitted persons to bring liquor from other states and it allowed drinking.

Dow proceeded to travel and lecture widely in the USA and Canada to advocate state prohibition laws. By 1855 twelve states and territories, all in the north, had enacted the so-called 'Maine Law' and embraced prohibition. These measures were controversial, however. German and Irish immigrant populations, now numerically important in those same northern areas, joined with other portions of the population not swayed by the beliefs of the Second Great Awakening to oppose prohibition. Maine repealed its law in 1856 but re-enacted it in 1858 after supporters won a referendum by a large margin; in 1884 the state added prohibition to its constitution. Elsewhere, however, the 'drys', as prohibitionists were known, were less successful, and by the end of the Civil War in 1865 their opponents, the 'wets', had killed prohibition in most places.

The industrialisation of alcoholic beverage production

Immigration not only had a profound impact on the politics of prohibition, it also led to economic changes that would eventually fuel a revival of prohibition as an economic policy. Especially important in this regard were German-Americans. German migration to the USA was very substantial in the middle decades of the nineteenth century, and sizeable German-American communities sprang up across the nation. Typically, wherever they settled, Germans supported a local brewing industry. German brewers also brought with them the techniques of making lager, or stored, beer, a beverage that required cool temperatures for brewing and for storage. This was unlike the English-style beers that had hitherto prevailed in the American market, and lager beers proved popular, especially in the hot climate that was so common across much of the nation, especially in the summer months.

The German-American brewers prospered. During the nineteenth century, beer was distributed in kegs and sold by the glass in retail places commonly called saloons. The local brewers tied their firms with saloons that, in turn, stocked their beer (as well as distilled spirits). Given the technologies available and the scale of the operations, these saloons typically sold only one brand of beer.

In some of the larger German-American communities, most notably Milwaukee, St Louis and Cincinnati, local brewers saw opportunities to develop larger-scale factories and national marketing systems using the improving railroad system and freight cars refrigerated with ice. These brewers became 'shipping brewers' seeking national and international markets. They employed scientists to improve the brewing process and to ensure uniformity in a high-quality product. They built larger factories to take advantage of the economies of scale. They developed brands and advertising campaigns to promote their beers as special premium products. These so-called shipping brewers needed to establish ties with retailers, saloons, in order to sell their beer. The result, as they expanded, was the establishment of more and more saloons (Kerr, 1998).

These retailers expanded in number dramatically. The marketing efforts of the brewers were successful in one important respect: beer replaced distilled spirits as the principal source of alcohol for American drinkers in 1890. This dominant position persisted into the 21st century. There were, however, problems in the long run. Brewers financed saloons, supplied them with fixtures and sometimes even owned them. But competition within the trade was also increasing. Competition increased further by the end of the nineteenth century as other brewers decided to ship beer regionally. As competition increased, so did the number of saloons, so that some communities had as many as one saloon for every 80 persons.

In this competitive environment it was difficult for saloon-keepers to earn profits just from beer and whiskey sales. Competition kept the price of a glass of beer at 5 cents, even as the American economy experienced inflation after 1900, making the saloon business even more precarious. Saloon-keepers offered free 'lunches' – salty foods – to encourage more liquor sales. They had every incentive to violate local laws regulating their hours of operation. Worse, commonly saloon-keepers entered other lines of business, such as gambling and other vices, including prostitution. To stay in business saloon-keepers entered partisan politics, making strategic donations to sympathetic politicians, and they bribed police not to enforce regulatory laws.

As the saloon became an evermore ubiquitous institution, its presence offended larger and larger numbers of citizens. Civic leaders like Neal Dow had long been appalled by the drinking institutions of their communities. During the nineteenth century the number of reformers grew, and after the dawn of the twentieth century dry support exploded. All over the USA 'respectable' citizens were seeking means of controlling saloons, drinking and the illegal activities that they so often housed.

In the meantime, the organisation of the distilled spirits industry had also changed. There were efforts among producers in the late nineteenth century to control competition through various forms of horizontal combination, none of which was lasting. Eventually, a large, vertically integrated firm, the Distillers Securities, emerged. It combined liquor production and wholesaling and was the nation's largest producer until national prohibition began. The distillers, however, had no incentive to enter the retail business directly in the ways that the brewers had done. In fact, distillers and brewers were bitter commercial rivals (Chandler, 1976: 328). Nevertheless, they had powerful economic incentives to avoid prohibition, or even other severe restrictions on their sales.

The rebirth of prohibition and the emergence of a modern reform movement

These business developments, combined with a resurgence of alcohol consumption, led to a rebirth of the prohibition movement. Prohibition made some gains at the local and state levels in the post-Civil War decades, and it rose to commanding heights in American politics in the second decade of the twentieth century. The rebirth began in 1869 with the formation of the Prohibition Party, dedicated to electing candidates committed to prohibition. It gained momentum through the efforts of women during the 1870s and 1880s.

Although women were often concerned with public affairs and even involved in trying to shape public policy in this period, they were disenfranchised as voters. Women concerned about the problems associated with drinking and convinced that liquor businesses were abetting those problems thus took direct action by demonstrating outside saloons, imploring customers to stay away and saloon-keepers to enter other lines of business. These demonstrations culminated in the winter of 1873/74 in a great 'woman's crusade'. Across much of the nation large bands of women gathered to try to end the alcohol business through prayer and public exhortation. They enjoyed modest successes, and in 1874 decided to form the Woman's Christian Temperance Union (WCTU) to maintain pressure on behalf of dry laws. The WCTU was an important prohibition organisation for the rest of US history. Organised and controlled by women, the WCTU launched various efforts at reform. In the 1880s prohibition legislation again began to be adopted at the state and local level.

In 1893 a new male-dominated organisation, the Anti-Saloon League, joined the effort in the state of Ohio. The Anti-Saloon League was formed not as a political party but as a non-partisan effort to pressure elected officials to pass new prohibition laws and to enforce those already in the statutes. The League soon developed a national structure and by the early twentieth century had become the principal force behind prohibition legislation. It received substantial support from Protestant churches and received hundreds of thousands of small donations that it used to build a professional staff to work in the legislative arena and to mount an enormous educational and propaganda effort to end the liquor traffic through prohibition. After achieving the promulgation of a number of important laws at local and state levels in the first decade of the century, mostly in rural areas and city neighbourhoods dominated by Protestants, in 1913 the League announced its campaign to achieve national prohibition through an amendment to the US Constitution. In 1916 the League and the WCTU saw elected the two-thirds majorities necessary to initiate a constitutional amendment. When the USA entered World War I in 1917, the drys quickly worked to enact prohibition as a wartime conservation measure, and they successfully initiated what became the Eighteenth Amendment to the US Constitution. When three-quarters of the states ratified the amendment in 1919 and prohibition went into effect in 1920, the drys thought they had won a permanent victory, as no constitutional amendment had ever been repealed.

The amendment outlawed the manufacture, distribution and sale of alcoholic beverages. It authorised enforcement by statute at both the federal and state levels. In 1919 Congress enacted, over the veto of President Woodrow Wilson, the Volstead Act, which defined as alcoholic beverages drinks containing even a very low level of alcohol. The states followed with their own enforcement laws. A few states went even farther with so-called 'bone-dry' laws, outlawing the consumption or possession of alcoholic beverages.

Economic arguments about prohibition

Economic arguments played a powerful role in the drive for prohibition laws. In the early days of the reform movement, the drys pointed to the over-consumption of alcohol as inhibiting personal success and achievement, and thus damaging the autonomy of the drinker and the prosperity of the larger community. As industrialisation progressed, with a growing reliance on complex technologies in the economy, these economic arguments expanded. Timberlake (1963: 67) quotes the Committee of Fifty in 1899, a group of prominent business and civil leaders concerned about alcohol misuse but which stopped short of supporting prohibition in this regard: 'As more things are done with machinery, ... as implements of greater precision and refinement take the place of cruder ones, as the speed at which machinery is run is increased, the necessity of having a clear head during the hours of labor becomes imperative, and the very conditions of modern business life necessitate sobriety on the part of the workers.'

Industrial safety and efficiency thus became core economic arguments on behalf of prohibition. While at the turn of the century three-quarters of employers surveyed still allowed workers to drink, these views were changing as safety became a larger and larger concern. By the twentieth century all the large railroad firms were requiring complete sobriety in their employees as a key to safer operations. And by 1910 more and more business executives were arguing that efficient operations required sobriety. Labour leaders sometimes endorsed these views, although the union movement was always divided on the subject of prohibition.

The Anti-Saloon League and other dry organisations promoted

these views. They also advanced the notion that prohibition and the resulting abstinence from drinking would boost the overall prosperity of the economy. Money spent on drink, in this view, was wasted money: if drinkers saved their drink money not only would they become more industrious and efficient when sober, but they would also become wealthier. Savings would facilitate the purchase of homes or other durable goods and benefit the social good (ibid.: 67–99).

Prohibition's opponents, the 'wets', were led by the brewing and distilling industries, helped by the trade unions of their employees. They largely ignored the arguments regarding safety and efficiency, concentrating instead on the economic contributions of their industries. At all levels, manufacturing to retailing, firms provided employment, purchased goods from suppliers, including farmers, and paid taxes to government bodies. In fact, brewing alone was by the early twentieth century the nation's sixth-largest industry in terms of capital employed and eleventh in product value. Tax revenue from alcoholic beverages was the third-largest source of funding for the federal government at this time, and the wets pointed out that it was funding that prohibition would eliminate, thereby placing a burden on other taxpayers. They appealed to other business leaders that allowing prohibition would only encourage the development of other undesirable forms of regulation. Finally, when prohibition loomed, the liquor interests appealed unsuccessfully to class interests, suggesting that the elimination of their firms was anti-capitalist (Kerr, 1985, 1998).

The economic arguments continued in the 1920s under prohibition. Although marred by a sharp recession early in the decade, those were generally years of substantial economic expansion prior to the collapse of stock prices near the end of 1929. The drys saw this prosperity as vindication of their policy. In their view, instead of wasting their money in needless consumption in saloons, funds were going to support family life. One result was a real estate boom. Another was higher earnings as sober, more efficient workers helped boost American productivity. These were powerful arguments that seemed to conform to experience, and the popularity of prohibition, if anything, grew during the decade. In fact, all evidence pointed to a more sober population.

The wets, however, continued to resist. At first they were not especially effective. The brewing, distilling and retail businesses were gone, or driven underground as criminal activities, and unable thereby to provide the political and monetary support as was previously the case. Prohibition opponents formed the Association Against the Prohibition Amendment (AAPA), but in its early years it was ineffective. Then, in 1925, some of the nation's wealthiest men began to contribute to the organisation. Eventually, in 1928, Pierre du Pont, who had made a fortune in the chemical and automobile industries, assumed leadership of the AAPA and it became much more adept at advancing wet arguments. These capitalists were especially concerned about the loss of alcohol tax revenue to the government and the pressures resulting to raise funds from progressive taxation of the wealthy. They lent not only their money but their organisational skills to the fight against prohibition (Kyvig, 1979).

The onset of the Great Depression after 1929 gave the wets their golden opportunity. No longer could their opponents claim that prohibition promoted prosperity. Instead, the wets argued that repeal would actually boost the economy. Legalised businesses would increase employment, buy raw materials from depressed farmers, obtain supplies from bottle manufacturers and the like, and provide governments with desperately needed tax revenue. Moreover, all these benefits would have a ripple effect through the economy, helping to lift the nation from its worst-ever economic calamity (ibid.).

The depression provided the wets with persuasive arguments. The political mood of the country shifted, furthermore, with the depression. No longer did drinking seem the social scourge witnessed by earlier Americans; it actually could be a socially beneficial act. The result was that in 1933 the nation repealed the Eighteenth Amendment with the Twenty-First Amendment. Prohibition continued in some states and localities but the national policy had changed. The economic arguments on behalf of repeal had proven powerful indeed.

The economics of prohibition in perspective

Much denial accompanied the repeal of prohibition. Propagandists for the AAPA had argued that prohibition had failed to reduce markets for alcoholic beverages, instead driving them underground and creating a crime wave as a result. Investors in the renewed brewing and distilling industries believed this situation to be true, as did many government officials. They were disappointed initially, however, because in fact prohibition had substantially reduced markets for alcoholic beverages and those markets were not quick to recover after 1933. In fact, consumption rates did not grow to their pre-prohibition rates until about 1970 (Pennock and Kerr, 2005).

All modern societies have public policies that regulate both the marketing of alcoholic beverages and the behaviour of drinkers. Prohibition was not confined to the USA, moreover. As a reform movement, it spread with more or less success throughout the English-speaking world. In this context, American prohibition was the most important form of the policy. It was also at the extreme end of a continuum of economic and personal regulation. The national law was a policy intended to stop the marketing of alcoholic beverages. Some state governments, furthermore, enacted laws banning drinking. And not all states repealed their prohibition laws immediately. The last state prohibition statute, that of Mississippi, was repealed in 1964. Some local laws persisted thereafter, however.

In the end, although prohibition was popular for some time, in part because of its success as an economic policy, the American people rejected it. There were efforts for the first four decades after repeal, largely unsuccessful, to enact federal measures controlling the marketing of liquor. Then, when drinking rates rose to their pre-prohibition levels after 1970, there was renewed interest in national policies of economic regulation regarding liquor. This renewed interest came mostly from health professionals who witnessed the harmful effects of alcohol abuse. The results were fairly meagre. Like the experiences of an earlier generation of reforms, the health professionals were branded as 'neo-Prohibitionists' by the powerful businesses involved in liquor sales. By the end of the twentieth century, at the national level, economic policies towards alcohol amounted to warnings on labels about the dangers of drinking while pregnant, and the setting of a national sobriety standard for motor vehicle drivers. In the meantime, however, the government effectively reduced taxation of alcoholic beverages as a proportion of the cost of doing business in them (Pennock, 2007: 12–165).

By the early years of the 21st century, national regulations on the marketing of alcoholic beverages were few in number and small in their impact. Nevertheless, concerns about the adverse human and economic impact of alcohol misuse nagged political consciousness, at least to a modest extent. The federal system of governance in the USA meant that controls over alcohol occurred in a fragmented and sometimes confusing manner through the complex layers of local governance. State and local regulations regulating hours of sale still existed in the patch-work of federalism. When the federal government repealed prohibition in 1933, eighteen states controlled the wholesaling of distilled spirits through government agencies in an effort to shape the marketing structure of liquor and ensure that zealous, profit-hungry firms did not over-stimulate sales and drinking; a smaller number restricted retail sales to state-run stores. With the passage of time, however, these state policies became less focused on marketing control and more geared towards raising revenue or promoting and protecting local liquor production. The relative prices of alcoholic beverages also declined after World War II as taxes on them failed to keep pace with inflation. Recognising that raising liquor prices led to reduced consumption, after 1950 reformers succeeded in having federal taxes on liquor raised only once, in 1991, and that increase did not include indexing the tax rate for inflation.

The focus on liquor control in the flowering of American consumer culture after 1933 rested on the individual. Apart from health professionals, few paid attention to the social and economic effects of liquor production and drinking. Nevertheless, efforts were widespread to punish those who drank too much liquor. There were also attempts to hinder opportunities to abuse alcohol by restricting its availability in the workplace. In 2007, for example, some baseball teams had removed beer from locker rooms to encourage greater sobriety among employees. There were also modest efforts regarding the economics of the liquor industries. The movement towards 'social investing', although representing only a small fraction of the capital employed in American industry, typically offered individuals opportunities through specialised investment pools to avoid placing money in business activities deemed socially and economically undesirable. 'Social investing' sometimes lumped together liquor firms with tobacco and gambling companies, among other 'undesirable' ventures.

Such individual efforts were a far cry from prohibition. The prohibition movement of the nineteenth and early twentieth centuries had focused on stamping out the economic and social systems that the brewing and distilling industries engendered. This sort of systemic approach had become but a historical memory in the prevailing American consumerist culture, which exalted the individual.

References

Chandler, A. D. (1976), *The Visible Hand: The Managerial Revolution in American Business*, Cambridge, MA: Harvard University Press.

Clark, N. H. (1976), *Deliver Us from Evil: An Interpretation of American Prohibition*, Philadelphia, PA: W. W. Norton.

Courtwright, D. T. (2001), *Forces of Habit: Drugs and the Making of the Modern World*, Cambridge, MA: Harvard University Press.

Kerr, K. A. (1985), *Organized for Prohibition: A New History of the Anti-Saloon League*, New Haven, CT: Yale University Press.

Kerr, K. A. (1998), 'The American brewing industry, 1865–1920', in G. Wilson and T. R. Gourvish (eds), *The Dynamics of the International Brewing Industry since 1800*, London: Routledge.

Kyvig, D. E. (1979), *Repealing National Prohibition*, Chicago, IL: University of Chicago Press.

Pennock, P. E. (2007), *Advertising Sin and Sickness: The Politics of Alcohol and Tobacco Marketing, 1950–1990*, Dekalb, IL: North Illinois University Press.

Pennock, P. E. and K. A. Kerr (2005), 'In the shadow of prohibition: domestic American alcohol policy since 1933', *Business History*, 47: 383–400.

Rorabaugh, W. J. (1979), *The Alcoholic Republic: An American Tradition*, New York: Oxford University Press.

Timberlake, J. H. (1963), *Prohibition and the Progressive Movement, 1900–1920*, Cambridge, MA: Harvard University Press.

ABOUT THE IEA

The Institute is a research and educational charity (No. CC 235 351), limited by guarantee. Its mission is to improve understanding of the fundamental institutions of a free society by analysing and expounding the role of markets in solving economic and social problems.

The IEA achieves its mission by:

- a high-quality publishing programme
- conferences, seminars, lectures and other events
- outreach to school and college students
- brokering media introductions and appearances

The IEA, which was established in 1955 by the late Sir Antony Fisher, is an educational charity, not a political organisation. It is independent of any political party or group and does not carry on activities intended to affect support for any political party or candidate in any election or referendum, or at any other time. It is financed by sales of publications, conference fees and voluntary donations.

In addition to its main series of publications the IEA also publishes a quarterly journal, *Economic Affairs*.

The IEA is aided in its work by a distinguished international Academic Advisory Council and an eminent panel of Honorary Fellows. Together with other academics, they review prospective IEA publications, their comments being passed on anonymously to authors. All IEA papers are therefore subject to the same rigorous independent refereeing process as used by leading academic journals.

IEA publications enjoy widespread classroom use and course adoptions in schools and universities. They are also sold throughout the world and often translated/reprinted.

Since 1974 the IEA has helped to create a worldwide network of 100 similar institutions in over 70 countries. They are all independent but share the IEA's mission.

Views expressed in the IEA's publications are those of the authors, not those of the Institute (which has no corporate view), its Managing Trustees, Academic Advisory Council members or senior staff.

Members of the Institute's Academic Advisory Council, Honorary Fellows, Trustees and Staff are listed on the following page.

The Institute gratefully acknowledges financial support for its publications programme and other work from a generous benefaction by the late Alec and Beryl Warren.

The Institute of Economic Affairs
2 Lord North Street, Westminster, London SW1P 3LB
Tel: 020 7799 8900
Fax: 020 7799 2137
Email: iea@iea.org.uk
Internet: iea.org.uk

Other papers recently published by the IEA include:

WHO, What and Why?
Transnational Government, Legitimacy and the World Health Organization
Roger Scruton
Occasional Paper 113; ISBN 0 255 36487 3; £8.00

The World Turned Rightside Up
A New Trading Agenda for the Age of Globalisation
John C. Hulsman
Occasional Paper 114; ISBN 0 255 36495 4; £8.00

The Representation of Business in English Literature
Introduced and edited by Arthur Pollard
Readings 53; ISBN 0 255 36491 1; £12.00

Anti-Liberalism 2000
The Rise of New Millennium Collectivism
David Henderson
Occasional Paper 115; ISBN 0 255 36497 0; £7.50

Capitalism, Morality and Markets
Brian Griffiths, Robert A. Sirico, Norman Barry & Frank Field
Readings 54; ISBN 0 255 36496 2; £7.50

A Conversation with Harris and Seldon
Ralph Harris & Arthur Seldon
Occasional Paper 116; ISBN 0 255 36498 9; £7.50

Malaria and the DDT Story
Richard Tren & Roger Bate
Occasional Paper 117; ISBN 0 255 36499 7; £10.00

A Plea to Economists Who Favour Liberty: Assist the Everyman
Daniel B. Klein
Occasional Paper 118; ISBN 0 255 36501 2; £10.00

The Changing Fortunes of Economic Liberalism
Yesterday, Today and Tomorrow
David Henderson
Occasional Paper 105 (new edition); ISBN 0 255 36520 9; £12.50

The Global Education Industry
Lessons from Private Education in Developing Countries
James Tooley
Hobart Paper 141 (new edition); ISBN 0 255 36503 9; £12.50

Saving Our Streams
The Role of the Anglers' Conservation Association in
Protecting English and Welsh Rivers
Roger Bate
Research Monograph 53; ISBN 0 255 36494 6; £10.00

Better Off Out?
The Benefits or Costs of EU Membership
Brian Hindley & Martin Howe
Occasional Paper 99 (new edition); ISBN 0 255 36502 0; £10.00

Buckingham at 25
Freeing the Universities from State Control
Edited by James Tooley
Readings 55; ISBN 0 255 36512 8; £15.00

Lectures on Regulatory and Competition Policy
Irwin M. Stelzer
Occasional Paper 120; ISBN 0 255 36511 X; £12.50

Misguided Virtue
False Notions of Corporate Social Responsibility
David Henderson
Hobart Paper 142; ISBN 0 255 36510 1; £12.50

HIV and Aids in Schools
The Political Economy of Pressure Groups and Miseducation
Barrie Craven, Pauline Dixon, Gordon Stewart & James Tooley
Occasional Paper 121; ISBN 0 255 36522 5; £10.00

The Road to Serfdom
The Reader's Digest *condensed version*
Friedrich A. Hayek
Occasional Paper 122; ISBN 0 255 36530 6; £7.50

Bastiat's *The Law*
Introduction by Norman Barry
Occasional Paper 123; ISBN 0 255 36509 8; £7.50

A Globalist Manifesto for Public Policy
Charles Calomiris
Occasional Paper 124; ISBN 0 255 36525 X; £7.50

Euthanasia for Death Duties
Putting Inheritance Tax Out of Its Misery
Barry Bracewell-Milnes
Research Monograph 54; ISBN 0 255 36513 6; £10.00

Liberating the Land
The Case for Private Land-use Planning
Mark Pennington
Hobart Paper 143; ISBN 0 255 36508 X; £10.00

IEA Yearbook of Government Performance 2002/2003
Edited by Peter Warburton
Yearbook 1; ISBN 0 255 36532 2; £15.00

Britain's Relative Economic Performance, 1870–1999
Nicholas Crafts
Research Monograph 55; ISBN 0 255 36524 1; £10.00

Should We Have Faith in Central Banks?
Otmar Issing
Occasional Paper 125; ISBN 0 255 36528 4; £7.50

The Dilemma of Democracy
Arthur Seldon
Hobart Paper 136 (reissue); ISBN 0 255 36536 5; £10.00

Capital Controls: a 'Cure' Worse Than the Problem?
Forrest Capie
Research Monograph 56; ISBN 0 255 36506 3; £10.00

The Poverty of 'Development Economics'
Deepak Lal
Hobart Paper 144 (reissue); ISBN 0 255 36519 5; £15.00

Should Britain Join the Euro?
The Chancellor's Five Tests Examined
Patrick Minford
Occasional Paper 126; ISBN 0 255 36527 6; £7.50

Post-Communist Transition: Some Lessons
Leszek Balcerowicz
Occasional Paper 127; ISBN 0 255 36533 0; £7.50

A Tribute to Peter Bauer
John Blundell et al.
Occasional Paper 128; ISBN 0 255 36531 4; £10.00

Employment Tribunals
Their Growth and the Case for Radical Reform
J. R. Shackleton
Hobart Paper 145; ISBN 0 255 36515 2; £10.00

Fifty Economic Fallacies Exposed
Geoffrey E. Wood
Occasional Paper 129; ISBN 0 255 36518 7; £12.50

A Market in Airport Slots
Keith Boyfield (editor), David Starkie, Tom Bass & Barry Humphreys
Readings 56; ISBN 0 255 36505 5; £10.00

Money, Inflation and the Constitutional Position of the Central Bank
Milton Friedman & Charles A. E. Goodhart
Readings 57; ISBN 0 255 36538 1; £10.00

railway.com
Parallels between the Early British Railways and the ICT Revolution
Robert C. B. Miller
Research Monograph 57; ISBN 0 255 36534 9; £12.50

The Regulation of Financial Markets
Edited by Philip Booth & David Currie
Readings 58; ISBN 0 255 36551 9; £12.50

Climate Alarmism Reconsidered
Robert L. Bradley Jr
Hobart Paper 146; ISBN 0 255 36541 1; £12.50

Government Failure: E. G. West on Education
Edited by James Tooley & James Stanfield
Occasional Paper 130; ISBN 0 255 36552 7; £12.50

Corporate Governance: Accountability in the Marketplace
Elaine Sternberg
Second edition
Hobart Paper 147; ISBN 0 255 36542 x; £12.50

The Land Use Planning System
Evaluating Options for Reform
John Corkindale
Hobart Paper 148; ISBN 0 255 36550 0; £10.00

Economy and Virtue
Essays on the Theme of Markets and Morality
Edited by Dennis O'Keeffe
Readings 59; ISBN 0 255 36504 7; £12.50

Free Markets Under Siege
Cartels, Politics and Social Welfare
Richard A. Epstein
Occasional Paper 132; ISBN 0 255 36553 5; £10.00

Unshackling Accountants
D. R. Myddelton
Hobart Paper 149; ISBN 0 255 36559 4; £12.50

The Euro as Politics
Pedro Schwartz
Research Monograph 58; ISBN 0 255 36535 7; £12.50

Pricing Our Roads
Vision and Reality
Stephen Glaister & Daniel J. Graham
Research Monograph 59; ISBN 0 255 36562 4; £10.00

The Role of Business in the Modern World
Progress, Pressures, and Prospects for the Market Economy
David Henderson
Hobart Paper 150; ISBN 0 255 36548 9; £12.50

Public Service Broadcasting Without the BBC?
Alan Peacock
Occasional Paper 133; ISBN 0 255 36565 9; £10.00

The ECB and the Euro: the First Five Years
Otmar Issing
Occasional Paper 134; ISBN 0 255 36555 1; £10.00

Towards a Liberal Utopia?
Edited by Philip Booth
Hobart Paperback 32; ISBN 0 255 36563 2; £15.00

The Way Out of the Pensions Quagmire
Philip Booth & Deborah Cooper
Research Monograph 60; ISBN 0 255 36517 9; £12.50

Black Wednesday
A Re-examination of Britain's Experience in the Exchange Rate Mechanism
Alan Budd
Occasional Paper 135; ISBN 0 255 36566 7; £7.50

Crime: Economic Incentives and Social Networks
Paul Ormerod
Hobart Paper 151; ISBN 0 255 36554 3; £10.00

The Road to Serfdom *with* **The Intellectuals and Socialism**
Friedrich A. Hayek
Occasional Paper 136; ISBN 0 255 36576 4; £10.00

Money and Asset Prices in Boom and Bust
Tim Congdon
Hobart Paper 152; ISBN 0 255 36570 5; £10.00

The Dangers of Bus Re-regulation
and Other Perspectives on Markets in Transport
John Hibbs et al.
Occasional Paper 137; ISBN 0 255 36572 1; £10.00

The New Rural Economy
Change, Dynamism and Government Policy
Berkeley Hill et al.
Occasional Paper 138; ISBN 0 255 36546 2; £15.00

The Benefits of Tax Competition
Richard Teather
Hobart Paper 153; ISBN 0 255 36569 1; £12.50

Wheels of Fortune
Self-funding Infrastructure and the Free Market Case for a Land Tax
Fred Harrison
Hobart Paper 154; ISBN 0 255 36589 6; £12.50

Were 364 Economists All Wrong?
Edited by Philip Booth
Readings 60; ISBN 978 0 255 36588 8; £10.00

Europe After the 'No' Votes
Mapping a New Economic Path
Patrick A. Messerlin
Occasional Paper 139; ISBN 978 0 255 36580 2; £10.00

The Railways, the Market and the Government
John Hibbs et al.
Readings 61; ISBN 978 0 255 36567 3; £12.50

Corruption: The World's Big C
Cases, Causes, Consequences, Cures
Ian Senior
Research Monograph 61; ISBN 978 0 255 36571 0; £12.50

Choice and the End of Social Housing
Peter King
Hobart Paper 155; ISBN 978 0 255 36568 0; £10.00

Sir Humphrey's Legacy
Facing Up to the Cost of Public Sector Pensions
Neil Record
Hobart Paper 156; ISBN 978 0 255 36578 9; £10.00

The Economics of Law
Cento Veljanovski
Second edition
Hobart Paper 157; ISBN 978 0 255 36561 1; £12.50

Living with Leviathan
Public Spending, Taxes and Economic Performance
David B. Smith
Hobart Paper 158; ISBN 978 0 255 36579 6; £12.50

The Vote Motive
Gordon Tullock
New edition
Hobart Paperback 33; ISBN 978 0 255 36577 2; £10.00

Waging the War of Ideas
John Blundell
Third edition
Occasional Paper 131; ISBN 978 0 255 36606 9; £12.50

The War Between the State and the Family
How Government Divides and Impoverishes
Patricia Morgan
Hobart Paper 159; ISBN 978 0 255 36596 3; £10.00

Capitalism – A Condensed Version
Arthur Seldon
Occasional Paper 140; ISBN 978 0 255 36598 7; £7.50

Catholic Social Teaching and the Market Economy
Edited by Philip Booth
Hobart Paperback 34; ISBN 978 0 255 36581 9; £15.00

Adam Smith – A Primer
Eamonn Butler
Occasional Paper 141; ISBN 978 0 255 36608 3; £7.50

Happiness, Economics and Public Policy
Helen Johns & Paul Ormerod
Research Monograph 62; ISBN 978 0 255 36600 7; £10.00

They Meant Well
Government Project Disasters
D. R. Myddelton
Hobart Paper 160; ISBN 978 0 255 36601 4; £12.50

Rescuing Social Capital from Social Democracy
John Meadowcroft & Mark Pennington
Hobart Paper 161; ISBN 978 0 255 36592 5; £10.00

Paths to Property
Approaches to Institutional Change in International Development
Karol Boudreaux & Paul Dragos Aligica
Hobart Paper 162; ISBN 978 0 255 36582 6; £10.00

Other IEA publications

Comprehensive information on other publications and the wider work of the IEA can be found at www.iea.org.uk. To order any publication please see below.

Personal customers

Orders from personal customers should be directed to the IEA:
Bob Layson
IEA
2 Lord North Street
FREEPOST LON10168
London SW1P 3YZ
Tel: 020 7799 8909. Fax: 020 7799 2137
Email: blayson@iea.org.uk

Trade customers

All orders from the book trade should be directed to the IEA's distributor:
Gazelle Book Services Ltd (IEA Orders)
FREEPOST RLYS-EAHU-YSCZ
White Cross Mills
Hightown
Lancaster LA1 4XS
Tel: 01524 68765, Fax: 01524 53232
Email: sales@gazellebooks.co.uk

IEA subscriptions

The IEA also offers a subscription service to its publications. For a single annual payment (currently £42.00 in the UK), subscribers receive every monograph the IEA publishes. For more information please contact:
Adam Myers
Subscriptions
IEA
2 Lord North Street
FREEPOST LON10168
London SW1P 3YZ
Tel: 020 7799 8920, Fax: 020 7799 2137
Email: amyers@iea.org.uk